FROM
FOOTBALL
TO SOCCER

SPORT AND SOCIETY

Series Editors
Aram Goudsouzian
Jaime Schultz

Founding Editors
Benjamin G. Rader
Randy Roberts

A list of books in the series appears at the end of this book.

FROM
FOOTBALL
TO SOCCER

THE EARLY HISTORY OF THE BEAUTIFUL GAME IN THE UNITED STATES

BRIAN D. BUNK

UNIVERSITY OF ILLINOIS PRESS
Urbana, Chicago, and Springfield

Chapter 3 was originally published in a different form in Graham Curry,
ed., *The Early Development of Football: Contemporary Debates*, Routledge,
Copyright © 2019. Used by permission.
Chapter 6 was originally published in a different form in Chris Bolsmann
and George Kioussis, eds., *Soccer Frontiers: The Global Game in the United
States, 1863–1913*, University of Tennessee Press, Copyright © 2021. Used by
permission.
Chapter 9 was originally published in a different form as Brian D. Bunk,
"The Rise and Fall of Professional Soccer in Holyoke Massachusetts, USA,"
Sport in History 31, no. 3 (September 2011): 283–306, reprinted by permission
of the publisher, Taylor & Francis Ltd., http://www.tandfonline.com.

Library of Congress Cataloging-in-Publication Data
Names: Bunk, Brian D., 1968– author.
Title: From football to soccer : the early history of the beautiful game in the
    United States / Brian D. Bunk.
Description: Urbana : University of Illinois Press, 2021. | Series: Sport and
    society | Includes bibliographical references and index.
Identifiers: LCCN 2020055747 (print) | LCCN 2020055748 (ebook) | ISBN
    9780252043888 (cloth) | ISBN 9780252085871 (paperback) | ISBN
    9780252052781 (ebook)
Subjects: LCSH: Soccer—United States—History—19th century. | Soccer—
    United States—History—20th century. | Soccer—Social aspects—
    United States.
Classification: LCC GV944.U5 B86 2021 (print) | LCC GV944.U5 (ebook) | DDC
    796.3340973—dc23
LC record available at https://lccn.loc.gov/2020055747
LC ebook record available at https://lccn.loc.gov/2020055748

To my family with gratitude.

CONTENTS

ACKNOWLEDGMENTS

Without the original research of Roger Allaway, Colin Jose, David Litterer, and Mel Smith this book could not have been written. Before the digitization of newspapers and other materials, this group of researchers scoured archives and spent countless hours poring over microfilm. Working almost like archaeologists, they excavated the long-forgotten history of soccer in the United States. I thank them for their generosity and willingness to help me when I first began researching this topic and when I had questions along the way

My colleagues in the History Department at the University of Massachusetts Amherst sustained this project in a number of important ways from providing research funding to reading drafts. I especially want to thank Sam Redman for his comments on an early version and Joel Wolfe for his general advice. When I began this project, I knew only a little about the history of soccer in the United States or globally. My colleagues at UMass encouraged me to develop and teach courses in sport history, and this helped me to learn the field and fill gaps in my knowledge. The enthusiasm of my students for the history of sport and for soccer more generally also contributed to the book in a number of positive ways. As with any project of this sort, archivists and librarians made much of the research possible. The late Rob Cox and Kirstin Kay from the Special Collections and University Archives at UMass warrant special mention.

I was honored to be part of a group of researchers who reformed the Society for American Soccer History in 2018. The organization has provided a community of scholars whose comradeship has improved this book immensely. Tom McCabe has always been a great supporter of the project, and his comments on the manuscript were invaluable. I'd also like to thank other folks, including Steve Apostolov, Zach Bigalke, James Brown, Steve Holroyd, Les Jones, David Kilpatrick, George Kioussis, Gabe Logan, Kurt Rausch, Patrick Salkeld, Patrick Sullivan, and Kevin Tallec Marston. Ed Farnsworth and Grant Czubinski shared my obsession with the 1894 professional leagues. Jack Huckel, formerly of the National Soccer Hall of Fame, was one of the first people I met when I started on this project. He has always been incredibly helpful and patient, even with some of my more ambitious ideas.

Just as soccer itself is a global phenomenon, there is a worldwide community of researchers on the game. It was a privilege to engage with this informal collective through publications, conferences, and conversations. Even when I was a neophyte in the field, many researchers, including Tony Collins, Graham Curry, Roy Hay, Dilwyn Porter, Matthew Taylor, Wray Vamplew, and Jean Williams, were incredibly supportive. Participating in the International Football History conferences has been a great pleasure, and I thank Gary James for his tireless efforts at organizing them. I very much appreciated Andrei Markovits's enthusiastic comments on the manuscript and Dan Nassit's persistent interest in publishing the book. I also thank Shireen Ahmed, Peter Alegi, Chris Bolsmann, Matthew Brown, Brenda Elsey, Christian Hesle, Alex Jackson, Roger Kittleson, Matt McDowell, Shawn Stein, and Stefan Szymanski. Even though Twitter can sometimes be a bit overwhelming, I found it also can be a source of great inspiration, and I thank all of the folks who contribute to making the site something positive.

In the course of the research for this project and others, I've been in contact with some family members of the players I write about. Special thanks to Clyde Behrendt, Andrew Smith, and others who helped make the sometimes impersonal process of historical work a bit more human. This book would not have been completed without the love and support of my family: Laura, Zoe, Clio, and Buster. Even though they are not big fans of soccer, or really any sport, they graciously listened when I reported on some new and exciting (to me, anyway) discovery.

INTRODUCTION

On September 18, 1866, the *Waukesha Freeman* reported on the first public appearance of Carroll College's new president, Walter Rankin. Located in southeastern Wisconsin, the small school was the state's oldest chartered college and enrolled about forty students. A graduate of the College of New Jersey, now Princeton University, he had been recruited for the position at the recommendation of a distinguished alumnus.[1] Rankin was born in India in 1841 while his parents served as Presbyterian missionaries in the country. Prior to arriving in Wisconsin, he had been a teacher and school principal in New Jersey. Although not an ordained minister like his father, Rankin nevertheless held strong religious beliefs and had a fierce "drive to Christianize the frontier."[2] In addition to strong spiritual convictions, the Rankin family had keen interest in sports. His father John, who stood six feet, four inches tall, promoted the value of physical activity and "was a genuine enthusiast for athletics as he was for intellectual pursuits." The elder Rankin taught his sons the type of football he had learned at Princeton in the late 1830s, about the time the sport became established at the school.[3] No direct evidence exists that Walter Rankin took part in football matches at Princeton, but records indicate he played baseball and some of the student body's top kickers were in his class.[4]

The newspaper article announcing Rankin's first visit to Carroll noted that he arrived "quietly and unostentatiously" to hear recitations in a variety of subjects. The new president impressed observers who praised his rapport with students as well as his abilities at "football playing." It was a rare educator, the article concluded, who could maintain discipline both in the classroom and on the athletic field.[5] Throughout his time in Wisconsin, Rankin keenly supported athletics, often participating in both formal and informal games. In June 1867, for example he captained a baseball team called Rankin Side and three years later was in the Waukesha Diamonds' lineup for a 28–16 win over the Dodge County Rangers.[6] In addition to competing in baseball, he enjoyed football and often played the game with his students. Former Carroll student Harvey C. Olin recalled how they exploited Rankin's fondness for the sport to extend classroom breaks: "the Professor could be inveighed into a game with the boys at the three o'clock recess—that he entirely forgot to call school, so great was his interest in the game."[7]

A month after Rankin assumed his office, a city paper reported that a group of students from the school had defeated a collection of town boys in a "match game of foot-ball." The event took place on October 11, 1866, when twenty-two players turned out for Carroll while the opposing squad fielded twenty-five "altogether larger men." Despite the seeming mismatch, the school boys triumphed winning five of seven matches in just over ninety minutes of play.[8] More details about the style of the game as played on campus later appeared in a school publication called *Students Offering*. The author of the story, writing as "Poor Pen," noted that "there was much running and kicking at the ball, and not a little kicking at air."[9] Fifty years later, a graduate of Carroll described the type of football played at the time as "the old-fashioned open game," and although tripping and pushing were common, there were "no mass formations."[10]

What type of football was played in Waukesha in 1866? The statement by a former student cites a lack of "mass formations," making it clear that it was not intercollegiate football. Despite a lack of information on the match, some researchers have concluded that the contest was the earliest documented game played in the United States using the 1863 association football code.[11] These rules, first drafted in England, formed the basis of the modern sport of soccer. The code had been published for the first time in the United States in 1866, but there is no evidence that anyone associated with Carroll had knowledge of the game.[12] Given the sparse description of the games and Rankin's presence, it seems more likely that the matches played in Waukesha were not soccer, but rather a similar type of kicking game developed at Princeton University.[13] The New Jersey college also participated in another event sometimes claimed as the earliest soccer game in the country—the 1869 contest versus Rutgers. Yet another match, this one featuring a group of Yale students facing off against a squad of alumni from England's Eton school in 1873, has also been suggested for the honors.[14] No concrete evidence proves that any of these games used the association or any other modern football code. Instead, the teams played these matches using traditional rules, or negotiated versions of them, that had developed at educational institutions over the course of the nineteenth century.

While the desire to locate "firsts" is understandable, such efforts reinforce the notion of an unbroken line of upward development from a sport's early varieties to a culmination in its modern equivalent. Historian Tony Collins calls this idea "the football historians' fallacy" and defines it as an overemphasis on the game's rules and a desire to see the past only through the lens of contemporary sports.[15] Long before the emergence in the late nineteenth century of various modern sports, including soccer, rugby, and the gridiron game, people in the United States enjoyed a pastime simply called football. Although the rules of the game differed from place to place, most of them emphasized kicking rather than carrying the ball. By the 1880s, the most prominent and important kicking game in the United States was called association football or soccer. This study examines the origins and development of kicking-centered football games from the earliest versions up to the reemergence of professional soccer after World War I. The book is not a comprehensive survey of the game, focusing instead on key themes and employing case studies to highlight important features of the early history of soccer in the United States. Throughout I use the term "football" to refer to the broad range of kicking and carrying games before the emergence of the modern versions. After the process of codification, I call the games by their more recognizable names (i.e., soccer and rugby) or use identifying qualifiers such as "association football" or "intercollegiate football."[16]

It's impossible to draw a direct line from the various types of early Native and European–North American games to modern soccer.[17] Nevertheless, the roots of the contemporary game lie in this diffuse and undifferentiated collection of activities known collectively as football. Codification is often viewed as the endpoint of traditional games and the beginning of modern ones, but historical actors didn't view the past that way. Instead, the emergence of formalized rules only gradually altered the lived experience of those who took part in football matches. By examining the long history of football both before and after the development of soccer, this book challenges the usual periodization of sport history into premodern (often dubbed primitive) and modern sport.

While the codes were important in motivating changes in the way the game was played, other social and cultural factors also influenced the historical development of kicking games. Such impacts were often driven as much or more by local concerns than by national or international developments. As a result, this book provides detailed examples to explain the significance of the sport for particular communities. Kicking games gave people the means to socialize and interact with those of the same ethnicity or social standing. Football helped groups reinforce communal identities and allowed for masculine sociability. Women used soccer as a way to develop new identities as athletes, initially as spectacle and later as serious players, coaches, and referees.

Formal research on the history of soccer in the United States is scant. Sport historians who focus on the United States have tended to concentrate on more popular pastimes, such as baseball, basketball, and boxing. Researchers who study the history of soccer internationally have had little to say about its origins and development in the United States. Since soccer did not emerge as one of the nation's dominant spectator sports, there seemed little reason to study its early history and development. Several important works have sought to explain why the sport has not been as economically and culturally successful in the United States as in the rest of the world.[18] By focusing on the ways the sport did not develop nationally, however, they minimize the importance of the game to particular cities and regions. In many ways the history of the sport in the United States is less about the development of a successful national league and more about its impact on local communities. Researchers of soccer in the United States have focused mainly on the important task of recovering knowledge of the game's history.[19] This is still a necessary undertaking, made increasingly possible thanks to the digitization of newspapers.

Other historians of US soccer have recognized that the sport's meanings are often to be found on the micro, rather than the macro level of analysis. The work of Roger Allaway explores the significance of the sport in the context of specific places and times. His *Rangers, Rovers, and Spindles* uses a comparative approach to explore the development of football in Fall River, Massachusetts, and Kearny, New Jersey.[20] The number of publications since about 2000 has increased as scholars have begun to explore the history of soccer in particular locales. Studies including Gabe Logan's book on soccer in Chicago, Steven Apostolov's investigation of Massachusetts, and George Kioussis's examination of the US Soccer Federation have produced work that analyzes the sport and its relationship to other aspects of community and global history.[21] The collection of essays titled *Soccer Frontiers: The Global Game in the United States, 1863–1913* includes early histories of soccer in New York, San Francisco, Los Angeles, and elsewhere.[22] Tom McCabe has written on the area around Kearny, New Jersey, while Steve Holroyd and Ed Farnsworth have produced numerous careful studies of Philadelphia's long and rich history with the sport.[23] Other works focus on St. Louis, Cleveland, and Louisiana.[24] Few researchers, with the notable exceptions of Jean Williams and Shawn Ladda, have tackled the early history of the women's game before the passage of Title IX in 1972.[25] The growing interest in soccer in the United States has also led to a veritable explosion of Web posts, podcasts, and other media chronicling the history of the sport.

The origins and history of European football have captured the attention of scholars, but indigenous football in North America has rarely been studied. Only a handful of indigenous accounts of their pastimes survive, and much of the existing literature on the topic was developed in the late nineteenth and early twentieth centuries. Chapter 1 argues that for Native North Americans and First Peoples, football served primarily a social and cultural role in building and sustaining extended communities. Football play generally occurred at moments when social groups larger than extended families gathered together, often to mark the beginning or end of a harvest or hunting season. Although competitive, the game play reflected the celebratory spirit of such occasions when the pressures of survival were temporarily abated. Playing football provided young men and women the opportunity to compete against others, thereby demonstrating their physical prowess and skill. Unlike lacrosse and some other pastimes, football did not appear to have religious or spiritual connotations for most groups.

Football had been played for centuries in Great Britain, and early colonists brought the game with them across the Atlantic. Because of the distinct economic and cultural context of the Americas, the sport assumed different meanings in the English colonies. The most common type of football play was loosely organized contests between groups of young people. Chapter 2 shows that the connection between football and childhood greatly influenced the historical development of the game in the United States. Unlike baseball, which by the 1850s had moved beyond its childish origins, football remained primarily a kid's game throughout the nineteenth century. A rise in the number of schools and colleges meant that young people were soon kicking the ball across campus. Football quickly became associated with educational institutions, consolidating its reputation as a schoolboys' game. From the limited information available about the rules of these matches, many of the schools favored a kicking-centered version of the sport. Nevertheless, the ability to handle, catch, or carry the ball never disappeared entirely, and rugby-style contests grew in popularity following the 1857 publication of the English novel *Tom Brown's School Days*. Eventually, college students at elite institutions in the Northeast sought opportunities to compete against their peers at other schools. After several efforts to produce a code to govern intercollegiate contests, they arrived at a version that emphasized carrying rather than kicking the ball; a game that would eventually develop into gridiron or American football.[26]

Although primarily known as a young person's pastime, adult men outside of the schools also played football. They gathered to compete for a variety of reasons: to relive educational or childhood experiences, to celebrate a particular ethnic identity or to reinforce connections brought on by employment or military service. These types of games often occurred when the usual social strictures on male behavior were loosened, such as during holidays or times of war. Chapter 3 outlines the four major types of football played outside of school settings. Players engage in nostalgia football to recall their schooldays or childhood. Holiday football is a version enjoyed on special occasions or as part of festivals. Military football was first played by soldiers during the Civil War (1861–65). Club football is organized by teams without direct connections to educational institutions. Games from the first three categories are the most common types to be reported during the nineteenth century, while the evidence for contests between clubs is almost nonexistent. A small number of published accounts give us the names of some football teams, but match reports or results are almost never recorded. The widespread development of organized soccer clubs and competitions did not occur in the United States until the 1880s.

After soccer emerged as a popular sport in Great Britain during the final third of the nineteenth century, people leaving those islands once again took the game with them across the ocean. In the United States, the influx of British immigrants combined with economic expansion to fuel the emergence of soccer clubs and competitions in many parts of the country. The process of growing the game did not always go smoothly, however, as many areas faced a variety of hardships. Some of these problems were the result of rivalries and conflict within the soccer community and some of them, such as poor weather, remained beyond their control. The phase of soccer's growth that began in the 1880s lasted until the end of the nineteenth century, when the internal and external challenges combined with broader financial difficulties to trigger a decline in the sport. Eventually soccer returned and even thrived, leading to an often dramatic expansion up to and after World War I. Chapter 4 uses Pittsburgh as an example of these general developments. Despite early problems, by the 1920s the Steel City had one of the most vibrant soccer communities in the United States.

A group of six baseball team owners centered on the East Coast formed the American League of Professional Football (ALPF) in 1894. The ALPF, however was not the only group to try their hand at the sport and a rival league called the American Association of Professional Football (AAPF) began operations at the same time. The AAPF had only four teams—Philadelphia, Trenton, Newark, and Paterson, New Jersey, but it was organized by people with roots in established soccer communities. I argue in chapter 5 that professional soccer emerged in 1894 as team owners sought to maintain their virtual monopoly over professional team sports and viewed the competition as an athletic enterprise that would generate profits outside of the traditional baseball season. The goals of the AAPF remain unclear, as do its links to the American Football Association (AFA). Although its influence was mainly limited to the East Coast, the AFA was the closest thing the country had to a national governing body until the formation of the United States Football Association, now called the United States Soccer Federation, in 1913. In the end, both experiments with professional soccer proved to be equally disastrous, and they shut down after only a few weeks of play. The leagues collapsed for three reasons: poor organization, low attendance, and higher than expected costs. Although from time to time in various regions talk began about the formation of another major professional circuit, none materialized until the American Soccer League began play in 1921.

While most early sources describe only men and boys playing football, women and girls also took part in the sport. Commentary on women's participation generally viewed it as a humorous undertaking or as a sexually suggestive performance. Despite such attitudes, many of the women who played the sport saw it as an opportunity to demonstrate their athletic prowess. This was the case for the players who competed in the earliest documented women's soccer games in the United States. Two matches between the Colleen Bawns and Bonnie Lassies were held in San Francisco in December 1893. Chapter 6 describes the games and profiles of some of the players in order to show how these matches reflected the growth of athletic opportunities for women in the second half of the nineteenth century.

Although the 1893 matches in San Francisco are the first documented soccer games played by women in the United States, they did not have a meaningful influence on the overall development of the sport. Instead, the growth of the game among women in schools and on college campuses had the greatest impact. For many educators, the violence of intercollegiate football made it inappropriate for female bodies, and as a result soccer was promoted as a less dangerous form of the sport. Chapter 7 traces the expansion of soccer playing among women and girls and identifies one of the earliest intercollegiate matches played in 1910. The chapter also uses the story of two pioneers—Doris Clark and Helen Clark—to illustrate two key points about the history of soccer in the United States. First, in addition to the growth of club soccer for men, women also began to play the sport during the first two decades of the twentieth century. Second, women did not just play soccer, they were also administrators, coaches, and referees.

Although the game had been played for decades prior to World War I, the experience of conflict helped launch the golden age of US soccer in the 1920s. How did participation in the war contribute to the growth of soccer in the United States? Chapter 8 uses the story of players Joe Cunat and Maurice Hudson to show how already-existing soccer clubs and leagues, like those in Chicago and San Francisco, laid the foundation for postwar development. Once they enlisted in the military, each had plenty of opportunities to continue playing the game they loved. Cunat and Hudson could do so because the government, in partnership with the

Young Men's Christian Association (YMCA), spent enormous resources encouraging soldiers to both play and watch soccer. Such investments meant that hundreds of thousands of men were, perhaps for the first time, able to watch and participate in soccer matches. After the war, many of these men returned home and contributed to the expansion of competitive soccer across the country.

In 1921, a little-known squad from western Massachusetts called Holyoke Falco Athletic Association Football Club joined the American Soccer League (ASL) for its inaugural season of play. The ASL was the first serious attempt to create a major professional soccer competition after the debacle of 1894. Although the region seemed an unlikely place for a professional sports franchise, I argue that the story of the Falcos reveals three major themes in the history of US soccer in the first two decades of the twentieth century. First, like many regions of the country, western Massachusetts had a long history of soccer playing. In many ways, the professional debut of the Falcos came about because the sport had experienced steady growth, especially in the 1910s. Second, industrial firms such as textile manufacturer Farr Alpaca, the sponsor of the Falcos, played an important role in supporting local soccer communities. Third, although soccer was extremely popular with certain ethnic groups, it often proved unable to expand outside of these enclaves and generally failed to find broader support.

1

INDIGENOUS FOOTBALL IN NORTH AMERICA

In August 1586, an English expedition led by John Davis in search of the Northwest Passage arrived off the west coast of Greenland at Nuup Kangerlua, a place known to English-speaking Europeans as Gilbert's Sound. The sailors encountered indigenous peoples and the resulting interactions were at times friendly and other times threatening. Soon after setting anchor, Davis and his men exchanged gifts with the Greenlanders and organized athletic competitions including the long jump and wrestling.[1] On August 21, Davis reported that a group of 130 local people attacked an English landing party but were driven off by the expedition's light boat. In the same journal entry, he recorded a different form of rough interaction: "divers times they did weave us on shore to play with them at the foot-ball, and some of our company went on shore to play with them, and our men cast them downe as soone as they did come to strike the ball."[2]

The account is noteworthy for two reasons: it is the earliest documented reference to football played in North America; it is also one of the few, if not the only account, featuring Europeans and indigenous peoples playing the sport together.[3] This brief description is all that Davis says about the game. One thing about the manner of play that can be gleaned from his account is that some form of tackling or pushing was allowed. Davis also used the more ambiguous word "strike" rather than the more specific "kick" or "punch" to describe how the players moved the ball. It may be that they both kicked the ball and/or propelled it with the hand or other parts of their bodies. When European explorers began to record their travels in the North Atlantic, they "tended to explain new phenomena through analogous reasoning," as Peter Mancall puts it, meaning that they compared their observations with what they knew from their own cultures. They also often portrayed themselves as smarter and more skilled in playing football.[4] In this case however, the fact that the two groups could and did play together indicates that something similar enough to English football was an established cultural practice for some indigenous groups. Evidence shows that both the Europeans and the Greenlanders had football-playing customs that emerged independent of one another.[5] Undoubtedly these traditions developed different rules, but there was enough commonality in the games to allow the groups to play together.

Contemporary scholars have focused more on European games than on indigenous football. Few indigenous accounts of football survive, and research by non-Natives largely began only in the late nineteenth and early twentieth centuries, well after initial contact with Europeans. European and North American researchers in the nascent field of anthropology investigated the early history of North American football in part because they felt a pressing need to document indigenous cultures they feared were disappearing.[6] Such efforts arguably culminated in 1907 with the publication of Stewart Culin's two-volume *Games of the North American Indians*.[7] Since then, research into the game has lagged behind that of other Native recreations, and Culin's statement that "information concerning the game of football is extremely meager and unsatisfactory" is in many ways just as true today as it was at the end of the nineteenth century.[8]

Culin began work on his study in 1891 and focused on cataloging activities that he divided into games of chance and games of skill.[9] He researched the two volumes by conducting fieldwork and citing the growing body of literature on Native American sport written by anthropologists, only some of whom were academically trained. Culin also relied heavily on thousands of objects held in museums and other collections as well as materials gathered on reservations and settlements. He classified football as a game of skill that involved moving a ball using only the feet. Although he failed to give a more expansive definition, he did differentiate the practice from other games that used either an implement or the hands to propel the ball. Because many North American cultures remain undocumented, it is uncertain how many tribes played football, though the available information suggests that, compared to other activities—especially variants of the sport now known as lacrosse—football was uncommon outside of a few regions.[10] No sources have survived to document that other groups played football. Remnants could have been destroyed along with other indigenous cultural practices, or it may be that football was of insufficient importance to be remembered or documented. The most widespread precontact football playing cultures and the best documented were the Eastern Algonkian, a language family extending from the Canadian Maritime Provinces through New England into Virginia and the Carolinas.[11] The evidence for groups outside this area include a relatively rich account of Washoe football from what is now California; vague references to games played by the Muscogee (Creek), Haudenosaunee (Iroquois) Confederacy, and Iswa (Catawba); and several accounts detailing Inuit and Eskimo cultures in Greenland, Canada, and Alaska.

Since no precontact documentary sources have come to light regarding football, scholars must rely on tribal accounts, a few early descriptions made by European observers and later anthropological studies by nonindigenous peoples generally conducted around the turn of the twentieth century. Such limitations inhibit our ability to reconstruct indigenous football because Native peoples may have explicitly hidden important meanings from outsiders and/or contemporary non-Native witnesses may not have fully understood what they saw.[12] The general lack of source materials also prevents a full understanding of the ways the meanings and functioning of indigenous kicking games varied across different communities within the same language group or nation. Finally, European, or North American observers may have allowed their own notions of football to inform or influence descriptions of Native American recreation.

One way to accurately consider indigenous games would be to incorporate storytelling and oral history since "indigenous understandings of sport do not slot into secularized Western perceptions."[13] Because of my position as a non-Native scholar and because this chapter is meant to offer an overview rather than an exhaustive treatment of indigenous kicking games, I have relied almost exclusively on textual sources. Such an approach however, does not imply that such materials are the only source of authentic knowledge.[14]

Employing "controlled speculation" may make it possible to identify and reconstruct the manner of play and some of the meanings that indigenous peoples assigned to the game of football. Controlled speculation is a research methodology that uses comparisons between similar cultural practices "to develop and support speculative inferences where information is lacking or obscured in the original sources."[15] Such an analysis acknowledges and honors each group's cultural distinctiveness while also providing a broad interpretation of the social significance of football for indigenous North Americans.

When Native North Americans and First Peoples came together in larger social groups, they played football, often at the beginning or end of a harvest or hunting season. The games helped build and sustain social and cultural ties between extended families that had limited interactions during the rest of the year. Although match play could be intense, it was less about violence and more in keeping with the festive nature of the gatherings. For unmarried men and women, football provided an opportunity to publicly demonstrate strength, stamina, and skill.[16] Evidence suggests that some football games played a role in the arrangement and celebration of marriages. The game was also an occasion for gambling, an important pastime for many North American tribes.[17] With important exceptions and unlike lacrosse and some other sports, football did not appear to have overt religious or spiritual connotations for most groups. Nevertheless, it is possible that the source material does not consider football's private or ceremonial meanings, making it difficult to evaluate how connected the game was to the cultural and spiritual values of the community.[18]

EASTERN ALGONKIAN FOOTBALL

Apart from the 1586 encounter recorded by John Davis, the earliest and richest firsthand accounts of Native American football deal with two Algonkian-speaking tribes: the Powhatan and Narragansett. The first description of Powhatan football in what is now the Commonwealth of Virginia describes games likely held sometime in 1609. Undoubtedly such matches also took place in the precontact period, but it is only after the founding and settlement of Jamestown by the English that any documentary record materializes. Two accounts of the Powhatan game survive; although both were written around 1612 they were not published until the nineteenth century. Henry Spelman and William Strachey each penned different but likely related accounts of the sport.

Spelman was born in England in 1595 to a poor family and left home by the age of fourteen.[19] In August 1609 he landed in Virginia as part of an expedition sent to Jamestown to reinforce the beleaguered settlement.[20] Soon after he arrived, the colony's leadership sent Spelman to join the Powhatan as a hostage, and he remained with them until the fall–winter of 1610–11. As a result of these experiences, Spelman learned Powhatan and eventually served as an interpreter.[21] A young man like Spelman probably would have seen and maybe even participated in football matches back in England, where such activities were often held in conjunction with religious or other traditional festivals.[22] Because of his age, Spelman may have been more inclined to record a brief description of the sport, or it may have been that he was more deeply integrated into Powhatan culture than most Europeans. Later authors had financial or literary reasons to highlight cultural similarities between Europeans and Native Americans (see Strachey and Wood below), but the relatively unschooled Spelman had no obvious reason to fabricate such a connection.

Due to his presence in a Powhatan community, Spelman had unprecedented and unique access to tribal customs and soon "developed a sensitive, appreciative understanding of the Patawomeke language and lifeways through daily contacts in a peaceful atmosphere of mutual trust."[23] His knowledge and interactions likely were a factor in his witnessing football being played. Spelman temporarily returned to England in 1611, and at some point in that year or the next wrote an account of his experiences in Virginia. As it appears in the published version released only in the nineteenth century, Spelman's report of football comes at the very end of the book as part of a simple one and a half-page chapter titled "The Pastimes." The entire account consists of only a few lines: "They use beside football play, wch wemen and young boyes doe much play at. The men neuer They make ther Gooles as ours only they neuer fight nor pull one another doune. The men play wt a litel balle lettinge it fall out of ther hand and striketh it wt the tope of his foot, and he that can strike the ball furthest winns that they play for."[24] Even this sparse account yields the information that the Powhatan played two types of football, one by women and young boys and the other by men. He characterized the Powhatan game as relatively nonviolent in comparison to the English version and indicated that players laid stakes on the outcome.

The second source for Powhatan football comes from William Strachey. Born in Essex in 1572 to a family of the minor gentry, Strachey attended the University of Cambridge before establishing himself in London as part of a literary crowd. Despite an inheritance, Strachey aimed to improve his financial situation and soon turned to North America as a place to make his fortune.[25] Like his young contemporary Henry Spelman, Strachey traveled across the Atlantic as part of the 1609 relief mission. His ship however, ran aground on Bermuda in a hurricane, and he spent the next eleven months stranded on the island. After constructing new vessels, the survivors landed in Virginia on May 20, 1610, and arrived at Jamestown a few days later. Because the settlement's previous secretary had died, Strachey was appointed to the post and took up his place within the colony's new leadership council.[26] Ultimately, he returned to England in the fall of 1611, having failed to make a significant amount of money.

His position meant that Strachey spent most of his time at the fort and made only a handful of trips outside. As a result, he had fewer direct interactions with Powhatans than Spelman, although Strachey reportedly conducted interviews with two Native men.[27] In addition, relations between the English colonists and the Powhatan deteriorated after the arrival of the group Spelman was in. According to historian J. Frederick Fausz, the period following the arrival of the relief fleet marked the start of the First Anglo-Powhatan war, 1609–14.[28] As the Native American way of life faced increasing "instability" due to the growing numbers and belligerence of the Europeans, it makes sense that previous cultural practices may have become unsustainable. When Spelman likely witnessed football games in the fall of 1609, it might have been one of the last times such activities could have been practiced without significant alteration. By the summer of 1610, English policy included the sacking of Powhatan villages and the destruction of crops, further upending the traditional rhythms of Native social and cultural life.[29] Since he was part of the English colony's leadership during this period, it seems unlikely that Strachey would have been able to personally witness a football match. Instead, he probably heard from Spelman and possibly others about the game and may have gleaned additional details from his conversations with the two Native men.[30]

Strachey's educational background and the time he spent in London literary circles resulted in a far more polished report than Spelman's. The account is longer, although still sparse, and contains several additional details. Strachey carefully notes a distinction between football and the sport bandy, which required a stick. By doing so he shows that football was a Powhatan sport and not some other activity that needed to be transformed into a familiar pastime for his British readers. The only significant divergence from Spelman's description is that Strachey makes no distinction between games played by men and those of women and children. He notes that only kicking the ball was allowed and that the players took pride in demonstrating "dexterity and swift footmanshippe." Strachey confirms Spelman's description of a less violent game and notes that, unlike in English football, striking the heels of an opponent was considered a dishonorable way to gain an advantage.[31]

The Narragansetts lived in the area that is now the state of Rhode Island. According to Stewart Culin, other surrounding tribes also played a version of football, but sources exist only for the Narragansett game. As was the case with the Powhatan version, just two major early descriptions of Narragansett football have survived. Little is known today about William Wood, the author of *New England's Prospect*, first published in 1634. Based on the writing style, he must have had some education, although it is doubtful he came from a family of much standing. Wood apparently arrived in New England around 1629 and departed by 1633. His text was "promotional literature" designed to entice and perhaps reassure new colonists about the region's possibilities.[32] The book is notable for its descriptions of Native life and culture, although it is unclear just how much interaction the author had with local tribes. Since earlier English accounts of football in North America had not yet been published, it is unlikely that Wood based his version on the works of Spelman and Strachey. He did admit to writing the book in a lively style and deliberately sought out similarities between the new world and the old; describing a football game allowed him to do both.[33]

Wood's account is the longest and most detailed early seventeenth-century account of Native American football anywhere on the continent. In a chapter devoted to Narragansett games, he explains how large groups played football on a smooth stretch of beach and that they also sometimes played in smaller groups on other occasions. Only men took part in the game, while boys played pipes and women sang encouraging songs praising the skill of their partners. The participants wagered large amounts of pelts, wampum, and other items of value on games that could last for days. Wood praised the skill and dexterity of the men, although he assured his English readers that one Englishman could easily defeat ten Native players. He suggested that the action could sometimes be rough and that the men painted their faces in order to make it harder to identify individuals so that any violence would not continue beyond the boundaries of the game. Wood characterized each match as rugged yet full of laughter and playful wrestling. After the game, the whole community gathered for a feast.[34]

The second account of Narragansett football is from Roger Williams's *A Key into the Language of America*, published in 1643. Williams sailed to Massachusetts in 1631, but disputes with the colony's leadership eventually led to his banishment from the community. He settled at Narragansett Bay after receiving permission from the local Native leader or sachem. Williams established himself as a trader and interpreter, because while living in Plymouth he had learned a neighboring dialect that allowed him to communicate effectively in Narragansett. His knowledge of the language gave him the opportunity to develop a familiarity with tribal culture.[35]

By the time Williams left Britain, Wood's *New England's Prospect* was considered "typical reading for prospective immigrants," but it is impossible to know for sure whether or not he had read that book. He claimed, however, that his own book was based on direct experiences and not hearsay or legend, although he deliberately avoided observing ritual ceremonies that he considered to be in service of the devil.[36] Perhaps having previously learned of the activity from Wood or some other source, Williams inquired about it during his interactions with Narragansetts. His account of the game was similar to Wood's but less detailed. He includes the term *pasuckquakohowaûog* in his dictionary and gives the meaning as "they meet to foot-ball." Williams repeated items about the field, players, and gambling on the outcome, while also describing the action as generally good-natured.[37] Although both Wood and Williams call the Narragansett game football, Chief Clearwater writing in the July 1935 edition of the *Narragansett Dawn* newsletter defines *pasuckquakohowaûog* as "they meet to play ball." He notes that the game had changed over time and cited lacrosse as one example of "the games of the great Algonquin nation." It is unclear from that article if Clearwater felt the older Narragansett game was closer to football as described by the English writers or to contemporary ball games including lacrosse.[38]

Sources for the Powhatan and Narragansett games are the earliest and most detailed portraits of football played by members of the Eastern Algonkian language group. Other accounts often describe the games in passing and with little or no detail. Many of them also originate from non-Native sources during the period when European colonization had become relatively established, making it difficult to untangle the original indigenous games from later ones that may have been influenced by foreign traditions. Two descriptions of Lenape (Delaware) football illustrate the challenges posed by these sources. A relatively early mention appears in Daniel Denton's *A Brief Relation of New York*, published in 1690. The author describes his experiences traveling in the region during the seventeenth century and like Williams claims that he wrote only about things he witnessed himself. In his description of Long Island, Denton remarks on the Native people who lived there calling them nonthreatening and generally "serviceable to the English." Denton notes that the population had declined significantly due to the "Hand of God," so that only two small villages remained. After giving details about their diet and housing, he records that the tribe's "Recreations are chiefly Foot-ball and Cards." The passage continues by explaining that individuals often gambled so much on the outcome they were left with nothing but a loincloth although it's unclear if this refers to wagers on football, cards or both.[39] Despite being an early and possibly eyewitness account, the text offers no other details beyond the fact that the group played a sport that Denton called football and may or may not have gambled on the result. Given the population loss and the fact that only two small settlements remained, it is likely that the football matches would not have involved large numbers of participants.

A later and more detailed description of Lenape football indicates that both men and women played the game. Almost one hundred and fifty years after Denton penned his account, Jacob Brunet described football as practiced by the Lenape in northwestern Ohio. His narrative is among the most detailed descriptions of Native football available before the late nineteenth century. Brunet was a lawyer who often traveled from his home in Cincinnati to attend court in distant places, including Detroit. On one of these journeys conducted sometime between 1786 and 1803, he and his companions stopped at a Native American settlement along the Auglaize

River. An elderly chief Brunet calls Bu-kon-ge-ha-las received the party and helped organize a football game "in the true aboriginal style" for the visitors.[40] The men of the tribe were on one team and the women were on the other. Women could both run with and throw the ball, while the men could only use their feet to kick it. The game took place on a field near the town, and two stakes six feet apart were set up at opposite ends as goals. The two sides, each numbering about one hundred players, faced off at the center of the grounds, where the village leader spoke a few words in the local language before throwing the ball into the air to start the game. During match play, men could grab hold of women carrying the ball and twirl them onto the ground in an attempt to dislodge the ball. After some time, a powerful woman grabbed hold of the ball, held off would-be tacklers, and ran through the goal posts to score and win the game. Brunet makes clear that the game was put on expressly for the entertainment of the visitors and that the women were clearly delighted both with winning and for doing so in front of white men.[41] Such details make it difficult to know how much of the game was based on precontact versions and how much developed in response to or through direct contact with European Americans.[42]

In the twentieth century, a member of the Unami tribe of the Delaware nation named Nora Thompson Dean recorded the rules of a traditional football game called *pahsahëman*. The description is similar to Brunet's account but supplies additional details. In 1971 Thompson Dean wrote that the game required a nine-inch-diameter oblong ball made of deerskin and stuffed with hair. She confirms that the teams were divided by gender and that the game began when the ball was thrown into the air at the center of the field. The size of the playing field could vary, but the goals consisted of two posts set six feet apart. Her account includes an additional detail that men who caught the ball in the air were allowed a free kick toward the goal or another male player. Unlike Brunet's version where a single goal won the match, *pahsahëman* had an elder keeping score using twelve sticks and whichever team scored the most goals won the match. Ties were decided by an extra game. Wagering on the result was allowed, but the stakes did not seem to be terribly high. The season for playing the game generally began in March or April and concluded in June.[43]

Early European explorers observed Mi'kmaqs (Micmacs) living in the Canadian Maritime provinces and down into Maine. Unfortunately, there are no descriptions of football from the pre- or early contact period in these regions. The key source for information on the game comes from fieldwork done by Stansbury Hagar in the late nineteenth century and published in 1895.[44] Hagar was a non-Native lawyer who developed an interest in indigenous cultures and conducted studies in Peru, Canada, and several regions of the United States. Like many early ethnologists, he seems to have had little formal training in the newly developing field. As the discipline of anthropology emerged, Native Americans became one of the key subjects of study, although they were generally perceived as "undifferentiated parts of tribal groups and little more than the sum of the inherited patterns of their behaviors." Scholars thus proceeded under the belief that cultural traits described at the moment of study generally captured features that had historically remained essentially unchanged.[45] Hagar followed such a pattern in his article, relying on interviews with two elderly men residing in Nova Scotia to catalog some of the tribe's recreations. The football game called *tooādijik* was played between teams of about a dozen men who tried to kick the ball into goals made of two sticks lashed together slantwise. A player could grab, clutch, and "catch his opponent by the neck" in order to prevent a score. According to Hagar's informants, the game had been even more violent in previous periods.[46]

MUSCOGEE AND ISWA FOOTBALL

The early accounts of Powhatan, Narragansett, and Lenape football are the earliest and in some cases the richest documentary accounts of Native American football. Most other descriptions date from the nineteenth century, with a few scarce mentions coming before that time. Unfortunately, the versions from the 1790s contain little descriptive content, making it difficult to judge the veracity or accuracy of the information presented. William Bartram was a US naturalist who wrote about his travels through the southwestern United States in the late eighteenth century. In his "Their Dress, Feasts and Divertissements" chapter he describes the recreational activities played by Muscogees. He concludes that ball games provided "the most noble and manly exercise" and gives a fairly detailed account of a version of lacrosse that pitted boys and girls from one village against another. Heavy wagering was often a part of the challenge, and Bartram writes that sometimes the stakes included "their whole substance." After this section, he notes that "football is likewise a manly diversion with them" and that feasting and dancing in the village square took place at the end of every game.[47] The Muscogee game shared many of the same characteristics as other indigenous football types, including its links to feasting and other types of celebration. If the cultural context of football was near to the lacrosse-style game practiced by the same people, it would be similar to the Lenape game in that both genders participated and that gambling was an important part of the spectacle. In addition, by indicating that the Muscogee had two distinct ball playing traditions, one similar to lacrosse and the other a version of football, Bartram makes clear that both the tribes and outside observers could distinguish between them.

Given the long history of Muscogee interactions with Europeans, it is difficult to know what if any elements of the game remained from precontact cultural traditions. Another account from around the same time makes clear that by this period some Europeans believed that their sporting traditions had already been adopted by Native American groups. George Henry Loskiel was a Moravian preacher born in Latvia who wrote, before he even traveled to the United States, a history of the church's missionary activities in North America. Loskiel relied on missionaries' letters and journals along with secondary materials to generate his depictions of Native life. In describing Lenapes and Haudenosaunees, he notes that they loved to gamble and that communities often competed with one another in dice games. He also claims that ball games and some other recreational activities had been introduced by the Europeans.[48]

Later, Edward H. Dewey argued that the English translator of Loskiel's original German text substituted "football" for the more ambiguous German word *ballspiel* (ball game) because football was clearly meant. Dewey may have come to that conclusion because Loskiel also describes a version of Haudenosaunee football that he calls *O-tä-dä-jish´-quä-äge*. Teams of six to ten players were chosen by kinship groups called phratries. The ball, roughly the same size as a modern soccer ball, was made of deerskin and the goals or "gates" were set up eighty rods apart in a field whose boundaries were marked with posts. The game play was organized into periods, and overall the sport had "evolve[d] from an antecedent game of soccer." Elements of the sport including the social aspects of the game, and wagering on the outcome reflected common features of other forms of Indigenous football. Dewey also reviews accounts of Native American football including those by Spelman, Wood, Williams, and Bartram and argues that in general the game as played in North America was "not dissimilar to the English rugby."[49] Dewey's account is problematic for several reasons. To begin with, he uses the Iroquois word for lacrosse to describe football.[50] Later in the article he differentiates the two games, and while some of the characteristics of what he calls the Iroquois game reflect elements of Native American football played elsewhere (gambling, goals), several other qualities (the small number of players, the marked field boundaries, periods of play) seem to be taken from European games. The information from Loskiel and Dewey indicates that for the Haudenosaunee at least, the influence of European games has likely obscured knowledge of any authentic Native traditions that may have existed.

Evidence for football among Iswas of the Carolinas comes from a single reference cited in volume 2 of Culin's *Games of the North American Indians*. His information was wholly derived from a letter sent to him by R. E. Dunlop in March 1901. A Presbyterian missionary, Dunlop claimed her information came from "the old Indians" who spoke of "a game played with the foot and a ball" that was not much practiced anymore. She sounded out the word of this game as "wah chip, pú," which Culin then turned into "wachippu."[51]

Washoes from the eastern slope of the Sierra Nevada mountains along the current border of California and Nevada are the only group from the western United States to have a documented football tradition. Epidemics and the encroachment of white settlement beginning in the mid-nineteenth century proved devastating to the Washoes and their culture. As a result, little can be definitively said about the games played in the area before the group attracted the attention of non-Native scholars in the late nineteenth and early twentieth centuries.[52] One of the most important food sources for the tribe was the pine nut and its annual harvesting was a time of celebration that lasted four days. The people gathered to feast, gamble, and play games, including archery contests, running races, and football. Men's football called *palo'yapi* was played by teams representing different kinship groups of five to six players each on a field marked with goals at each end. One team put white paint on their bodies with two straight lines under each eye. The opposing team used the same pattern but with red paint.[53] The object was to be the first side to kick the buckskin ball between the sticks, and scoring a goal meant winning the game. The small number of players despite the gathering of people for an important annual festival likely resulted from the low overall population. In the mid-nineteenth century, numbers had fallen to around nine hundred, and a hundred years later were recorded at between four hundred and one thousand.[54] Another type of football for young men seventeen to eighteen years old was called *palo'yapi teli''liwa palóyap*. In this version, teams of three attempted to score at goals made of two sticks about ten to fifteen feet in height.[55] Despite the lack of early sources, the importance of football among Washoes echoed that of other tribes. It was played between squads composed of "complementary patrilineal" groups as part of an important social and cultural gathering and likely included wagering. The pine nut festival and dance was also a time when marriage contracts would be agreed to before becoming finalized at the following year's festival.[56]

FIRST NATIONS FOOTBALL

The problem of uncovering precontact football among indigenous North Americans becomes especially acute when dealing with the aboriginal peoples of Canada. Establishing an independent footballing tradition in the region is complicated by several factors: the lack of textual and material sources for the precontact period; the early, albeit limited exposure of at least some groups to European-style football games; and the fact that much of the research and recording of indigenous football games occurred during the nineteenth century, when the process of colonization had already begun to influence tradition patterns.

A 1991 essay from *Tumivut*, the cultural magazine of the Nunavik Inuits, reveals the challenges in uncovering the roots of aboriginal football. The essay, titled "Inuit Games" details a number of pastimes by drawing on a variety of source material from different time periods. The oldest-described activity is an 1884 game called *ajuttaq* that involved either kicking or using a leather whip to move the ball. People of all ages and genders played with seal or deerskin sewn into a ball three to seven inches in diameter and stuffed with moss or feathers. Later, "in the times of our grandparents and great-grandparents," groups of people from one village would compete with another in a variety of contests including *ajuttaq*.[57] The article also cites interviews with Inuits conducted in 1984 and 1988 in order to discuss popular recreations. One reports that the groups played "soccer" on the lake ice in the evenings when the moon was bright. Although the article uses the term "soccer," the rules did not include scoring goals; instead a team won the match when the other side gave up and refused to play any longer. The second subject stated that "people played football like the white people play." At games held in early March, the participants often sewed material on the bottom of their boots to help avoid slipping. The players took the contest seriously and practiced beforehand. The contests also involved women singing and the distribution of stored food to both people and dogs.[58]

Anthropologist Franz Boas observed and recorded accounts of Inuit football that are similar to the *ajuttaq* game described in *Tumivut*. He conducted fieldwork on Baffin Island in 1883–84, publishing the results as *The Central Eskimo* in 1888, after he emigrated to the United States from Germany. According to Boas, the people living on the island met nightly to talk, share stories and wager on activities such as dice and cup and ball games. In the summer, the groups played games including one that involved keeping a sealskin ball in the air as long as possible and another where teams of men employed small whips to prevent the other side from getting the ball. Another football-type game called *igdlukitaqtung* had players attempting to keep a ball in the air by kicking first with one foot and then the other.[59] The latter game resembled one also described by Spelman in Virginia. Games such as these likely did not require large numbers of players and so could have been played by relatively small social groups. Although the game play differed somewhat from other versions of football, the Baffin Island contests had a similar social importance. By specifically noting that the *ajuttaq*-like game was for men only, Boas allowed for the possibility that women could and did participate in other forms of the sport. The whip ball game was played at the end of the fall feast designed to protect the people from the spirits of the dead.[60]

Although most studies focused on the eastern part of the arctic region, Edward William Nelson traveled to the other side of the continent near the Bering Strait to report on the footballing activities of local indigenous people. At the end of winter or in early spring, young men and children played football with a leather ball (*ûñ´kak*) five to six inches in diameter and stuffed with deer hair or moss. Goals were marked out, two captains alternated in picking sides, and the ball was thrown into a scrum until one team scored. Nelson also described a type of contest that he called women's football or *ûñ-käl´-û-g'it*. The activity, however was closer to a type of hand ball, where four players standing in a diamond shape used their hands to strike a ball that was slightly larger than the *ûñ´kak* used in the other game.[61]

In general, little evidence suggests that most of the indigenous forms of football played in North America had important religious content. In fact, one of the only recorded direct links between a football-type game and spirituality comes from descriptions of the game as played in Greenland by the people living in what is now the Canadian territory of Nunavut. In 1721 Norwegian missionary Hans Egede traveled to western Greenland, eventually publishing an account of the area and its peoples.[62] Egede includes a detailed account of the local football game, calling it the group's

FIG. 1.1: An eighteenth-century European depiction of football in Greenland. Credit: Hans Egede, *Det gamle Grønlands nye perlustration . . .* (Copenhagen, 1741), 93. (Courtesy of the John Carter Brown Library)

"most popular diversion." He writes that it was played between two teams on a long open space three to four hundred paces long. The match began at the center of the field when the ball was thrown in, and players tried to kick the ball toward "barriers" set up at opposite ends of the field. The game ended when "the most nimble and dexterous" kicker reached the opposing team's barrier first. He also reports that Greenlanders told him they believed that the dead also played football and that such play manifested itself on earth as the Northern Lights.[63]

About two centuries later, Danish anthropologist Knud Rasmussen conducted a series of expeditions in the same region. Rasmussen had been born in Greenland, grew up speaking the indigenous language, and spent much of his career collecting information about the local Inuits and their culture. His investigations expand on the spiritual connection, first recorded by Egede, between football and the Northern Lights. Rasmussen notes that the people believed that after death a person's soul could either travel up toward the dawn or down to the bottom of the sea. Although neither place was unpleasant, those who moved upward toward *Udlormiut* could play football. An untethered soul who played the game became an *arsatoq*, or football player, and to the living people below the game appeared in the sky as the Northern Lights, or *arsarnerit*—"football players."[64] The activity of the souls differed from the "Eskimo's favorite game" in that it used a walrus skull in place of a ball and the goal was to get it stuck in the ground by its tusks.[65] Drawings of people playing football that are included in Rasmussen's volume appear to show both men and women playing football, and Rasmussen interviewed a woman named Takornâq, who confirmed that she was allowed to take part in games with young men.[66]

OUTLINE OF INDIGENOUS FOOTBALL

Reviewing the sources and employing controlled speculation makes it possible to sketch the outlines of what indigenous football in North America might have looked like during the initial stages of European colonization and maybe even before. As with other forms of recreation, different types of football had been played at various points among the tribes. Women, boys, and men practiced versions of the sport, some of them informal games played among small groups at various times of year and others more deliberately organized matches that involved larger numbers of exclusively male players.

Because these last football games drew the attention of observers, we have more information on them than the other contests.[67]

Although North American indigenous groups played football at different times of the year, the choices made reflected larger patterns of tribal life centered on times of plenty involving larger-than-usual gatherings of people. Neither Spelman nor Strachey gives any sense of when Powhatans played football, but one likely time would have been in the fall when the crops had been harvested and other foodstuffs gathered, hunted, or fished.[68] Freed for a time from the labor required to obtain food, people also used the season as a time for ritual and war.[69] A similar period called *keesaqúnnnamun* by Narragansetts fell in late May and early June.[70] For Mi'kmaqs, who relied less on planted crops than the semi-agricultural tribes farther south, the richest time of year came during the spring, which was when they likely played the games.[71] Inuits of Canada and Greenland may have played the games at *aasivitt*—summer hunting camps when people from various communities gathered together. The game was part of a series of social interactions that included exchanging news, knowledge, and stories. The practice of having communities compete with each other may have been a reason why Greenlanders were comfortable inviting John Davis's crew to play with them. Such times were also when disputes could be resolved, so football became part of the general process of reaffirming and strengthening community identities.[72] Procuring resources was a fundamental component of life for most indigenous groups, making it necessary to maintain harmonious social relations because group discord threatened the survival of the whole community.[73]

Periods of communal gathering featured games partly because of shifting settlement patterns and population densities. During certain times of the year, the tribes lived in much smaller communities of family groups; only during bountiful periods did the populations grow to sufficient numbers to support the large games of football described in many of the sources. As the dispersed Mi'kmaq families relocated to coastal areas during the spring, for example, the number of people in each community could rise to around two hundred.[74] The reunion of these kinship bands after living apart for the winter was cause for celebration as well the exchange of information, items, and gifts. They held feasts at which long speeches recounted the tribe's history and genealogy. Some groups felt that success in games led to success in attracting a mate, so larger gatherings also allowed young people the opportunity to meet and perhaps find a spouse.[75] Stansbury Hagar reported to Stewart Culin in a 1907 letter that wedding celebrations lasted four days. The first day featured a dance, and on the second day all the guests participated in a football match.[76] Like other ball games, football undoubtedly played a role in reinforcing gender roles and supporting social and cultural cohesion at such events.[77] The football matches also provided an opportunity for gambling. This wagering was not about monetary gain but rather was embedded in a culture of reciprocity and gift giving.[78] The fact that the games were held during times of plenty meant that even large losses were not irreplaceable and the cultural values of generosity and sharing ensured that nobody became destitute.[79]

The relationship between football and religious ritual is largely undocumented but would not have been unusual. Many other Native American games were associated with religious ceremony, and the line between ritual and sport could be unclear especially for outsiders.[80] An absence from the sources does not mean the game served no ritual purpose, as indigenous peoples often performed sacred actions in private, away from the eyes of European observers.[81] It may also have been the case that nonindigenous peoples simply failed to recognize or record the significance of what they saw. Reneé Fossett confirms such possibilities, noting that "some non-Inuit observers of past events simply could not grasp the logic of what they were told, or comprehend the practicality of what they saw." There is also evidence that some groups may have taken exception to questioning by outsiders and set out to deliberately mislead them.[82] William Wood claimed that the singing and music accompanying Narragansett football were songs boasting of player accomplishments. An alternative explanation is that Wood, who had little meaningful contact with the Native peoples he described, may have been mistaken about the content of the songs. Most other accounts give no indication that the game served a larger purpose or was directly connected to any other cultural practice. In the case of Spelman, there is reason to believe this may be accurate because he had lived among the Powhatan, making it more difficult to keep such activities from him. As a whole, it seems most likely that the purpose of football was more social than anything else, an idea confirmed by the good-natured play of the game itself.[83] It may also be that, as in Europe, games were played at the same time or in conjunction with religious rituals but were not religious in and of themselves. Instead, they may have been part of a broader celebration offering relief from ordinary day-to-day life but were not spiritual actions in the same way as church activities or processions.

All of the accounts indicated that indigenous football was fast and rough but not overly violent, although it must have been a young person's game since many men developed arthritis by the time they entered their thirties. Players likely wore nothing other than simple loincloths, possibly combined with face painting and hair decoration particular to each tribe. Powhatan men had the lean physique of distance runners and stood on average five foot, seven inches—about an inch taller than the typical male Londoner of the time. They cut their hair in a distinctive pattern: shaved on the right side, longer on the left, with a roach along the center of the head.[84] Mi'kmaq footballers applied white to their eyebrows, along with red coloring on the face combined with black or blue lines along the forehead and nose. The hair was worn long but tied into a knot at the back of the head, often with feathers, shell beads, or porcupine quills woven through. They sometimes coated the skin with animal fat as a protection from insects, which when combined with the sweat generated during a match likely helped to prevent opponents from holding or tackling.[85] Washoe players likely wore their hair long, dressed in minimal clothing like other non-Arctic tribes, and employed specific designs of red and white face and body painting.[86] The game was played using a small ball made of deer or moose skin filled with hair or a plant material, such as moss or leaves.[87] This physically taxing game would have required speed, dexterity, and stamina. Although not excessively rough, it featured a great deal of grabbing, pulling, and body contact. Injuries seem likely even if the sources make clear that the players aimed to demonstrate their prowess through slick and skillful play rather than through brute strength or physical domination. Overall, the game was enmeshed in the social and cultural lives of all groups and would have been an important and no doubt enjoyable part of community life.

Like the young men of indigenous groups, European colonists in North America also played football. Although the format may have been different, the pastime often served the same purpose of reaffirming social bonds while taking part in friendly competition.

2

THE SCHOOLBOYS' GAME

Sources for Native American football during the colonial period are scarce but are still more common than records of European settlers playing the game. Although football activity had taken place for centuries in Great Britain, it did not make a perfect transition to European North America. As a result, the sport took on different meanings in colonial society. Off the field, "football" was widely used as a metaphor for a contentious issue or debate, demonstrating basic universal knowledge of how the sport is played— roughly and against an opponent.[1] The game on the field developed as a largely informal one played mostly by young men. Child-rearing manuals published in Great Britain and the United States advertised football as an appropriate pastime for children. Often such texts described the sport as a manly recreation that inculcated boys with appropriate masculine qualities.

The link between football and childhood had important and lasting impacts on the development of the sport in the United States. Football was simple to play, required no elaborate equipment, clothing, or even set rules. It was chaotic, democratic, and could be practiced anywhere there was open space. These qualities mimicked the experience of upper-middle-class white male childhood and youth, a time generally free from the cares and responsibilities of adulthood.[2] Baseball also began as a child's game, and until the nineteenth century the two pastimes held similar positions in US sporting culture. They were played all over the country using a variety of local rules and were given little attention by the press and other observers. When they were written about, it was often in nostalgic terms recounting an idyllic period of childhood. By the 1850s, however, baseball had become ordered, codified, and rationalized, with adult men increasingly playing the sport.[3] Research by baseball historian John Thorn shows that at least five clubs had organized before 1845; by 1856 the number had grown to twelve. Discussions about the formation of a standard set of rules soon began, and the first national convention took place in 1857. Efforts to create a similar structure for football in the United States did not emerge until the 1880s. Baseball also supported organized gambling, an activity Thorn calls "the vital spark" that allowed the sport to overcome social resistance to adult men competing at a children's game. Two teams played for dinner in 1805, and by the 1850s wagering included propositional betting, such as whether or not a certain player would hit a home run.[4] Baseball's organization and quantification was modeled on that of cricket. In contrast to football, the bat and ball sports had codified sets of rules that organized play and specified an exact number of participants. The nature of the sports also highlighted individual contributions, thus allowing statistics to be gathered that then enabled propositional betting. Mob or folk football matches often had larger numbers of players and this, combined with a free-flowing, less regulated style of play, made it more difficult to assess individual contributions. Simply put, football allowed for fewer betting opportunities since in many ways only goal scoring or the final result seemed easily counted.

Baseball eventually required special equipment and playing fields while quickly becoming a mark of social standing. The men who formed the earliest known teams generally graduated from relatively elite schools and enjoyed comfortable white-collar jobs. When the Olympic Club formed in Philadelphia sometime in the 1830s, the team constitution stated that no members could be under the age of twenty-five.[5] Such a rule could be seen as a deliberate effort to distance the organization and the sport from juvenile pastimes. As a result of these developments, baseball emerged as a sport played by men, while football remained a young person's game. It was only in the late nineteenth century that football also came to be seen as an appropriate sport for men. Adults would at times play football, but generally only on special occasions, such as at festivals or during wartime.

These types of contests are discussed in the next chapter. Crucially, the time when football became recognized as a game for adults was also when it began to become more Americanized.

Although likely played on a regular, if not daily, basis by boys across the country, football matches were rarely documented. The lack of publicity and attention from newspapers may have contributed to the game's low reputation relative to baseball.[6] Notice of these games mostly appeared in laws prohibiting play on city streets or in newspapers when some noteworthy accident occurred. The constant need to revisit such regulations indicates the popularity of the sport throughout much of the late eighteenth and early nineteenth centuries. The expansion of educational facilities in the nineteenth century meant that boys took the game with them to schools and colleges. These institutions emerged as the most visible and well-documented sites of football play. The available sources skew our knowledge of the past toward the types of football played at academic institutions, almost exclusively those on the East Coast. The mostly elite, white males attracted media attention, later publishing memoirs and reflections of their school days. As a result, there is little concrete information on the ways that boys and young men played football outside the boundaries of academic institutions. At the same time, we know virtually nothing about when or if people of color played the game.

Youths did sometimes form clubs that may or may not have had direct links to educational institutions. Such is the case with the Oneida Football Club (FC), often called the first football club in the country. The main organizers were students of a private academy in Boston run by Epes Sargent Dixwell, although the team was not an officially sanctioned school club.[7]

During the nineteenth century, different types of football contests emerged at the country's most prestigious colleges, including Harvard, Yale, and Princeton. Ritualized competitions between classes, often scheduled early in the new year, resembled traditional mob football or rush-style games. These games placed few limitations on physical contact or in the ways in which the ball could be moved. The lack of regulation meant that these contests were incredibly violent and allowed for both carrying and kicking the ball. Most schools also played more informal and less chaotic versions of football, but the rules for these games are more difficult to pin down. Running with the ball during informal games seems to have been generally outlawed, although by the 1850s and 1860s Harvard adopted a style of play similar to the game played at Rugby School. The popularity of *Tom Brown's School Days*, with its depiction of football as played at the English public school, might have influenced the development of a carrying game.

Eventually the rough-and-tumble nature of the rush-style version of the game played on college campuses began to attract negative attention from the press. In response, faculty and administrators sought to reform or eliminate the violence associated with the contests. Officials at many schools banned the highest-profile and well-publicized versions of the game on campus. The sport regained popularity in the late 1860s, with students forming clubs and formalizing collegiate rules in the early 1870s. Many of the schools, with the notable exception of Harvard, produced codes that resembled the association rules, although there is no evidence that the students were directly influenced by the English code. A growing desire for intercollegiate competition in the sport eventually led to the development of a common version of football, one that would be called intercollegiate, gridiron, or American. Inspired in part by the rugby code, this new style of football emphasized carrying over kicking the ball. The kicking games developed in US schools such as Princeton, Dartmouth, Trinity, and Yale eventually gave way to the intercollegiate game.

FOOTBALL IN BRITISH AMERICA

In *People of Progress: Sport, Leisure, and Labor in Early Anglo-America*, Nancy Struna begins chapter 4 with a description of a football match played at Rowley, Massachusetts, in the late seventeenth century. Calling it "an unusual event," she acknowledges that "outside of Southern New England, there is no evidence that colonists played football."[8] Struna was right to question the account of European settlers playing football, because the game in Rowley probably never took place. Struna relies on a secondary source for the account, thereby replicating an error made by that previous history. The description of the football game did not come from an English bookseller Struna and her sources called "John Dutton" but rather one named John Dunton.[9] Born in 1659, Dunton published in 1705 an account of his visit to the colonies between February and April 1686. His source for the book was letters he had written to his sister as well as a journal he kept during his stay in North America. His goal was to publish a book of his travels that would attract a wide readership and earn him substantial profit. The fact that Dunton visited the colonies is not in dispute, but his reliability has been questioned, including by the editor of his book, W. H. Whitmore, who wrote in the introduction that "the character of John Dunton is not easily understood except upon the supposition that he was partially insane."[10] In his book, Dunton often copied directly from previous writings, especially those of Roger Williams, making it unlikely the match in Rowley happened. After describing a game of football among colonists, Dunton asks his companion, "Mr. Stewart," about Native American games. The account of indigenous football given by Stewart is nearly identical to Dunton's description of the game at Rowley and in turn was heavily influenced if not directly copied from Williams's description of the Narragansett game *pasuckquakohowaûog*. Indeed, Whitmore drily comments in the notes for this section that "Mr. Stewart, like Dunton's other interlocutors, had a marvelous facility of quoting Williams verbatim."[11]

Struna's mistake, however confirms her larger findings. She argues that the process of relocating across the Atlantic had removed the colonists from the cultural context of traditional British sports. The challenges of colonization meant that settlers could choose which recreational activities to retain and which to discard. Such a pattern remained in place until after 1680, when subsistence conditions improved, colonist populations grew and a more complex system of sports could be imagined. The expansion of recreational activities at the end of the seventeenth century included the revival of English ball games, especially among young people.[12] Evidence showed that European Americans had resumed the practice of playing holiday football. By the early eighteenth century, revelers in Georgia made football part of the activities on festival days such as Christmas, New Year's, and St. George's Day.[13] A few years later, in 1736, a group of Virginians planned to celebrate St. Andrew's Day with horse racing, dancing, football, and other pastimes.[14]

During the American Revolutionary War, soldiers sometimes used such sports as a way to pass the time. Soldier and spy Nathan Hale recorded in his diary that he played football on November 8, 1775, and a friend later reported that Hale enjoyed the game and was quite good at it.[15] Other officers also noted dates and times when they sometimes joined the enlisted men at "ball play," although it is unclear if this referred to football or some other sport.[16] By the end of the eighteenth century, the game had become a common recreation at least in some areas of the new nation. Geographer Jedidiah Morse wrote that across New England a great many pastimes, including football, were "universally practiced in the country."[17]

Along with the growth of recreation came efforts by those in power to assert greater control over the sporting activities of both children and adults.[18] Many officials disliked the crowds that gathered to watch such contests because they felt that games took people away from productive economic activity and had the potential to disrupt existing social hierarchies. In the case of football, authorities enacted rules and regulations designed to outlaw play on the Sabbath and to protect people and property from the damage caused by wayward balls.[19] In Charleston, South Carolina, for example, the penalty for playing football or other "publick sports or Pastimes" on Sunday was a fine of five shillings.[20] Philadelphia went a step further and included football along with cock fighting, bull baiting, and dice on a list of unlawful games.[21] Towns across the colonies also passed regulations specifically banning football in city streets. In 1701, for example, the bylaws of the city of Boston stated that playing or kicking a football in the street was punishable by a fine of one shilling. By 1758 the maximum penalty had been raised to four shillings, and in 1844 the rate was set between fifty cents and two dollars.[22]

That such laws were widespread and that they persisted into the nineteenth century indicate not only how common it was for young men to kick around a football but also how often such play drew the ire of other citizens. By 1818 Hartford, Connecticut, like many other towns, passed an ordinance banning football on "the highways and streets," imposing a fine of one dollar for anyone who violated the law. Perhaps in an acknowledgment that many of the football players were young men, the law specified that parents, guardians, or masters were liable if the violator was a minor or apprentice.[23] Seven years later, the mayor created a new position of street commissioner, whose duties included issuing parking violations, ensuring that the roadways were clear, and enforcing regulations "relative to playing at or with any ball."[24] Although Struna found few court cases showing the impact of the laws, brief newspaper reports indicate that at least by the nineteenth century, municipalities sometimes did enforce them. In Boston, for example, authorities charged John Murphy with fleeing a police officer and fined him one dollar plus costs for "kicking football" on Sunday.[25] A Louisville, Kentucky, court in 1859 imposed a penalty of ten dollars on

Thomas Hayden for the same crime, although with various fees and expenses the total eventually came to almost twenty-three dollars.[26]

The motivation for laws against football in public streets was partly to assert greater control over recreation but also reflected a desire to limit the potential dangers posed by uncontrolled play in public spaces. In some cases, the decision to outlaw football was made in order to preserve social tranquility. In Springfield, Massachusetts, the city banned football games on Court Square in part because they "blemish the Pimlico order of the place."[27] Such measures seemingly did little to remove footballers from public areas, so townspeople wrote to the newspaper to complain about them. An 1859 letter to the *Hartford Courant* warned of the "incalculable danger" posed by the kicking of footballs on city streets. The author claimed to have witnessed two incidents, including one resulting in serious injury, when horses bolted after being frightened by the ball.[28] A few decades later, another correspondent wrote to complain about how groups of youths playing football blocked access to his premises. As if to make matters worse, the young people responded rudely when asked to leave the area.[29] Similar problems arose in New Orleans when some ladies denounced the "rude full-grown boys of sixteen and eighteen years that have adopted Jackson Square as a fit place for a foot ball game." The players jostled women and younger children and damaged plants and flowers.[30]

Newspapers also published stories insinuating that women's complaints about the sport were cause for amusement. Such attitudes reinforced the perception that football was a sport for boys and that the boisterous nature of play was unsuitable for women and girls. The tone of the articles indicated a sort of boys-will-be-boys attitude among the largely male newspaper writers. A story in the *Brooklyn Daily Eagle* reported that the residents of Nantucket Island in Massachusetts tried to ban the sport because a wayward ball had destroyed a young woman's bustle. Unlike the angry letter writers in Hartford, the newspaper sided with the players, exhorting them to "Go it, boys!" The notice also blamed the victim for the incident writing it "Served her right—what business had she to wear a bustle? They are altogether out of fashion."[31] Another account of a clothing related mishap took place in Cincinnati when a woman's silk bonnet was ruined after being struck by "a filthy foot ball."[32] One verse of a humorous poem published in the *San Francisco Chronicle* in 1868 described how at the end of the day South Park was quiet

Save that from yonder jealous guarded basement
Some servant-maid vehement doth complain,
Of wicked youths who, playing near her casement,
Project their footballs through her window pane.[33]

Other incidents resulting in serious injuries or death explain why authorities regulated where and when football could be played. A nine-year-old boy playing football in the street in Taunton, Massachusetts, died after he went to retrieve a ball from underneath a baggage wagon and was run over.[34] In 1857 a Connecticut newspaper reported that Mrs. Van Ness was seriously wounded by broken glass after players accidently kicked a football through her carriage window.[35]

YOUTHFUL FOOTBALL

By the early part of the nineteenth century, child-rearing manuals consistently promoted football as an appropriate game for boys. Many of these texts were originally published in England, but those made in the United States deviated little from the imports. These manuals either explicitly or implicitly reinforced two main ideas about football: moderate exercise was important for children, and football was a game for boys.

The chapbook *Youthful Recreations*, published around 1818, argues that childhood was the best time to "obtain a stock of health" and "prevent bodily weakness and infirmity." The pamphlet claims that "playing at Foot-Ball is a manly exercise, and though not proper for girls, it affords good exercise for boys on a cold day." The author provided no rules for play except that care should be taken not to kick other players' shins. An image titled "Foot Ball" shows three boys, one of whom seems to have just kicked a small ball. Another boy has his arms at his sides, while two more are holding their arms and hands in a manner suggesting they might be preparing to catch the ball.[36] William Clarke's *The Boy's Own Book* from 1829 describes a football game that closely resembled later codes. The game should involve an even number of players per side using a ball made of lightweight material—an inflated bladder enclosed by leather was best. The field should be one hundred yards long, and the object is to kick the ball across your opponent's goal.[37] The book was reprinted many times over the course of the nineteenth century, but the description of football remained unchanged until 1881. The

FIG. 2.1: Young boys playing soccer, circa 1904–8. (Author's collection)

new edition kept the basic description of the game but added an image and a more detailed code that was very similar to the association rules. The text, however reflected the fact that various football codes existed: "the great contention now is whether the players shall be allowed to touch the ball with their hands or not."[38]

Perhaps reflecting its childhood origins, youth football remained an informal game without organized teams or competitions. Writing in 1902, Clarence Deming described the "old-fashioned football game" played at New England schools circa 1855 as "an all-round breezy and 'open' sport." No set field or boundaries existed, and the play was generally improvised. The game encouraged dribbling or "puggling" the ball because running with the ball was forbidden. In many ways the game resembled early versions of English kicking games, as carrying the ball was banned but catching it in order to claim a free kick was allowed. Deming praised the sport as "so well adapted to cold weather, so effective in its culture of muscle, speed, and a wind which made the stripling of those days like a young hound." He dated the demise of traditional football to the 1860s, when more formalized games appeared on college campuses.[39]

Many newspaper reports on youth football lack detail and are similar to a brief story in the *Daily Illinois State Journal*, which simply noted that "scores of young men" played on a prairie south of town.[40] By the middle of the nineteenth century, however, there is evidence that some young people began to form clubs. The lack of information on such groups makes it difficult to make broader generalizations about their activities. As with Oneida FC, some of these sides were organized by school boys but were not sanctioned by educational institutions. The Mount Vernon football club appeared in Baltimore in 1860 with J. S. Lemmon and Joseph L. Toy listed among the officers. Lemmon and Toy had recently been students at the University of Maryland, although it is uncertain if they had graduated by the time the club was formed.[41] Younger boys also participated in clubs outside of Baltimore. In Buffalo, New York, the Quick-Step Foot Ball Club organized on September 29, 1858. The *Buffalo Commercial* reported that the paper was generally "against giving immortality to juvenile Ball Clubs" but relented this time due to the "manly bearing" of the ten-year-old boy who delivered the notice.[42] The *Springfield (MA) Republican* reported in 1860 that the "Maple St. Boys" had organized a team and were actively seeking opponents.[43] At times these activities took on a more formal character, especially when adults became involved. In November 1860 the Hannibal and Atlantic Football Clubs played at Hampton Park in Springfield, Massachusetts. Myron Williams of the Massasoit Base Ball Club served as umpire. The presence of adults and a referee implies a level of organization beyond informal status and indicates that there was an established set of rules that needed to be enforced.[44]

Clubs also appeared at boarding schools, where students played on a somewhat more formal level than was common in urban public spaces. Historian Axel Bundgaard studied elite private schools in the Northeast and determined that students practiced a range of different leisure activities, including football. Evidence from many of these institutions indicates that football was a common pastime as early as the 1810s. Students at Exeter had been playing since at least 1811 and even formed squads based on where they sat in the classroom. By the middle of the nineteenth century, such activity became more organized as the pupils began to emulate sports clubs and college students.[45] Perhaps the most celebrated example of this is the formation of Oneida FC. The boys closely followed the development of cricket clubs and rowing competitions across the city, especially at Harvard.

James D'Wolf Lovett, one of the original Oneidas, later wrote about how they idolized the rowers and how on regatta days "merely to catch a glimpse of them I have squirmed between the legs of a crowd and all but crawled over their heads; but these were state occasions and occurred, alas, like angel's visits."[46] Undoubtedly the young men who formed the club would have been aware of Harvard's annual interclass football game eventually known as Bloody Monday. It is not impossible as Bundgaard suggests that they learned to play football by watching Harvard students.[47] Such imitation had happened before as Oneida FC chose to wear red scarves wrapped around their heads during matches, probably not by coincidence the same color that Harvard crew members wore at the Beacon Cup race in 1858.[48] Indeed, the very name of the football club itself may have been taken from the Harvard boat *Oneida* that had bested rival Yale in the first intercollegiate sporting competition in 1852. Given that the boat "had great renown" at the time and the extent to which the Oneidas followed Harvard crew they could have picked the same name for their football club.[49]

The earliest games played by the boys at Williston Seminary in Easthampton, Massachusetts, included football. Joseph Henry Sawyer, who published a history of the school in 1917, wrote that the sport "had more kicking and running and less wrangling than the game has now. If one party could force the ball across a two-acre lot and get it over the fence, they were not molested with fouls and foul line, and numerous other 'scientific' regulations, which have made this jolly game of our fathers a rough and tumble squabble within a few square yards of turf." Students formed a football club and elected officers in 1860, but there is no record of them playing any games. In the years that followed, the school competed against other institutions, but the game remained uncodified and Sawyer noted it had "few bothersome rules" that were from neither the association nor the intercollegiate code.[50]

Matchups between preparatory and high schools predated intercollegiate football games. The *Boston Herald* reported that students from Woburn High School defeated a team from Warren Academy in December 1857.[51] At times the young men who played football at schools competed against nonstudents often referred to as "town boys." In October 1858, a group of twenty Hartford boys challenged an equal number of Trinity College students to a football match. The notice published in the local newspaper, the *Hartford Courant*, instructed the students to send three men to meet at the

United States Hotel if they accepted the challenge.[52] The rendezvous may have allowed the two sides to agree on a set of rules and perhaps even set stakes on the outcome. Poor weather postponed the match for several weeks until the two sides finally met on South Green on November 9. The rules governing the contest, the earliest original football code published in the United States, appeared in the *Hartford Courant* on November 6, 1858.[53] The rules made no mention of what sort of physical contact was allowed, but the newspaper observed that "a good spirit and courteous tone was preserved, with some unimportant suggestions." The match attracted significant media attention, with between two and three hundred spectators turning out to watch. The teams played three matches—all won by the town boys. Overall the event seemed to be a success, with the only negative being the tendency of onlookers to encroach on the field of play. The newspaper wrote with some irritation that such action "embarrasses the combatants in their manly and invigorating sport."[54] A few days after the game with Trinity, two groups of town boys returned to the field to play another game of football.[55] The town-gown rivalry was scheduled to be renewed a few weeks later, but the match was canceled after the college faculty disapproved.[56] It is unknown what caused such resistance, but it could be the potential roughness of the game or it may have been the fact that it attracted unwanted attention, both problems that would have an impact at other institutions.

CLASS CONTESTS AND INFORMAL GAMES ON COLLEGE CAMPUSES

Football had been played on campuses before the nineteenth century, but the earliest clear evidence of the sport at one of the major elite colleges comes from 1827 at Harvard.[57] What became known as "the Battle of the Delta" is described in an article of the same title about the annual contest between freshmen and sophomores. The match took place on the first day of the new term on an open patch of ground near where Memorial Hall now stands. The description of the game took the form of an epic poem celebrating the battle between the first- and second-year students:

> The Freshman's wrath, to Sophs the direful spring
> Of shins unnumbered bruised, great goddess sing;
> Let fire and music in my song be mated,
> Pure fire and music unsophisticated.[58]

Little is known about the exact rules of such contests, but the main purpose was to drive the ball over the opponents' goal line. It is likely that both kicking and carrying the ball were allowed. Following the start, the game proceeded as a rush-style football game that favored physical force over strategy.[59]

Allusions to classical literature and characters are not surprising, given that Greek and Latin remained important parts of the educational curriculum. Such references undoubtedly appealed to juvenile players, but they also reveal the seriousness with which they took such matches. In 1858 the *New York Clipper* published a long poem called "The Foot-ball Game" on its front page. The work describes a match that took place at Spring Hill College in Mobile, Alabama, and was written by a student named John Augustin. Like Harvard's epic ode, the poem is full of classical imagery, including the names of the two sides: Thebans and Spartans. The game play was similar to other colleges because carrying the ball was allowed and violent collisions were commonplace.[60] A year later the Union Club of Boston played three games against the Aristonican Foot Ball Club.[61] Although there is no indication that these clubs were formed by school boys, they were likely organized, or at least named, by someone with knowledge of classical literature. Aristonicus was one of Alexander the Great's companions who was celebrated for his abilities as a ball player. In fact, some reports indicate that a Greek city state commissioned a statute to celebrate him.[62]

Other schools developed class contest traditions similar to those at Harvard, and by the 1840s clashes between first- and second-year students were commonly held at Yale and Brown. These games appear to have been equally as violent as those taking place in Cambridge. In 1888 a historian of Yale athletics wrote that once a student took control of the ball—carrying was allowed—his teammates formed a wedge around him and the contest devolved into "a question of mere physical strength."[63] An alumnus of Brown characterized the annual matchup between classes at the school as "nothing but a prolonged rush, or series of rushes." These games often included entire classes eventually numbering sixty to seventy-five players on each side.[64]

In addition to battles between classes, students commonly participated in informal matches.[65] While the rules permitted some use of the hands in these games (mainly to make a fair catch or punch the ball) they were essentially kicking and not carrying games. Columbia College students gathered in the "hollow" on the Battery to play "an irregular game," while at Brown "monster mob games" of football took place behind Manning Hall, with nearly half the college taking part. Dartmouth's version of the sport began in the 1820s and lasted into the 1880s.[66] At Yale the class contest seems to have emerged from earlier, more loosely organized activities characterized as "mere kicking of a ball about the Green" and the sport at Princeton during the 1820s was described simply as "old-fashioned football."[67] Little is known about the informal matches played at the schools, but early versions may have been nearly as violent as the class contests. A few months after the epic Battle of the Delta, the *Harvard Register* described students who joined in football matches: "it could tell how many pedal members began the game with white, unspotted skins, but limped off at its conclusion tinged with variegated hues."[68]

At Harvard accounts of football in the period after the Battle of the Delta are rare. There are more descriptions about the sport as it was played in the 1830s and 1840s, but most were written years later. One of these remembrances observed that running with the ball was not an important part of the game. Players arranged themselves as "rushers" who attempted to kick the ball over the opponents' end line and "protectors" who tried to stop them. Hacking and tripping were allowed but "hindering" was not. In general the laws were fluid, with a student who graduated in the 1850s calling football at Harvard "an artless game without elaborate hard and fast rules." Questionnaires sent to students who attended in the 1840s through the 1860s generated "a goodly number of replies." The results of the survey indicated that the objective remained to kick the ball over the end line and that there were no rules banning offside, holding, or tripping. Importantly, the replies were in agreement that carrying the ball was not allowed, although catching it earned the player a free kick.[69]

Yale also had distinct versions of the class contest and regular football. As with the game at Harvard, carrying the ball was permitted during the class game, though, like their great rivals, the faculty ended the practice in 1859. The termination of the class contest combined with a city ban on playing football on the Green led to the virtual abandonment of the pastime. Beginning around 1870, the sport was revived at Yale due to the efforts of a class that enjoyed outdoor sports. A key figure in the process was David S. Schaff, who is sometimes claimed to have studied at Rugby School in England.[70] Although Schaff helped popularize the sport at Yale, he did not attend the English public school but instead was enrolled at a private academy in Germany, where several English students taught him Rugby's version of football. Once at New Haven, Schaff ordered a rugby ball from England, but when it arrived the students initially preferred the traditional round ball. Schaff helped draft Yale's football code and despite his affinity for the sport of rugby the rules included a law declaring that no player shall pick up, throw, or carry the ball.[71]

During the nineteenth century, a football game centered on kicking developed at Princeton. Changes in the social organization of the school along with broader cultural shifts both within the institution and in the larger society made the playing of such a game more acceptable, especially with the faculty and administration. A more positive outlook on athletics began in the 1820s, in part due to the influence of Philip Lindsley. In 1817 the Princeton alumnus and former tutor was appointed vice president of the college. Lindsley urged reform and favored allowing some sports to be played on campus. He argued that the educational experience at Princeton should mirror that of the ancient Greeks and aim to strengthen both the mind and body. Without proper outlets, Lindsley argued that the students' "spare moments were often wasted in lounging, talking, smoking, and sedentary games, if not in dissipation, drinking, and gaming."[72]

Over the next few decades, the administration relaxed its supervision of the students and allowed them more free time. By the 1840s, such changes contributed to the formation of an increasing number of competing student organizations that led to internal divisions and rivalries.[73] By the early 1850s, two literary organizations—the Whig and Cliosophic societies—had entered into an "intense rivalry" for members, honors, and rank. Another factor that may have fueled organized competition was the growing numbers of students at the college: seventy-three young men graduated in 1858, eighty-one in 1860, and the class of 1863 saw the largest in the history of the college: eighty-five.[74] Princeton students had also become involved in a nascent intercollegiate rivalry with Rutgers (the two were only twenty miles apart) as they vied for a revolutionary-era cannon.[75]

The more relaxed atmosphere combined with the growing competition between student groups and neighboring Rutgers helped lay the groundwork for the development of organized athletics. Other measures channeled the energies of the young men into specific sports including cricket, baseball, and football. In 1846 the college banned students from taverns and other exhibition spaces within three miles of campus, and in 1853 the state outlawed bowling places, tennis courts, shuffleboard, faro, cock fighting, and pistol shooting in the same radius.[76] The restrictions cut down on potential recreational pursuits and helped locate allowed activities primarily on campus. In the second half of the 1850s, a rapid growth in organized sports took place; as one student publication put it, "we have long thought that there was too much stress laid upon our mental and moral culture, (perhaps) at the expense of our physical development."[77] In 1853 a book by James Buchanan Henry and Christian Henry Scharf titled *College As It Is* stated that football, handball, and shinny were the most popular campus recreations. Shinny is a game similar to field hockey, and Henry and Scharf noted that players used wooden clubs rather than their feet to move the ball.[78] Students established the college's first athletic organizations, the Nassau Cricket Club and a baseball team, in 1857. Although the cricket club soon vanished due to an inability to field enough players, the baseball squad was reinvigorated in 1858 with the arrival of several first-years who had played with the Star Club of Brooklyn. A year later Princeton constructed a campus gymnasium, furthering the college's support for physical education.[79]

Evidence of early football at Princeton is limited. Researcher Parke H. Davis, however, claimed that around 1820 Princeton students adopted an old English pastime called ballown that involved batting the ball with the hands or fists.[80] It is unclear where the term "ballown" originated, though it may be a derivation of a traditional English pastime called balloon. In their respective surveys of such games, Joseph Strutt and Jehoshaphat Aspin each describe "Wind-Ball or Balloon." The rules involved using the hands, arms, or wooden bracers to strike the ball.[81] Davis also used the term in a quote attributed to Henry Spelman that claimed to describe the Native American version: "Football with us may be with them ballown. As they at tilt, so we at quintain run."[82] Such a description does not appear in Spellman's book detailing his experiences in North America. Davis may have known of Henry and Scharff's account of shinny and so may have changed the terminology in order to link the game more closely with English origins. Historian Tony Collins describes the development of gridiron football as "Anglocentric" and notes that Davis's book "stressed the enduring cultural and sporting ties between the U.S. White Anglo-Saxon Protestant (WASP) middle classes and their British equivalents."[83] As a result, Davis's claims about the origins of Princeton football must be treated with caution. No other early source on football at the school mentions ballown, including works that appeared before Davis published his account in 1911. In his text, Davis traces the history of intercollegiate football back to ancient times. Incorporating a dubious quote from Spelman and linking Princeton's early football to traditional British pastimes (Strutt even claimed that balloon ball had been played by the Romans) gave the intercollegiate game roots that stretched back centuries.[84] Rather than being a contemporary revision of a traditional childhood pastime, gridiron football acquired a patina of history and tradition unrivaled by other sports. The fact that ballown allowed for the use of the hands predicted the emphasis on carrying the ball in intercollegiate football. It also distanced the sport from association football even though the traditional Princeton game was quite similar to the English code. Later in his book Davis explains that, after playing ballown, "the transition to the feet soon ensued and an ingenious set of rules immediately followed, thus placing at Princeton a definitely organized game of football twenty-five years in advance of any other college."[85] It is noteworthy that Davis himself played football while attending the college and that a continued affection for his alma mater may have influenced his eagerness to make such claims.

Detailed accounts of Princeton football begin to appear around the middle of the nineteenth century. Edward Shippen, class of 1845, described a practice where students took up a collection to buy a football composed of a leather cover and beef bladder that would be inflated by an enslaved African American. The field was the space between East and West College, and whoever first kicked it to the wall scored a goal and won the game. Anyone was welcome to join the game, and the sides often numbered in the dozens. Shippen fails to provide many details about the nature of play apart from characterizing it as rough, with players continually dropping out due to injury. Although the game was still loosely organized and remained uncodified, there was "only one inflexible rule—you must not touch the ball with your hands—you must only kick."[86]

Formed in 1857, the first official football club had thirty members by 1863.[87] The rules varied over time, and the authors of a 1901 history of athletics at the college quoted one former student who stressed that the game played in the 1850s was not rugby or association football but rather "football as is football—the genuine *kicking* game, when the ball got the kicks instead of the players, and the ball *must* be *kicked* to the goal instead of being carried there at the risk of somebody's life." Sometimes a match began with the round, rubber ball placed at the center of the field; players would rush up to kick it, while at other times it was thrown into the air to start. There was no set number of participants as long as the teams were roughly even, and at times the squads were divided by classes or alphabetically. The play was described as a free-for-all, featuring violent action and many "barked shins." The teams had little organization or tactics, although there were two preferred methods of advancing the ball: "nursing the ball in open field" and "kicking it long." When competing classes took to the field, they kept score by notching elm trees.[88] Although the game resembled traditional mob-style contests with an emphasis on rushes and rough play, the description of distinct modes of action indicates that kicking rather than carrying predominated. By the end of the 1850s, football was one of the most popular games on campus.[89]

Despite its popularity in the 1850s, the sport "languished" for much of the next decade due to smaller classes and muted rivalries.[90] In 1867 a group of students challenged their colleagues at the Princeton Seminary to a two-legged tie, but only the first match was played, with the college side winning 7–5.[91] The contest may have sparked a resurgence of the game on campus, because by the fall of 1868 there was "much playing" of football, with games held between teams representing different classes, societies, dining clubs and political parties.[92] As competition between different campus groups intensified, Princeton students also reactivated their rivalry with Rutgers. After losing a baseball game to Rutgers in 1868, Princeton students challenged them to a football game. The resulting match played on November 6, 1869, was the first football game played between colleges in the United States.[93] Despite claims by both adherents of the gridiron game and followers of soccer, the rules more closely resembled traditional-style football games than any of the modern codes. Although Princeton acquiesced in all rules conflicts, most notably giving up the notion of allowing free kicks after catching the ball, the game seems to have resembled those played at Princeton for decades.

THE CODIFICATION OF COLLEGIATE FOOTBALL

Even as class contests were banned at many institutions, the evidence suggests that other, less violent football games continued to take place on campus. By the end of the 1860s, the sport had been revived and the elite New England schools began to formalize their individual codes. In the period after 1860, several factors promoted the expansion of athletic opportunities at schools and colleges. One notable influence was the rise of the muscular Christianity movement in Great Britain and in the United States. Initially developed in the 1850s, muscular Christianity aimed to use sport to reinvigorate Christian churches while instilling a kind of vigorous nationalism. For author Charles Kingsley, whose books became one of the most important vehicles for disseminating muscular Christianity, its three basic elements were "athleticism, patriotism, and religion." Such notions proved especially popular in the urban Northeast—the site of Ivy League colleges.[94] The growth of newspapers and magazines and their rising interest in sports also helped disseminate notions of muscular Christianity beyond the upper classes.[95] This was done in a variety of ways, including reviewing or excerpting influential or important books published abroad.

Efforts to reactivate football play on campus or return to a previous, more authentic form of the game were often put in terms of building masculine virtues. The decline of the sport at Yale led one concerned alumnus in 1863 to publish an essay titled "A Plea for Football." The author praised football as a great outdoor activity: "it is unscientific, requires little apparatus, is not exclusive nor expensive, is hearty, uniform, facile, easily begun or let off, and self-sustaining." Football of this type shaped previous generations and "helped to build the manly forms of those days, needing no such grasshopper gymnastics as we spindling moderns have instituted."[96] Thomas Wentworth Higginson, who graduated from Harvard in 1841, characterized the football during his time at school as "a manly, straightforward game, rough and vigorous, but without the unnecessary brutality to which this match-game afterwards descended."[97]

Perhaps the key event in promoting the return of football to schools was the 1857 publication in the United States of Thomas Hughes's *Tom Brown's School Days*, which had already appeared in England. This fictionalized account of life at Rugby School sold over ten thousand copies in the United States by 1859.[98] Thomas Wentworth Higginson penned his influential essay, "Saints, and their Bodies," in the same year that *Tom Brown* appeared in the United States. Higginson approvingly cites the work of authors such as Kingsley and Hughes and argues directly that men should renew their affection for boyhood games, including "the joyous hour of crowded life in football."[99] On Christmas Day 1858, the *New York Clipper* carried a long excerpt from *Tom Brown's School Days* centered on an account of a football match.[100] During his 1870 tour of the United States, Hughes spoke at Harvard; two years later, students formed the first organized football club.[101] Even if Hughes's appearance at the school was not the direct inspiration for students to form a football club, it is likely that the visit was part of a series of developments that made sports more acceptable and more visible at elite colleges. The impact of the book and of Hughes himself may have been a result of Boston's traditional affinity for British culture.[102]

The rebirth of football on Ivy League campuses, along with the codification of these games, fueled students' desire for more intercollegiate competition and encouraged the development of a single unified code. During the early 1870s, college football appeared or was restored at a host of institutions, including Cornell, the University of Pennsylvania, Columbia, Harvard, and Yale.[103] After publishing a school code in 1873, Princeton students extended challenges to Columbia, Yale, and Rutgers. Columbia could not play, and Yale faculty objected that the students would be off campus too long, so the only matchup that took place was with Rutgers.[104] Later that year, representatives of Princeton, Yale, and Rutgers met in New York City to negotiate a common set of rules. The versions of football played at the schools were generally similar, although there were some important differences. The size of the field and the numbers of players varied, as did the distance between the goal posts. Despite the challenges, the students successfully negotiated a new set of rules and established an Intercollegiate Football Association.[105] The new competition did not include Harvard. In a letter declining to meet with the others, Henry K. Grant, captain of Harvard's football team, wrote that he believed that the new code's ban on carrying the ball made any effort at negotiation pointless. Furthermore, he disparaged the game as played at Yale, saying it was all about "brute force, weight, and especially the 'shin' element," while Harvard's "depends on running, dodging, and position playing."[106] Instead of playing against the other Ivy League schools, Harvard faced off against students from McGill University in Montreal. The matches proved influential on the Cambridge boys, who soon adopted a modified version of the rugby code. After a series of failed efforts, Yale and Harvard finally agreed on a set of compromise rules to play each other in 1875. By the next year, all of the major schools

FIG. 2.2: Stereoscope image of the Lawrence University football team, circa 1882–84. (Lawrence University Archives, Lawrence University, Appleton, WI, https://library.artstor.org/asset/25237329)

had agreed to a rugby-style game that ultimately led to the development of intercollegiate gridiron football.[107]

Although intercollegiate rules would soon come to dominate football at educational institutions, some evidence suggests that traditional-style games continued to be played. A stereoscope of a team from Lawrence College in Wisconsin likely taken between 1882 and 1884 shows a group of young men posing with a round ball. Most of the men wear uniforms with a dark shirt and pants, pillbox baseball style caps, and belts adorned with an initial representing the college. The back of the images record the names and positions of the players. Six of the men are listed as "field," one as captain, and the others as advanced goal left, advanced goal right, goal left, and goal right. The man holding the ball is named as the referee, and there is one substitute.[108] The positions listed indicate that eleven players took the field at a time. This, along with the lack of padding or other protective gear as well as the shape of the ball, implies that it was an association football team. The description of the players' roles, however, fits no known formation, including those published a few years later in the 1893 Spalding rule book. Early reports of association football in other parts of the country more clearly correspond to the established 2–3–5 formation. It is hard to know what to make of the images, since, on the one hand, they seem to suggest the sport was soccer, but on the other hand the player roles and details correspond with no known tactic. Perhaps the students played a version of traditional football that, like versions developed elsewhere, resembled the association rules even if they were not directly inspired by them. It could also be the case that the young men were following the association code but developed their own unique formation. Whatever the situation at Lawrence, the formation of the Intercollegiate Football Association and its carrying-style code marked a turning point in the development of youth football. With the establishment of a formal set of rules, the type of football played by the schools ultimately diverged from traditional games. Although football had been and to some extent would remain a young person's game, adults had also played the sport during the nineteenth century and earlier. Such games and the circumstances under which they were played are the subject of the next chapter.

3

MANLY GAMES OF CELEBRATION AND ESCAPE

Throughout the first half of the nineteenth century, football in the United States was an established pastime for children and had also been popular at schools and colleges. In certain circumstances, adult men outside of the schools played the sport, using it as means of confirming social bonds centered on educational experience, occupation, ethnic identity, and military service. Generally, these types of matches fall into four categories, although there was often considerable overlap between them: nostalgia football played as a way of recalling schooldays or childhoods; holiday football, a popular version of mob football generally played on special occasions or as part of ethnic festivals; military football played by soldiers during the Civil War (1861–65); and club football organized by teams outside the schools. Although games from the first three categories were not uncommon, matches between formal established clubs were rare.[1] Some newspaper articles mention the names of football clubs, but almost no documented match reports exist until after the Civil War.[2] In fact, formal organized clubs detached from educational institutions do not begin to form until the 1880s.

Despite the absence of match reports, sources suggest that adult football games of all types became more frequent, or at the very least received more attention from newspapers during the 1850s and 1860s. Therefore, at the same time that some colleges tried to end mob-style football on campus, it appears that the game had begun to grow outside of educational institutions. One reason for this is that the period of the early to mid-nineteenth century saw a change in notions of proper masculinity, at least among middle-class white men in the Northeast and Midwest. As noted in the previous chapter, much of the source material about football during this period comes from this same relatively privileged class. An earlier stress on "communal manhood" switched to an emphasis on the "self-made man," where "ambition, rivalry, and aggression drove the new system of individual interests."[3] For young men who were transitioning between childhood and adulthood, football provided a space to help navigate a process that often invoked confusing emotions. The camaraderie of the playing fields "returned a man to a boys' world in its hedonism, its boisterousness, its frequent cruelty, and competition, and its disdain for polite, "feminine" standards of behavior."[4] Because a young man's return to a comfortable approximation of childhood could only ever be temporary, such matches often occurred at times and among groups where the usual standards of social propriety were suspended or did not apply. This included class reunions, holidays, and the fraternal worlds of the firehouse and military camp.

When rules for these types of matches are known, they generally resembled the loosely organized contests common in educational settings, or they came from England and were especially influenced by the sport as practiced at Rugby School. At a time when baseball was being actively promoted as an authentically American sport, formal football's clear dependence on imported models may have limited its attractiveness.[5] On a structural level, baseball had begun to establish itself before the Civil War and so gained in popularity both during the conflict and after hostilities ended. In the prewar period, football did not develop in the same way, as there was virtually no tradition of adult clubs outside the schools and the process of forming a national organization only began in the 1880s.

NOSTALGIA FOOTBALL

One of the longest running annual football games played by adults illustrates how many alumni saw the activity as a way of reconnecting with old friends (and sometimes old rivals) while fondly recalling their school days. Woodward College was an educational institution founded in Cincinnati, Ohio, by William Woodward in 1831. Originally from Connecticut, Woodward relocated to the Midwest in 1791 and made his fortune in real estate and by marrying his former ward, who had inherited money. Five years after the institution began as a high school in 1831, the trustees obtained a college charter. Between 1836 and 1851, when it shut down, the college enrolled 1,377 pupils, although most did not complete a formal course of study.[6] A few years after its closure, Woodward alumni organized a reunion and formed an association open to any student who had attended either the high school or the college. The first meeting of the group occurred on September 27, 1855, with a football game part of the events. Over one hundred men of all ages participated in the match on an unused field near an Orphan Asylum. As with most versions of youth football, the rules of the game were not stated but it seemed to allow both kicking and carrying the ball. The description of that first match recounts how a clergyman caught the ball before kicking it away and that the first of twenty games ended when the "the ball at last [was] carried home."[7] Despite the fact that the men were adults with established positions in society and business, the game nevertheless resulted in ripped clothes, a nosebleed, and plenty of players falling to the ground.

This first meeting of the Woodward association sparked a long-running tradition that brought former students back to Cincinnati annually for at least the next several decades. Each year's activities included speeches and a banquet, but the first day always began with a football game except on a few occasions when war or inclement weather forced its cancellation. In the Woodward case, the adult men played football games as a form of nostalgia for their school days. Often the speeches and other activities included fond reminiscences of former teachers and classmates; other pastimes included mumblety-peg and shinny.[8] Despite its regularity, the annual game remained an informal contest, played by adults as a way of recalling and re-creating their childhood experiences. No record survives of attempts to formalize the rules or to organize into anything but rough sides. It was in some sense an extension of youth football played into adulthood, and did not indicate an increased level of organization.

Although the football games played by the Woodward alumni were well planned and continued over the course of many years, most types of nostalgia football were less frequent and even more informally organized. In 1855, for example, graduates from Fall River High School in Massachusetts used the

Thanksgiving holiday as an opportunity to rekindle their rivalry with New Bedford. Around forty past and present Fall River students challenged an equal number from New Bedford to a holiday football match.[9] A similar occurrence took place in Amherst, Massachusetts, in August 1857. Twenty students of the Mount Pleasant school returned to town in order "to shake hands again upon the spot of their boyish studies and boyish sports." Much to the amusement of current students at the school, the "Old Fellows" took part in a football match.[10]

Football games could also develop spontaneously, and sometimes these matches implicitly or explicitly harked back to childhood when the men had fewer cares or responsibilities. In October 1857, levee workers in New Orleans began a game despite lacking a clear playing field. The *New Orleans Daily Delta* reported that even though some players walked away with bumps and bruises, "it brought back, no doubt, to many their boyhood's days, when free from care and school, they sent the foot-ball flying o'er the campus, and whiled away the hours 'till evening's shades stopped the play." The article concluded on a melancholy note by observing that the adult men themselves were now like the footballs of their youth—buffeted about by an uncaring world.[11] The notion that the childhood sport of football could provide a temporary respite from adult responsibilities, especially the need for work, can also be seen in Indiana. In October 1859, groups of "citizens" in Indianapolis quit work at 2:00 p.m. in order to play a game of football.[12]

HOLIDAY FOOTBALL

Perhaps because holidays often meant a break from labor, they were also a time when men gathered to play football. Often such activities were very public and involved large numbers of players. On Thanksgiving Day 1853, for example, "hundreds" of men and boys engaged in football play on Boston Common.[13] At other times, the holiday game was a much smaller and more intimate affair. Such matches are generally only known to us when mention of them emerges as part of a larger story unrelated to sports. As a result, it is impossible to know how often such games were played or what rules they followed. One example from 1855 surfaced only because of newspaper stories reporting on the murder of William Sumner in Boston. The victim met two "candy-Shop Coquets" at a teahouse and was convinced to follow them home. Once there, two men accused him of improper advances toward the women and savagely beat him. Summer later died as a result of his wounds. Testimony from family members during an inquest into the crime revealed that, despite his injuries from the assault, he had played football on Thanksgiving with family members.[14]

A detailed examination of an 1848 match played in Chelsea, Massachusetts, shows that, in addition to its connections with holiday festivities, football also performed a role in the masculine culture of the time. Fire Company Four, based in Chelsea and nicknamed the Hamiltons, played a Thanksgiving Day football game in Winnisimmet Square. The original newspaper report on the match shows that it was a one-off contest for this particular occasion; it does not indicate how many players took part or what type of rules may have been involved.[15] Like firemen in other large cities during this period, the men of Company Four socialized together and had a sometimes contentious rivalry with other local fire companies.[16] These companies became bastions of a certain type of brash masculinity and "formality and restraint, which grew increasingly important as markers of status among urban Americans of the emerging middle class, were anathema to firemen." Physicality, rowdiness, and a resistance to evangelical Christian norms also emerged as important to firehouse culture.[17]

Understanding the broader context of the 1848 football game allows us to better gauge its significance. In the absence of hard evidence, I surmise that on Thanksgiving the members of Fire Company Four had a holiday feast that included drinking. In keeping with the established tradition of having a football match, the men decided to play in the town square. Given the nature of fire culture, the play may have been especially boisterous and/ or physical, which the newspaper described as "fast and furious." Eventually the constable arrived, ordered them to stop, and attempted to grab a boy holding the football—at the time, it was common for boys to socialize at the firehouse and to tag along with the men.[18] At that point, a member of the Hamiltons seized the ball and "gave it a mooner" while exclaiming "Alone, and on my own responsibility, I set this ball in motion."[19] As the action continued unabated, the constable left the scene to report the men to the city selectmen for prosecution. During the course of the game, other members of the community—including deacons from neighboring churches as well as other pious citizens, referred to as "saints" in the original article—walked through the square. Given the belligerent male culture and anti-Christian sentiment associated with firemen, it seems they began to throw the ball at the interlopers' feet and shout derisively that they would be fined by the constable for kicking the ball away.

The masculine world of the firehouse also collided with the raucous football games of students one Saturday afternoon in 1841. On the day, various companies of New Haven's fire department turned out for inspection and review. During the event, the companies showcased their ability to pump water and "exhibited their various powers by playing upon several of our tallest buildings." In order to reach the heights of Centre Church, they wanted to snake their hoses across the green, where "the young gentlemen of Yale college" were "engaged in the exercise of kicking a foot-ball." The students resisted attempts by the firemen to cross the yard, and even refused the requests of both municipal and college officials, who ordered them to stand down. After tensions escalated, only the efforts of town officers prevented the irate firemen from attacking the students. In anticipation of further trouble, the department posted guards at the firehouse to prevent damage to the equipment. Just past midnight, and after the watchmen had retired, a group of students rushed the firehouse with axes, severely damaging the engine and destroying two hundred feet of hose.[20] A town magistrate fined one student twenty dollars, along with additional fees of eighty dollars—likely restitution for the firemen's damaged equipment.[21] The story reflects typical town-gown hostility but also suggests the tensions that could develop between two groups engaging in very public displays of rough masculinity: the students playing at football, and the firemen demonstrating their physical prowess at the water-pumping engine. It also showcased two areas where conceptions of manly behavior encouraged the display of raucous emotion and violence: the firehouse and the campus football field.

Holidays gave men an opportunity to revisit youthful recreations while also indulging in friendly rivalry with men from other schools or workplaces. Such events could also be a means of socializing with those of similar social standing. In 1859, the printers of the *New Bedford (MA) Mercury* newspaper challenged those of the *Standard* to a best-of-three-out-of-five football contest, with the losing team providing the Thanksgiving feast.[22] The *New York Clipper* published stories about Christmas Day football games organized in several states. A group of twelve men from the neighboring New Jersey towns of Elizabethtown and Rahway had arranged to play football during the holiday season of 1857. Since the notice was published

FIG. 3.1: Contests between married and single men, sometimes dubbed Benedicts vs. Bishops, could be considered a form of holiday football. Such match-ups also took place in other sports, including tug-of-war, baseball, and cricket. (Author's collection)

after the game was scheduled to take place, it is possible the match never was played. In any case, there is no other detailed information about the event. During that same year, the Kensington Foot Ball Club of Philadelphia played what appeared to be two inter-squad games, each lasting three hours. Teams of eight men each met on December 25, 1858, in Richmond, Virginia, and although the headline called it football, the final score was given as 21 innings to 19.[23]

Other informal games took place on special occasions, such as outings sponsored by ethnic associations. In these cases, football was a part of the celebratory experience, a break from everyday life, and did not represent any sort of formal sporting organization. The list of recreational activities scheduled for a German Volksfest held in New Orleans in May 1858 included "foot balls." An advertisement for the festivities invited all to participate and noted that some of the sporting events offered prizes.[24] Another newspaper described the scene that took place on May 16, including a parade featuring authentic German costumes as well as "a portly Saxon, astride a beer barrel, representing, as best he could, the god of the beer drinkers." Although primarily a German cultural festival, the event attracted a large crowd and "the grounds swarmed with jovial life, and the flying horses, the dance, gymnastic exercises and sports of almost all descriptions became separate centres of attractions."[25] With no surviving description of the match play, the nature of the contest and its rules remain unknown.[26]

Various ethnic groups in other regions of the country also sponsored athletic festivals that included football. The Boston Scottish Club held annual games featuring a variety of sports, both traditional and modern: tossing the caber, shinty, and wheelbarrow races. The activities also included football matches played for prizes. Results for 1861 indicated that a team captained by Juo. C. Gibson took the prize. Two years later, the British consul donated a medal valued at ten dollars to be awarded to the winning team. In the end, Chief Kerr's team defeated former Chief Ross's side to capture the prize.[27] Although it was not generated by a formal ethnic society, a December 30, 1854, notice in the *New York Clipper* invited the general public and "especially Englishmen from Lancashire" to play "some good old Lancashire sport" including five-a-side football matches.[28] Such an event displayed elements of nostalgia, childhood, and holiday football.

In addition to matches played on holiday excursions, football could also be part of a series of events designed to make money. Profit-driven matches in the United States were more closely related to the types of games put on by ethnic associations than they were to more organized developments in England that may have showed early indications of commercialization.[29] Instead of being celebrations of community and heritage, however, the games promoted by entrepreneurs were designed as commercial entertainments that city dwellers could attend as spectators or compete to win prizes.

An early example was the opening of the Cricket and Archery Grounds in East Boston in 1843. Beginning in September of that year, George H. Andrews and John Sheridan began advertising that they had recently leased the grounds and would be holding a three-day athletic festival to celebrate the facility's inauguration. According to the *Boston Evening Transcript*, the location had previously been a racecourse and was centrally located near the Maverick House tavern. Despite being situated near a drinking establishment, there is no indication that the owners of the pub were involved in organizing or sponsoring the football game or other activities, something that occurred with small-scale games in England.[30] Instead, the driving force was likely Sheridan, who was an athletics instructor, proprietor of the Boston Gymnasium, and later operator of a "pistol gallery."[31] The scheduled events included a variety of games and recreations, such as cricket, archery, running, wrestling, and football. Admission to the athletic festival was twenty-five cents for adults (half price for youths), and prizes were awarded to the victors. The final event listed on each day's schedule was a football match between teams of twelve men each.[32] While football appeared on the list, it was not the main focus of the event but rather part of a diverse program featuring a range of different competitions.

Only one account described results and only for the first of the three days of competition. Published in the *Boston Evening Transcript* on October 20, it noted that a large crowd attended the previous day's events and that Mr. Dearing's party won the football match. Neither the nature of the match nor notice of the sides involved appears in the article.[33] Since anyone could apply to compete in the event and because the report called the winning squad a "party," this was likely a temporary association, perhaps a group of friends or maybe random players led or organized by Dearing.

The original advertisements called for three small-sided football games to be played, but only one actually took place and there is no information about the rules or scoring. What is clear is that a subsequent advertisement for the second day of the three-day festival in 1843 contained an important change in the description of the football match. Instead of a contest between two teams of twelve men, the game was now listed as "a general Football Match in which all persons can join; two Footballs on the ground."[34] This change could indicate that there was not enough interest in having a small-sided game, so people instead preferred a more traditional mob-type contest. The lone match report of the event from October 20 noted the festival "gave universal satisfaction, and went off with spirit" but suggested the proprietors needed to do a better job of managing the crowd to allow for better viewing of the various competitions.[35] Such reports support the notion that the large crowds in attendance made a mob-style football match preferable to small-sided games. A few weeks later, an advertisement for another set of activities planned for November 2, 1843, included notice that "a general Football Match" would be played, making no mention of the number of players or offering any prize.[36]

The following year, the promoters once again placed advertisements in the newspaper for athletic competitions in East Boston, but only once did they mention football. The program was for an Independence Day celebration and listed a variety of entertainments including a foxhunt, greased pole climb, pigeon shooting, and football. The paper offered no other information and no description of the event as it took place exists. The ad indicates only that some type of football was scheduled to be played and that its status as a pastime was on a par with activities such as catching the pig. Instead of football, the marquee event of the day was a foot race with a $500 prize. None of the other events held at the Cricket and Archery Grounds in 1844 or 1845 included any further mentions of football, and instead the sponsors seem to have shifted to organizing less participatory events.[37]

Another commercial venture reveals the ways that youth, holiday, and military football could be combined into a single spectacle. In August 1863, the *Buffalo Commercial* newspaper ran advertisements for "the Great Festival of the Flower Queen." The ad copy promised that "500 young ladies and gents" would be participating in "the Sports of Olden Times." The first day of the event would feature a football game in which ten young men would compete for the prize of a football valued at four dollars.[38] A voice coach and music teacher named George C. Rexford promoted the event.[39] The festival was named for "The Flower Queen," a popular song in the 1850s and 1860s, and Rexford mounted several productions of the event in Buffalo with each more extravagant than the last. The first notice of performance appearing in June 1856 promised that "one hundred young ladies and misses" would assist in the show. A year later the event featured only eighty singers, though this time they also had appropriate costumes, stage tableaux, and other decorations. Finally, the festival of 1863 stretched over three days and included a number of different events along with the performance of the celebrated cantata. Now over five hundred young men and women would take part and the entire festival was subtitled "The Sports of Olden Times." Along with the football match, the activities included many of those present at the East Boston Cricket and Archery Grounds as well as Civil War army camp holiday celebrations: climbing the greased pole, catching the pig, sack races, and shooting contests (bow and arrows for the young people, firearms for the soldiers.)[40]

MILITARY FOOTBALL

Accounts from the Civil War provide some of the earliest and most plentiful depictions of football outside of the schools. These contests had features that resembled the mob-style games played in the schools and often took place on holidays. The federal government felt the sport was beneficial for both the men's bodies and their minds. In outlining the best ways to protect the health and morale of its soldiers, the US Sanitary Commission wrote that "when practical, amusements, sports, and gymnastic exercise should be favored amongst the men" and named football as one possible recreation.[41] Near the end of the first year of war, a survey of army units reported that 42 regiments practiced "systematic athletic recreations" including football while 156 did not.[42] During the preparations for operations, the military at times made special efforts to provide soldiers with the opportunity to play football. When US forces set out to capture Port Royal Sound, South Carolina, one of the conflict's first large-scale assaults, newspaper reports stated that "several hundred foot-balls for the amusement of the troops" were among the supplies.[43] Reports from other units throughout the war years confirm that troops originating in different parts of the country, including the southern states, played football.[44] Given that these were informal games, it seems likely that these contests had few if any specific rules, with the size of the playing field and even goals dictated by local conditions. Military football—as with other events, such as the games held in East Boston

FIG. 3.2: Members of New York's Thirteenth Heavy Artillery Division posing with a football, somewhere near Petersburg, Virginia, circa 1864. (Library of Congress, Prints and Photographs Division, Civil War Photographs, LC-DIG-cwpb-01820)

in 1843—was often part of a general program of activities that could be played by large numbers of people, especially during holiday celebrations. In his history of the Vermont Tenth Regiment, for example, E. M. Haynes describes a scene from the unit's Thanksgiving Day activities. The day began with "a grand game of foot-ball" followed by running races, pistol shooting contests, and the release of a greased pig.[45]

The textual sources on football during the fighting are not the only way of understanding how the game was played during the Civil War. Three images taken between May 1864 and April 1865 outside Petersburg, Virginia, may represent some of the earliest known photographs of people playing football anywhere in the world. The negatives were used to create a stereographic card titled "Camp Sports, 13th N.Y. Artillery Playing Ball, before Petersburgh, Va." that appeared as part of a series called "War Views." The cards were published by E. and H. T. Anthony and Company of New York City from images produced by Brady and Co. of Washington, DC. The name of the individual who took the images is unknown, but the company was founded by well-known Civil War photographer Matthew Brady. The negatives show a member of New York's Thirteenth Heavy Artillery Regiment preparing to kick a slightly deflated football held by a comrade (fig. 3.2).[46] The unit organized in 1863, two years after the start of the Civil War and served in a variety of operations across North Carolina and Virginia. By May 1864, Companies A and H found themselves camped outside of Petersburg, Virginia, a major port and key supply center for the Confederate capital at Richmond.[47] Commonly known as the Siege of Petersburg, the action was part of a broader campaign aimed at isolating Richmond while forcing General Robert E. Lee into an open confrontation with US forces. Ultimately it degenerated into nine months of grinding trench warfare, presaging the destructive campaigns of World War I. During the long siege, the New Yorkers, like many other soldiers serving in different campaigns, had a fair amount of free time once they had completed their duties and drilling. One of the activities they used to pass the time was football. Due to the technical limitations of Civil War–era photography, however, the image does not show much in the way of action, but instead captures one man kneeling to hold a football while another moves to kick it.

Popular newspapers the *New York Illustrated News* and *Harper's Weekly* published three prints depicting football games during and shortly after the war. The photographs and prints confirm that soldiers could and did

FIG. 3.3: Detail of fig. 3.2 showing a soldier about to kick a football. (Library of Congress, Prints and Photographs Division, Civil War Photographs, LC-DIG-cwpb-01820)

play football especially during holidays such as Thanksgiving, Christmas, and Independence Day. The pictures also show at least two distinct types of football games: a direct competition between two teams, and a mob style, free-for-all that appeared to have little in the way of organization. The visual and textual sources also record that violence, including life-threatening injuries was often a part of the game.

The earliest published image of military football appeared in *Harper's Weekly* on August 31, 1861, and shows Confederate soldiers of the First Maryland Regiment engaged in a game.[48] The print depicts the main part of a camp in the background, with shrubs, brush, and sections of fence forming a half circle in the foreground. In the oval space at the center of the picture two groups of men appear facing each other. The total number of figures is around eighty, but the men are not evenly distributed between the sides. A figure stands between the two groups, his leg raised as though having just kicked the airborne ball a short distance away. The artist may have captured the very start of the game, since the two sides have not yet made contact. The team kicking off is rushing forward, while some of the receiving side stand ready to meet them and others run toward the ball. The print is the only Civil War football image to show two distinct sides, although there are no obvious features to distinguish one team from another except their positioning. No goals or boundary lines to the playing area can be seen other than the camp tents at the rear and the material boundary of the foreground.

CAMP JOHNSON, NEAR WINCHESTER, VIRGINIA—THE FIRST MARYLAND REGIMENT PLAYING FOOT-BALL BEFORE EVENING PARADE.

FIG. 3.4: Descriptions of Confederate soldiers paying football are not as common as those of U.S. troops. This image shows a football match played by members of the First Maryland Regiment. Credit: *Harper's Weekly* 5, no. 244 (August 31, 1861): 557. (Courtesy of the Lincoln Financial Foundation Collection)

The title indicates that the game took place after parade, an event that usually concluded in the late afternoon.[49] The image likely illustrates the type of football played on a regular basis in military encampments. Although seemingly organized into two teams, the large number of participants and the lack of obvious goals makes it likely that the play resembled the class contests that took place at colleges. How such matches differed from the more generalized mob-style football games is difficult to fully determine given the lack of detailed sources on the modes of play.

Artist and illustrator Alfred Waud's sketch of a football match became a print published in the *New York Illustrated News* on January 11, 1862. Waud's title makes clear that the football match took place on a special occasion "Holiday in the camp of the 23rd Penn[sylvania]. Vol[unteers] near Bladensburg [Maryland]." The image captures a number of different pastimes, all appearing to take place simultaneously, including chasing a shaved and greased pig, climbing a smooth pole, and playing football. The group of men playing football is much smaller than the crowd chasing after the pig. Waud captures one person at the moment of kicking the ball in front of a group of about a dozen men. Three people stand a distance from the kicker, but it's unclear whether they are taking part in the game or just spectators. In the foreground of the drawing, Waud placed groups of figures watching the events, including soldiers in uniform and women in long dresses. For the version printed in the newspaper, the printmaker has split the original drawing into two distinct images while adding more men to the group playing football.[50]

The final Civil War print depicting the sport appeared a few months after the conclusion of hostilities and is titled "Holiday in camp—soldiers playing 'foot-ball'" (fig. 3.5). The print was based on a drawing by Winslow Homer and likely depicts activities that took place on the Fourth of July holiday.[51] The image shows two distinct football games: the first takes up the majority of the frame and shows a large group of soldiers engaged in what looks more like a fight than a football match; the second game is visible along the upper edge of the picture as a sketch featuring three tiny figures chasing a large ball. The football used in the foreground match appears just off center, although its round form is nearly hidden within the tangled masses of the soldiers. The man nearest the ball is bent slightly at the waist with his arms flung out at the elbows. He does not appear to be making any move to catch the ball, but his right arm could be in a position to punch it clear. Just behind the man nearest the ball, two soldiers have squared up to one another using the stance typical of boxers of the era. Next to them, another pair have their fists raised above the crowd, although it's impossible to tell if it is simply exuberance or if they are preparing to throw a punch. Directly in front of the boxers, a man has thrust out his leg in an attempt to kick the ball while another figure just behind him grabs hold of his shoulder. Although it looks as though the man is trying to reach out toward the ball, his boot is actually closer to the head of a man who has fallen to the ground at the bottom of the frame. Nearby, another soldier is in the process of joining him in the dirt even as he clutches the shoulder of the man next to him in an effort to remain on his feet. The falling man wears the billowy pants and tasseled hat characteristic of a Zouave unit, as does a second man farther back in the crowd.

Three figures in the group have a Maltese cross used as the badge of the V Corps of the Army of the Potomac on their kepis. Another man stands

FIG. 3.5: Winslow Homer's depiction of camp football. The game likely took place as part of Fourth of July celebrations in 1865. Credit: *Harper's Weekly* 9, no. 446 (July 15, 1865): 444. (Courtesy of the Lincoln Financial Foundation Collection)

near the ball, although his attention is focused elsewhere as his fist slams into the face of the soldier next to him. Several nearby figures rush toward the ball, passing by a soldier standing with his mouth open in pain as he clutches his leg. Such a depiction recalls the barked shins often described as a characteristic feature of early football matches, especially as practiced in the schools and colleges. Behind these figures, the crowd recedes nearly to the top of the frame, becoming a dark mass of indistinguishable heads, bodies, and roiling dust. Overall, the impression is one of uncontrolled violence, with no indication of teams or tactics.

The intense physical nature of Homer's print shows that, like many mob-style versions of the sport, military football could and did devolve into actual violence. Early in the war, several newspapers reported an incident that took place between men from Rhode Island. While training at Camp Stevens in Massachusetts, a group of soldiers "were kicking football with some citizens, [when] an altercation commenced between them." After Lieutenant George H. Tabor and the post commander rushed to stop the melee, one of the soldiers knocked Tabor down and stomped on his head, breaking his cheekbone. Soon other members of the unit rushed to grab the offender and his friends. After he came to the officer's aid, nineteen-year-old drummer James Simmons was stabbed in the abdomen and died of his wounds a few days later.[52] From the newspaper reports, it seems that the most seriously wounded men, Tabor and Simmons, were not originally part of the group involved in kicking the football. As a result, Simmons's murder only indirectly resulted from the football match, but the incident still shows that such games could become quite heated, sometimes turning into brawls.

CLUB FOOTBALL

While informal or ad hoc matches occurred with some frequency, formal organized football games played between clubs were rare. As the sporting press grew during the 1850s, coverage of football expanded, although it received considerably less attention than other pastimes. Efforts by the *New York Clipper*, one of the country's leading sporting publications, to encourage the growth of the sport reveal the limited spread of football outside youth games, the schools, and the informal matches described above. English publications such as *Bell's Life in London* had long been popular in the United States, and soon native sporting periodicals began to appear, including the *Spirit of the Times* founded in New York City by William Trotter Porter in 1831. Initially, coverage of sports featured horse racing and cricket, but stories on baseball and prizefighting became increasingly common. George Wilkes began publishing the *Police Gazette* in 1845 and in 1856 purchased the *Spirit of the Times*.[53] Despite a growing interest in a wide variety of pastimes, Wilkes's publications made virtually no mention of football until after the Civil War.

Harrison Trent Fulton published the first edition of the *New York Clipper* in 1853. Although the editor, Philadelphia-born Francis "Frank" Queen, had little formal education, he had previously worked in the newspaper business and eventually purchased ownership of the paper in 1855.[54] Like his competitors, Queen's paper wrote about sports such as pedestrianism, cricket, and prizefighting, but soon the focus was on baseball. The *Clipper* first mentioned baseball in 1853, but it was mentioned with much greater frequency after Henry Chadwick became the field sports editor in 1858.[55]

The newspaper distinguished itself from its rivals by encouraging the playing of football and by reporting, although in a limited and piecemeal way, on the results.

On December 13, 1856, the paper attempted to encourage football organizations by asking "Who is up for a 'Foot Ball' Club?"[56] According to a follow-up story a week later, some young men in Philadelphia had developed an interest in the sport but "never having seen any instructions concerning the correct mode of playing" requested more information.[57] In response, on December 20, 1856, the *Clipper* published the earliest football rules for adults in the United States. The code was copied directly from the 1856 *Manual of British Rural Sports*, with only the mention of Rugby School excised from the original text.[58] The rules were simple and consisted of only two numbered laws. The first declared "The ball itself is the only thing required by this game, except a large field to play in." The ball was constructed using an inflated bladder eight or nine inches in diameter covered with calf leather. The second rule explained how to mark off the field and the general style of play. The boundaries of the field were to be set at fifty to sixty yards apart, extending up to one hundred if there was enough room. The result was a square rather than a rectangular playing area. The rules did not call for any sort of goal markers; instead, a team scored by propelling the ball across the opponent's end line.

The assembled players chose two captains, and a coin toss determined who would first pick someone for his squad. The rules did not stipulate a certain number of players for each side, declaring only that the leaders took turns selecting participants until all had been assigned a squad. Afterward, the two teams faced off in the middle of the field before one captain began the game by kicking the ball toward his opponents' side of the field. The receiving team was allowed to return the ball "either by a kick, or carrying it, if preferred." This was a key feature of the rules, as it clearly allowed for both kicking and running with the ball. As the game continued, the team without possession could "throw down the ball-carrier or kicker by any means in their power." This is another important feature because it allowed for virtually any type of physical contact, including tripping and tackling. In fact, the code stated that tripping from behind was the most commonly employed way to bring down a rival player. Although it is not spelled out in the rules, it would follow that once brought down, the player would likely have to give up possession of the ball. Nothing in the regulations indicated whether the ball carrier was required to kick it away to his opponents as at the start of the match or had to relinquish the ball in some other way. Likewise, the code was silent about the ways that teammates could pass the ball or if there was anything like an offside rule. The object of the game was to propel the ball over the other team's end line, resulting in the conclusion of the match. The article clearly stated that the ball had to be kicked over the goal line, thus implying that carrying it across was not legal.[59]

The efforts of the *Clipper* to promote the growth of the sport proved largely ineffective. A year after publishing the first set of rules, the paper concluded that football "does not seem to meet with much favor in this vicinity," presumably meaning New York City, where the periodical was based. The paper did claim, however, that the sport was popular in Massachusetts, where "clubs were forming in great numbers."[60] The story may have been referencing school teams, since football at Harvard had already attracted some attention from the press, and the only Massachusetts clubs mentioned by name in the *Clipper* were the equivalent of high school sides.[61] In addition, contemporary Massachusetts newspapers made no mention of the supposed large number of football clubs that had been or were in the process of forming. Taken together, football's yearly mentions in the *Clipper* show that while the game remained popular among schoolboys and college students, it made little headway outside of educational institutions. In 1858, as if to emphasize that the game was largely one for young people and students, the *Clipper* published the long poem describing a football game at Spring Hill College in Alabama, and in a later issue reserved an entire page for an excerpt and illustration of a match from *Tom Brown's School Days*.[62] By December 1859, almost three years to the day after first advancing the idea of formal football clubs, the newspaper continued to promote the game as an ideal winter sport. As if to demonstrate the lack of existing teams, the *Clipper* once again asked readers "Who is to have the honor of organizing the *first* foot ball club?" In order to facilitate the growth of such groups, the newspaper published two English public school codes—Rugby and Eton.[63]

Four years after printing the Rugby and Eton codes, the *Clipper* took notice of the early meetings of the Football Association (FA) in England, declaring "we anticipate the code, as digested, in a couple of weeks."[64] When the newspaper printed a set of football rules nearly a year later on December 3, 1864, it did not credit them to the FA but instead presented them simply as the "revised Rules for Football."[65] Curiously, the laws that appeared in the *Clipper* were not the final FA rules but instead was the original code as determined by the meetings in late November 1863 and subsequently published in British periodicals, including *Bell's Life in London* and the *Sporting Gazette*.[66] That is to say, the association code as first published in the United States included both the carrying and hacking provisions that had been expunged from the final FA version. The reasons for publishing the original rules are unknown but could indicate that the editors favored a Rugby-style code over the alternatives.

Although the editors of the *Clipper* seemed to prefer a carrying type game, an 1864 article in the *Evening Post* offered an alternative description of traditional football rules in the United States. The author lamented the fact that football had fallen out of favor but noted it was experiencing a resurgence in England. The story acknowledged the debate in England between the Eton and Rugby codes and concluded that the Eton game that banned carrying the ball was closer to traditional US rules than to the Rugby code. In fact, the article declared that the idea of running with the ball was anathema to the spirit of the game: "in our younger days, when foot-ball was a favorite school-game, an attempt to pick up, carry or throw the ball would have excited as much horror and disgust as the English fox hunter experienced when his French guest shot a fox."[67]

The majority of published accounts of football games in periodicals such as the *Clipper* are of informal contests, and virtually no press reports of formal matches have surfaced. In addition, the country's top sporting newspaper exhibited little knowledge of such games, and the earliest published rules allowed for both kicking and carrying the ball. A few tantalizing mentions indicate that a handful of football clubs had been formed, but they are often named in only a single report and there are no stories describing the rules or results of any matches. Some of the teams emerged from existing ethnic or other sporting associations while others may have been purposely formed to play football, but there is no evidence they ever played games against other clubs.

Several notices from New York City show that established cricket clubs also played football.[68] One of these, first organized in 1838, was the St. George's Cricket Club, an organization closely connected to the social association of the same name.[69] Newspaper accounts from the 1840s show that the club played cricket teams from Philadelphia and Toronto and that these contests often involved quite large stakes. At one game versus Toronto in 1844, for example, the clubs reportedly played for between $500 and $2,000, with another $50,000 wagered on the outcome.[70] Although the cricket club had been organized in 1838, evidence that they also played football doesn't appear until 1854. The source was a communiqué, likely composed by a member of the organization and published in slightly different forms by the *Spirit of the Times* and the *Clipper*. The brief notice asserted that the St. George's Foot Ball Club had been in existence in New York since 1842 and although it had previously met only once each year, the club was now preparing to play more regularly.[71] Historian David Kilpatrick concludes that such information may have been given with the goal of "showing itself" in order to attract more members and/or spectators to the club. Nevertheless, the only further mention of the football club so far discovered appeared in the *New York Herald* in November 1854 alerting "members and friends" that the annual Thanksgiving match would kick off at ten o'clock.[72] The St. George's cricket club had an established history of playing against other teams, including contests featuring high-stakes wagers. Yet, their football club either chose not to compete against outsiders or was unable to find opponents. Instead, the football match occurred annually during Thanksgiving celebrations and appeared to involve only members of the club and their friends.

The second known club to emerge out of a previously established baseball and cricket organization was the Clover Hill Foot Ball Club. In late 1859, the *Brooklyn Daily Eagle* ran notice that it had formed and would meet on the evening of December 7 to elect officers and make arrangements for the upcoming season.[73] No further mention of the Clover Hill club has surfaced, although they may have played games against school teams. Young men already out of school may have been involved in the formation of neighborhood sides. In 1859 the *Clipper* gave notice that the New York Foot Ball Club had been organized on December 1 and was made up of "the young men residing in the neighborhood."[74] A year later the *Springfield (MA) Republican* announced that the "Maple Street Boys" of the city had formed a "Rough and Ready" football club and were seeking challengers. Although many of the club notices come from the northeastern United States, there is some evidence of clubs being formed in other regions. In 1859, newspapers in New Orleans noted that Southern Athletic FC and Jefferson City FC had organized, but no match reports or further accounts of their activities have been found.[75]

The city of Baltimore presents an intriguing case involving non-schoolboy football teams. The local press printed meeting notices for five clubs between

1859 and 1860: Cottage, Mount Vernon, Waverly, Olympics, and East Baltimore Hurling and FC. Three of the four (Mount Vernon, Waverly, and East Baltimore) were likely organized in specific neighborhoods of the city. Most of the announcements listed club officers and directed members to convene at an established place of exercise on a particular day or days.[76] Such detail implies a continuous existence along with a level of organization. Nevertheless, there is no evidence of what rules may have governed club activities, whether or not the clubs had any connection to one another, or that they ever played games against other sides. Indeed, most of the notices describe the activity as "exercise" rather than an organized match, which may indicate that only members of the club participated. When Baltimore's earliest baseball teams formed around this same time, they only played games among club members for the first year or so.[77]

It has proven difficult to identify members of the football clubs with any certainty except John Southgate Lemmon, president of the Mount Vernon Foot Ball Club. In the 1860 US Census he appears as a nineteen-year-old clerk living with his family.[78] Lemmon and the club secretary, Joseph L. Toy, both attended the University of Maryland and may have still been students when the football club formed.[79] If that was the case, it would be similar to Oneida FC organized by schoolboys in Boston in 1862 and often called the country's first football club. The Oneida's only known matches were against other schoolboy teams. Although Lemmon was reported to be the president of the Mount Vernon Foot Ball Club, he may also have turned out for the Waverly Base Ball Club. A "Mr. Lemmon" was singled out for his fine play at shortstop in a game between the Waverly and Excelsior clubs on September 10, 1860, and the box score of the rematch on October 17 included the surname Lemmon.[80]

Newspapers, illustrations, and early photographs indicate that small-sided mainly kicking games between formal football clubs were not widely played in the United States before 1863. Most of the match reports describe informal contests between loosely organized squads that were usually played on special occasions and holidays. Although some team names are known, no descriptions survive of games. It is also unclear if these groups competed with other sides or simply played football among club members. Only in the 1880s would soccer clubs and competitions take hold in many communities around the country.

4

STEEL CITY SOCCER

In 1866 the FA code was first published in the United States as *Beadle's dime book of cricket and football: Being a complete guide to players, and containing all the rules and laws of the ground and games.*[1] The appearance of soccer's official rules did not spark an immediate rise in the number of organized clubs. Instead, as happened earlier, informal games continued and variations of football experienced a resurgence in schools and colleges during the 1870s. It would take a decade or more before formal, organized club soccer appeared on a major scale. During the 1880s, soccer clubs and competitions formed in cities around the country; this trend accelerated in the 1890s before dropping off in many places around the beginning of the twentieth century.

A number of factors contributed to the enormous growth of the game in the final two decades of the nineteenth century. In the years after the formulation of the association rules, soccer's rise was slow and unsteady even in Great Britain. Only with the creation of the FA cup competition in 1872 did the sport begin a rapid ascent in popularity. Such growth eventually led to the legalization of professionalism in 1885 and the establishment of regular league play three years later. Thanks to the circulation of popular British periodicals such as *Bell's Sporting Life*, along with sporadic coverage in local newspapers, sports fans in the United States could follow the growing development of association football during these years. The rising popularity of the sport in Great Britain also meant that emigrants from those islands took the game with them as they traveled to locations around the globe, including the United States. Immigration from the United Kingdom to the United States rose between 1850 and 1890, with the greatest increases coming in the decade between 1881 and 1890.[2] The popularity of soccer in many cities and regions expanded steadily over this same period before falling away around 1900 as economic recession slowed the influx of British immigrants. The turn-of-the-century decline, however, did not mean that soccer disappeared—it would return and, in many ways, grow stronger in the years leading up to and after World War I.

Contributing to the expansion of soccer in the late nineteenth century were changes in the conditions of labor as well as general economic growth at least until 1893. Shifting social and cultural attitudes also helped boost the popularity of association football. Many laborers' weekly work hours were reduced, giving them more recreational time. Saloons emerged as spaces for men to gather outside the home and workplace, and these drinking establishments soon became a place to talk about sports.[3] At the same time, urban dwellers of a higher socioeconomic status became more interested in active recreation at the end of the nineteenth century. Historian Roy Rosenzweig describes the 1890s as "the years in which America's middle and upper classes passionately embraced competitive sports and outdoor recreation."[4] In Pittsburgh, the 1890s saw a growth in both middle- and working-class leisure activities.[5] The influential Spalding sporting goods company also helped boost soccer even before the firm began publishing its yearly national surveys, *Spalding's Official Soccer Foot Ball Guide*. In 1893, just as the game had begun to take off in many cities, the firm published *The Official Guide to Gaelic and Association Football*. The short pamphlet summarized the rules of the game, included diagrams showing the outline of the field, and illustrated the basic tactical alignment of the players. At the back of the book were advertisements for various Spalding products, including their official association football.

The influx of British immigrants combined with economic and cultural developments to produce conditions that led to the growth of amateur soccer in the United States. Many of the English and Scottish workers who came to the United States in these years tended to be "experienced craftsmen" who arrived with specialized skills that could command higher wages than immigrants from other parts of Europe.[6] In many cities across the country, these newcomers were instrumental in forming the earliest soccer associations and in making sure that they remained amateur endeavors. Soccer provided a means for Anglophone men from around the world to express sociability through participation in masculine leisure. Taking part in soccer organizations as players and administrators helped them build social capital and sustain ethnic identities. The game also allowed the men to assert a distinct class identity, one that differentiated them from lower-paid members of the working classes, who tended to favor other sporting pastimes.

The teams and competitions that proliferated across the country in the final decades of the nineteenth century shared several common features, including their origins, development, and ultimate decline by 1900. Although each city had its own unique story, many followed a similar pattern. In most cases, Scottish-born players and ethnic organizations played a key role in founding and sustaining association football communities. Immigrants from England also made important contributions, as did native-born players in some areas, but Scots were consistently involved in nearly all major soccer-playing regions of the country. One reason for this is the propensity of Scots to form ethnic societies, especially sporting clubs. Another factor is that, by the 1870s, soccer had become a key part of Scottish self-identity, in part due to the intensity of the country's sporting rivalry with England.[7] Historian Tanja Bueltmann argues that immigrant organizations allowed the Scottish diaspora to form its own ethnic identity rather than have it defined by others. By the mid-nineteenth century, many organizations including Caledonian societies began to focus less on mutual aid and more on sport and leisure activities. As part of this process, soccer clubs and competitions emerged as organizations designed to promote and preserve a sense of Scottish identity.[8] Perhaps as a result of the influence of the Scottish game, amateurism also became a strongly engrained value to many competitions.[9]

Organized clubs and competitions faced a number of challenges, including disputes, infighting, and protests.[10] Conflicts took place between individual players, teams, and spectators. The arguments sometimes escalated into physical confrontations. Soccer communities also had logistical issues to overcome, such as inclement weather and trouble finding and maintaining places to play. Since the associations were amateur groups largely run on a volunteer basis, they had difficulties putting together sustained competitions, scheduling individual matches, and even making sure that teams showed up at the appointed time. In western Pennsylvania and elsewhere, the sport also had to deal with the realities of industrial life, where employment was both precarious and dangerous.[11] Eventually the clubs and competitions encountered internal and external challenges that made it difficult to maintain themselves over the long term. Although soccer never completely disappeared from most locations nearly all of the clubs and competitions experienced a dramatic decline in the years approaching 1900. This chapter uses Pittsburgh and its surrounding region as a case study to explore the general developments outlined above.

ORIGINS

The earliest documented soccer match in Pittsburgh took place on October 6, 1885, when the Pittsburgh Wanderers defeated East Liberty FC 5–3.[12] The name East Liberty might refer to the city neighborhood, although there is no record before or after of a team based there, or it may actually have been East Liverpool FC from Ohio. Two weeks later, the Wanderers had been scheduled to play at East Liverpool in what may have been the return leg of the fixture, but the match was canceled when only three of the Pittsburgh squad showed up.[13] After these initial efforts, association football continued to be played in the region but without much organization and not in a way that newspapers bothered to write about. The next report appeared in 1887, when East Liverpool fell 7–1 to the Scotch Rangers of McDonald, another Pittsburgh area opponent.[14] The McDonald club, later known as Rovers, became one of the area's most successful teams when league and cup competitions began after 1890. A month later, a notice appeared that Braddock FC had been formed.[15] The establishment of these two clubs marked the beginning of organized soccer in Pittsburgh; in some form or another both clubs featured in many of the city's competitions throughout the rest of the nineteenth century.

A flurry of notices in 1888 showed that teams and individuals in Pittsburgh were interested in forming a variety of football teams including ones playing by the association rules. A short article from February reported on the results of two matches: the Eighteenth Ward beat Homestead 4–0, and Braddock defeated the Roscoe Rangers 2–0. Given the scorelines, the fact that a Braddock soccer team had formed in 1887 and that the Eighteenth Ward team would later be an important part of the first organized competition, it seems likely that these were soccer games. Other matches featuring Eighteenth Ward, Roscoe, Braddock, and another team called the Shireoaks could indicate the existence of an informal competition.[16] Indeed, by May 1888, the *Pittsburgh Daily Post* reported that Braddock and Lawrenceville would play on Memorial Day for the western Pennsylvania championship. The winning club would earn a $500 prize and the right to play the best club from the eastern part of the state. Later reports indicated that Braddock considered the holiday match to be an exhibition only and not a title decider. While the squad was open to facing Lawrenceville, they nevertheless claimed the championship by virtue of the fact that they had won more games in the spring and fall.[17] No record remains of the result of any championship match or if Braddock ever traveled east to play for the state title.

In June 1890, the *Dispatch* published a long article on soccer by Pittsburgh resident William J. Barr. Writing from Birmingham, England, he recounted the history and rules of the sport and remarked on its popularity in Britain citing a recent Aston Villa match he attended with a crowd of twelve thousand. After outlining some of the merits of the game Barr concluded "I hope some day to see the Association game of football firmly established as one of the American outdoor games."[18] The article along with a scheduled trip of the Scottish team Clyde FC to the United States a few weeks later stimulated interest in the city, and a meeting was held to discuss the possibility of bringing over an English side.[19] It may be that such discussions promoted the formation of new clubs in Pittsburgh and some of the surrounding towns. Clearly, though, soccer had grown since 1887 because, at the time talks began to form a league, at least eight soccer clubs already existed. The league proposed including clubs from Pittsburgh and surrounding communities as well as East Liverpool from Ohio.[20] A few weeks later, representatives of nine teams—Allegheny Athletic Club, Eighteenth Ward, McKeesport, Homestead, Eureka, Shaner, East End FC, and New Castle—formally established the league and elected officers. They left open the question of how many teams would eventually be a part of the group but suggested it would be eight, ten, or twelve.[21] Twelve clubs ultimately petitioned to join the competition, with two rejected because they were deemed too far from Pittsburgh. One team representative noted that a previous competition had collapsed because the distance between teams had been too great.[22] Calling the new organization an experiment, the clubs hoped to avoid excessive costs associated with longer trips. League play was scheduled to begin on Christmas Day 1890, and the clubs—Allegheny Athletic Club, East End FC, Eighteenth Ward, Homestead, Braddock, Eureka, McKeesport, Shaner, Allegheny Thistles, and McDonald—would compete for a pennant donated by sporting goods firm A. G. Pratt and Company. Although not initially mentioned in early reports, the organization was eventually christened the Western Association Football League (WAFL).[23] The sheer number of clubs in the region demonstrates the rapid growth of the sport in the area. Nevertheless, organizers almost immediately faced challenges that delayed the beginning of league play into 1891. The problems facing the new organization served as a preview of the types of conflicts that would plague soccer in western Pennsylvania over the next decade or more.

THE CHALLENGES OF ORGANIZED COMPETITION

Issues with the new league in Pittsburgh arose just days after it organized the competition in the fall of 1890. Leaders of the Allegheny Athletic Association (AAA) announced that they had not been informed about the plan to launch a soccer team under the organization's name. The committee decided that they would not pay rent for the team to play at Exposition Park, although one member remarked that the AAA would likely reconsider the decision if all members of the soccer team joined the association.[24] Later, the executive committee of the group held an emergency meeting to discuss the matter and decided to withdraw from the WAFL. In a statement, a member of the AAA explained that they did not oppose the idea of a league but felt it would struggle financially because of a predicted hard winter. As a result, the organization "cannot afford to pay the rent of the grounds and other expenses without getting it back in receipts. We feel sure that the weather will keep the receipts down to zero."[25] Around the same time, the *Pittsburgh Dispatch* published a letter from John C. Carlin of the New Castle Cricket and Football Club. He wrote to protest the "discourteous treatment" of his organization by the newly formed league and accused the group of using his team to help generate interest in the new competition and then dropping them in favor of other teams. He felt that travel costs had been used to exclude his club, even though at least two other teams faced similar questions.[26]

Despite the withdrawal of the AAA and complaints of mistreatment by New Castle, the league moved forward with its plans, scheduling five games on Christmas Day and five more on New Year's Day. On January 8, however, the WAFL announced that league play would instead begin on February 14. Only one of the ten previously announced matches took place, and even that lone result was later nullified after a protest over the condition of the field. The combination of bad weather and poor organization afflicted the WAFL in that first season. The AAA team eventually rejoined the league, and the fact that its lineup had been reinforced by two players who had previously been with New Castle likely did little to soothe that club's hurt feelings.[27] Less than a month later, however, the AAA football club decided to change its name because it was severing all ties with its parent organization. No explanation was given for the decision, but it probably reflected the tensions that had characterized the relationship between the soccer club and the AAA from the beginning. The soccer team quickly reformed itself as Pittsburgh FC and elected a new group of officers.[28]

Even before league play began in earnest more conflict erupted. The day before a scheduled match between McKeesport and Shaner, the two teams could not agree on a referee and appealed to the league secretary to appoint one.[29] Things reached something of a climax at the WAFL's March meeting where a lively discussion took place and at least half a dozen protests were dismissed. The group also decided once again to postpone league play for two weeks due to poor weather. The meeting illustrated one of the major problems facing soccer in western Pennsylvania—a lack of responsibility on the part of both teams and players. At least one club had been sanctioned for not appearing for a scheduled match, and the league's officers "made some very opportune remarks regarding certain players manifesting a little more interest in the game." Without the full commitment of both clubs and players, the new league would never attract enough fans.[30] Despite such entreaties, the competition faced more obstacles. Players from Braddock either did not get the message about commitment or were just greatly outclassed when McDonald beat them 13–0. Near the end of the season, Pittsburgh canceled the rest of its games after several players left town, and the East End team abandoned the league due to an unresolved grievance.[31] Despite the rancor and bad weather, the *Pittsburgh Dispatch* optimistically summed up the WAFL's inaugural season: "while none of us can truly say the season has been a successful one, we can certainly argue that it has not been a failure by any means."[32]

THE SCOTTISH GAME

Despite a rocky first season, the *Pittsburgh Dispatch* seemed convinced that with some fixes a soccer league could be viable in the region and singled out league secretary George Macpherson for praise in what was likely a difficult role. As was the case in other regions of the country, immigrants from Scotland like Macpherson played a key role in managing soccer clubs and competitions in Pittsburgh. The organization of labor also played a role because often one nationality predominated in a particular mill. When the company needed to hire more employees, they relied on international networks to recruit workers from the same country. Such a practice strengthened social bonds, and immigrants arriving from places where soccer was already popular helped create conditions for the game to thrive.[33] Scots were heavily involved in Pittsburgh soccer, although the English influence was also important. Born in Scotland in 1865, Macpherson came to the United States in 1889 just a year before the WAFL formed.[34] Alec Macpherson was also active in the game, although it's unclear if the two were related, although family connections were not uncommon in Pittsburgh soccer circles.[35] Scottish-born William McVicker (b. 1863) and his brothers Charles (b. 1866), James (b. 1870), and Joseph (b. 1873) all lined up for league powerhouse McDonald.[36] The Liddell clan, Andrew (b. 1869), Robert (b. 1866), and John (b. 1870?), had been born in Scotland and played for East End FC of Pittsburgh.[37] Not all of the region's soccer families were Scots. The Partridge brothers—William (b. 1866), John (b. 1868), George (b. 1871), and Richard (b. 1873)—were iron molders who came from England in 1889 and played for McDonald.[38] Other English-born players included Joseph Pickard (b. 1867), William Wardle (b. 1865), and Thomas Parks, while another early Pittsburgh team from 1892 featured nine English-born and two Scottish-born players.[39] Despite the overwhelming numbers of English and Scottish players, some soccer-playing families came from outside the British Isles. In 1910, for example, the Beadling team included four coal miner brothers: Joseph, Charles, John, and George Luxbacher, whose family had roots in the Austro-Hungarian Empire.[40] Not all soccer players were immigrants, however, and the 1895 Rovers squad included eight US-born players on the team.[41]

THE CONTINUED DEVELOPMENT OF ORGANIZED SOCCER

After a sputtering start in 1890, the WAFL made a deliberate effort to improve the organization and functioning of the league. George Macpherson traveled to England, where he met with the secretaries of the Scottish Football Association and the English Football League. He returned with copies of their constitutions as well as other documents.[42] Ultimately the league reduced the number of clubs to six—Pittsburgh, Bloomfield, McDonald, McKeesport, Homestead, and New Castle—for the following season and aimed to play matches every Saturday between October 10, 1891, and January 1, 1892. The association also left some weeks open to fit in weather-postponed games, and it implemented a points system, two for a win and one for a draw, in order to prevent disputes over the championship.[43]

Despite efforts to take control of the game, the league continued to be dogged by controversy. Just a few weeks into the schedule, a match between Homestead and New Castle ended in protest because the referee "lacked firmness in his decisions." The dispute centered around a Homestead goal scored in the eightieth minute that the New Castle captain claimed had come off the player's arm. After the decision, "a wrangle ensued" as spectators rushed the field; by the time it was cleared, New Castle claimed it was too dark to finish the match.[44] The discord within the WAFL culminated in a contentious meeting of the organization in November 1891. Four protests were lodged and upheld, including three involving referees and one because a team showed up to the wrong field. Claiming that the organization had a grudge against the Pittsburgh team, the *Dispatch* declared "probably never in the history of athletic organizations were more stupid and illogical decisions arrived at." Secretary Macpherson threatened to resign over what he felt was a lack of respect for the authority of the league and its officials.[45] The Pittsburgh team held a meeting the next day to decide if they should withdraw from the league because "the general opinion is the Tuesday night's majority violated all rules of fair play and were not in any way guided by common sense and intelligence."[46] Eventually the WAFL smoothed over the differences and ordered that any team lodging a protest would put up five dollars, a sum that would be forfeited if the complaint was denied by the league.[47]

The conflicts across the WAFL showed how seriously most fans, players, and teams took the competition. One club reported that after an away win the losing side's supporters threatened to kill the winning team.[48] Sometimes the pressure to succeed had an impact on the relationships between team members. Early in the 1891 season, after Pittsburgh FC lost two games in a row, a meeting held to discuss the club's shortcomings produced "a good deal of bad feeling." The captain and manager both quit their posts, but the team convinced the former to withdraw his resignation.[49] In 1894 a dissident faction from the Homestead side met to form a new version of the club and demanded that the previous officers turn over the team's account books and cash. However, the remainder of the club's members held elections and named a separate list of officers. The two Homesteads even had a match scheduled for the same day on the same field. A *Pittsburgh Press* article sarcastically suggested that the two opposing Homestead clubs play a match to decide who would be given the accounts and the money. The rival factions did not respond to the newspaper and later forged a compromise.[50]

As in other cities, Pittsburgh players also competed and socialized off the field. Late in 1891 many prominent soccer players, including Alec Macpherson, became involved in a new cricket league.[51] The soccer games gave men the opportunity to spend leisure time with their peers. Employees from the Kaufmann Brothers department store were involved in the Pittsburgh Rovers team first organized in 1894, while the squad from Jeannette was largely made up of electrical workers from Westinghouse.[52] After a match between the Allegheny Thistles and Sewickley, the visitors were treated to a dinner where they were "waited on by the charming girls" of the home city.[53] The players on the Homestead football and cricket teams held a match featuring the Scottish versus the English players, with "a sumptuous banquet" served afterward. The event not only offered a means for club members to participate in friendly competition but it also attracted a large number of spectators and gave the British community an opportunity to gather together.[54] In general, different ethnic groups did not mingle with those of other backgrounds, especially outside the workplace. In Homestead, English speakers often had little connection with immigrants from Eastern and Southern Europe. In her 1910 study of the community researcher Margaret F. Byington, found that "the break between the Slavs and the rest of the community is on the whole more absolute than that between the whites and the Negroes."[55]

Generally speaking, the English-speaking community was tight-knit, brought "together by common interests and common ties."[56] Soccer also provided a way for people to unite in support of those in need. In February 1897, a match was scheduled to benefit the family of Homestead and Marchand player Moses Beddoes, who died of pneumonia. The proceeds from matches in 1893 and 1896 were pledged to striking miners.[57] The death of John "Jack" Robson in 1913 was a tremendous blow to the region's sporting community. After he was electrocuted while working in the mines, over five hundred people attended his funeral.[58] Robson had been born in England and reportedly played professionally there before arriving in the United

FIG. 4.1: Jack Robson was captain of the Beadling squad and the 1911–12 Press League All-Star team. A year later, he died in a mining accident. (Author's collection)

States. He lined up for Monongahela City and Beadling and in 1912 was named captain of the Pittsburgh Press League All-Star team.[59] A skilled halfback, a position equivalent to a midfielder today, he was a commanding presence who also had a degree of skill with the ball at his feet. A match report from 1910 noted that Robson "passed Westfield's half-backs all by himself and shot one into the net which was the prettiest piece of work in the game." He may also have had a hardness to his game; following one match, Westfield protested the result due to Beadling's use of foul language and dirty plays.[60] Columnist Ralph Davis deemed him "one of the greatest soccerites living."[61] After his death, the *Pittsburgh Press* went even further calling the over-six-foot Robson "one of the most magnificent specimens of physical manhood that ever lived" and "a modern Hercules."[62] Immediately the club made plans to hold a benefit for his widow and two sons. The April 1 event featured the Beadling brass band, an athletics meet, and a soccer match. Only a loss by the home side marred an otherwise successful day.[63]

Once regular competition began in the region, some Pittsburgh teams also hoped to test themselves against clubs from farther afield. Early in 1892, Pittsburgh FC challenged the Chicago Thistle team to a series of three matches—home, away, and a coin flip to decide the location if a third game was necessary. Pittsburgh offered to pay for gold or silver medals to be given to the winners and also suggested a side bet of between $250 and $1,000.[64] The match against Thistle never materialized, in part because the Chicago club responded by offering to play a match on Sunday, something the local squad refused to do.[65] Despite the problems with Thistle, Pittsburgh did schedule a game against the Chicago Cricket Club. The match ended in a 2–2 draw and attracted a crowd of around two thousand, including "a large number of ladies."[66] By the fall of 1892, Pittsburgh FC had decided to forgo the local competition and instead sought contests against teams from other cities. Perhaps due to Pittsburgh's absence, the local league gradually fell apart. It had begun in the fall of 1892 with just six teams and only three holdovers from the previous campaign. By December some of the better players from league teams had signed on with Pittsburgh due to the collapse of the competition.[67]

Pittsburgh FC's decision to bolt the local association seemed sound, as one report indicated that they had already received offers from Boston and another suggested they were arranging games against teams from Fall River and Toronto.[68] In a letter to the *Pittsburgh Dispatch*, the president of the club challenged any team in the country to a match with the following terms: the winners would keep all gate receipts, and the losing team would pay to rent the ground, print flyers, contract security, as well as other costs associated with the match.[69] The first confirmed game took place in October, when they trounced the Frankfords of Philadelphia 4–0. Before the match, the Pittsburgh squad had been strengthened with several experienced players, including one who had reportedly lined up for Notts County in England.[70] The win over the Frankfords along with victories over local squads New Castle and Homestead and a tie with Chicago caused the *Pittsburgh Dispatch* to proclaim them one of the best teams in the country. Despite these victories, the Pittsburgh team came back to earth after being thrashed 7–2 by a Toronto team. About one thousand people witnessed the defeat, and even the newspaper refused to dwell on the result—"to tell the story of how the goals were scored would be wearisome."[71] About a month later the local side again drew with a visiting team from Chicago in a match that attracted a crowd of only five hundred on a "wretchedly cold day." Although no specific prize was mentioned, the match report did note that hundreds of dollars had been wagered on the game.[72]

Despite such events, the notion of amateurism remained strong in the region and not all clubs believed in playing for money or gambling on the results of matches. After the *Pittsburgh Post* claimed that Bloomfield Rovers had challenged Homestead to play a match with $100 at stake, the team's treasurer Wilson McHarg was prompted to respond that "the Rovers most decidedly will not help to disgrace that most scientific and manly style of football by dragging gambling into it."[73] Later the club even refused to play for a supper and demanded that the gate receipts be donated to charity. The team's attitude must have been well-known within the soccer community, as a few weeks earlier the *Pittsburgh Press* had published the following poem:

WHEN
A $ Mark
IS put at stake
THE Bloomfield Rovers
REFUSE to play that kind
OF Association Football[74]

The Bloomfield club was not the only part of the soccer community insisting on the moral value of playing the game the right way. After a match drew a small audience of only 150, the *Pittsburgh Press* lectured the players claiming that if they hoped to attract more fans "better language must be used on the field."[75] Columnist "J.H.G." of the *Pittsburgh Daily Post* boasted that the local competition was organized only for the love of the game, unlike "its pretentious eastern brother" who was only interested in turning a profit.[76] Just a year later, the same paper again chided soccer teams after a series of Thanksgiving games degenerated into "quarrels and wrangles." Part of the issue was that the league's alleged refusal to hire good referees resulted in poor decisions that in turn led to complaints and protests. Such behavior harmed the reputation of the sport and gave the impression that soccer was on the same level as dog- or cockfighting.[77]

Once again developments outside the area, in this case the formation of the American League of Professional Football (ALPF), may have contributed to the revival of an organized soccer competition in Pittsburgh. In a meeting held on September 7, 1894, the Western Pennsylvania Football League (WPFL) was formed. The founding clubs included Pittsburgh, Bloomfield, Wilmerding, and Marchand Athletics; it was hoped at least four more teams would soon join.[78] By October the league roster was set (McKeesport, Bloomfield, Pittsburgh, Marchand, Homestead, and Youngstown), A. G. Pratt once again offered a pennant to the winning team, and a local clothing store pledged to give each player on the victorious side a hat.[79] As in previous iterations, the league soon fell into arguments and infighting. One story claimed that Pittsburgh wanted to keep all of the gate money from a match versus Marchand and the other teams eventually sided with the latter. A week later, the WPFL's grievance committee noted that Pittsburgh had refused to show up for its last three scheduled matches. Eventually the league expelled the club because of the previously reported incidents as well as for general "sulking and indifference."[80]

The 1895 season began with just six teams, and within a month of organizing the clubs decided to scrap the league structure in favor of an open-cup competition. Eventually six clubs agreed to contribute $12.50 each to cover the costs of paying referees and to purchase a trophy and medals for the winning squad.[81] Soon the same problems began to reappear, as a match between Homestead and Pittsburgh Athletic Club (PAC) turned chaotic after spectators rushed the field to protest a decision to award a penalty. Representatives of the clubs traded accusations in the newspapers as PAC declared "the way the spectators acted was a disgrace" and Homestead claimed the opposition "start[ed] all the slugging." Eventually, the league ordered that all three of the holiday games be replayed with match officials named by the organization's vice president.[82]

The 1896 season was slow to organize as various clubs pondered whether to enter the competition. The planning was further put off when league president Frank Holt resigned his position and moved to West Virginia.[83] Ultimately just five teams—Homestead, McDonald, Laurel Hill Rangers, Allegheny Standards, and Jeannette Swifts—competed in an abbreviated cup competition that began in late November and ended by early February 1897.[84] The following season witnessed a revived eight-team competition, although it took some time to determine which clubs would join the league. In September, newspapers reported that the newcomers would be East Liverpool (Ohio), Phoenix of East Pittsburgh, and the Roscoe Rangers of Lucyville, but by the start of play in November, Roscoe had been replaced by Marchand, who had previously captured the title in 1894.[85] Once again McDonald proved to be the cream of the crop, and once again the season was marred by squabbling. The decision of Jeannette to protest after losing to McDonald in the title decider prompted the *Pittsburgh Press* to respond: "it is a pity that there is so much protesting and so little real sportsmanship in association football." The article claimed that such attitudes hindered the growth of the game: "for several years the final games in the association championship series have been marred by protests and squabbles that should never have been allowed to see the light of day, and it is this spirit that keeps the game struggling along at the bottom of the heap, instead of being the popular sport that it ought to be."[86] The conflicts that tarnished the championship may have contributed to the region's dampened enthusiasm for the game. The league contracted to five entering the 1898–99 season and press coverage of the game also diminished.[87] Long-time participants Homestead Athletic Association declined to even form a side since the club's field had been reserved for the organization's rugby team.[88] Other teams continued to play each other in what were essentially friendlies rather than in a league or cup format. Teams continued to claim the championship of western Pennsylvania, but organized competition would not resume until 1904.[89]

REBUILDING SOCCER

The problems that plagued organized soccer in Pittsburgh, combined with difficult economic conditions, led to the collapse of leagues and cup tournaments. Even though formal competition ceased, it does not mean they stopped playing soccer in western Pennsylvania. In fact, the years around 1900 saw an unprecedented number of teams take to the field. These clubs used newspapers to arrange informal contests as a form of friendly competition and an opportunity to socialize with peers. In other cases, the teams played games for a monetary prize and individuals and clubs placed bets on the outcome. The lack of a league did not mean that the region stopped crowning champions. Such awards seem to have been granted to the most successful side or whoever won a series of matches designated as title deciders. The absence of an organizational structure did not end the problems that proved so disastrous in the past. It does seem, however, that the contentiousness and violence that characterized soccer in the region did lessen over time. By 1904 a new league began play, and its officials and the press seemed determined not to repeat the mistakes of the past. The establishment of the Pittsburgh Press League and the Western Pennsylvania Association Cup eventually created a stable pair of competitions that would last until the disruptions caused by World War I. The formation of the Western Pennsylvania State Foot Ball Association in May 1913 lent administrative structure to the soccer-playing community and through its affiliation with the United States Football Association (formed April 1913) linked the region to the national scene. By the time the United States entered World War I, the soccer community in Pittsburgh had become one of the most active in the nation.

Soon after the collapse of the WPFL in 1899, clubs began to advertise their desire to compete against other sides. Often these new teams included experienced footballers who had played with some of the most successful outfits in the region. One example is the Homestead Library Athletic Club, which formed in late November 1900. The squad included men who had previously turned out for Roscoe, Pittsburgh, McDonald, as well as previous Homestead teams. Initial discussions about forming an Allegheny County league took place, but it never materialized.[90] The fact that players changed clubs with ease was undoubtedly an effect of not having a governing body for the area. Over the next few years, new teams sprouted up around the

FIG. 4.2: The 1914–15 Beadling FC team. By this season the Pittsburgh region had twenty senior teams playing in two soccer leagues, a cup competition, and a public school boys' league. (Author's collection)

region. At times the clubs specifically requested matches against established sides, perhaps as a sign of their seriousness or a desire to test themselves against a higher level of competition. In the fall of 1901, the East Liverpool Rovers challenged no fewer than nine clubs by name, including local heavyweights such as Roscoe and McDonald.[91] Whether they were newly formed or had been playing for years, squads looking for games did not lack for competition, as more than twenty teams were active during the fall of 1901.[92]

In addition to the new clubs, many of the oldest and most successful teams of the region also continued playing. When two old rivals were scheduled to meet on December 14, 1901, the *Pittsburgh Daily Post* reminded readers about the history of such matches: "in the good old days, when the game was really flourishing in this section, until killed by grasping managers and foolish players, the announcement of a game between Homestead and McDonald would cause excitement all around."[93] Games between legacy clubs proved popular, attracting both press coverage and spectators. An estimated two thousand people witnessed a o–o draw between McDonald and East Pittsburgh on January 11, 1902.[94] Many experienced players continued to be involved, although the *Pittsburgh Daily Post* noted that a younger generation was also taking up the game. The paper expressed hope that this new group of managers and players would learn from previous mistakes.[95]

Generally it does seem that the matches became less contentious, or at least the press ceased reporting in detail on the discord.[96] One reason may be that, without an established league structure, no team was guaranteed matches against outside clubs. If a side developed a reputation because it played too rough, complained too much, or were not reliable, it would have trouble finding opponents. After Bridgeville failed to appear for a game against East Pittsburgh, the home club was forced to give refunds to six hundred people who had paid to see the match. The team depended on the gate receipts to cover expenses and due in part to advertising costs, they had reportedly lost a great deal of money. The fact that the information appeared in the newspaper meant that other teams would likely approach any future challenge from Bridgeville with caution. East Pittsburgh notified the *Pittsburgh Daily Post* that it would not schedule another match against Bridgeville until either the expenses were paid or the team agreed to put up $100 on the result.[97] It is unclear how often teams played for stakes, but evidence that betting on games was not considered remarkable is that newspapers openly acknowledged such wagering. When old rivals East Pittsburgh and McDonald were set to meet in late 1900, the *Pittsburgh Press* reported that "betting on the event is about even money." A similar notice accompanied a match between Monongahela City and Roscoe in 1906.[98]

The impetus for organizing a new league came from East Liverpool, Ohio, a small city along the West Virginia–Pennsylvania border about forty miles from Pittsburgh. As indicated above, East Liverpudlians had played soccer since at least the late 1880s. The East Liverpool Rovers team formed in 1895, and the squad participated in regional competitions including the Western Association Football League. In the fall of 1904, brothers Samuel and George Hancock pledged to donate a trophy worth $250 to the winner of an association football league. Continuing the key role that British immigrants played in local soccer, the Hancock brothers had been born in England and came to the United States in the 1880s or 1890s. It is unclear if they had been involved in the Rovers or other clubs prior to announcing the donation. The local newspaper called them well-known businessmen, with Samuel owning a saloon and later selling insurance, while George ran a grocery and drug store.[99] The organizers sent a letter inviting teams to join the new Eastern Ohio and Western Pennsylvania Association Football league.[100]

The response to the letter must have been positive, because within a few weeks the organization took shape, with elder brother George Hancock serving as president. The leaders of the nascent association must have been aware of the problems that had led to the collapse of older competitions in the region. No previous association had presented its regulations to prospective teams and the broader public. On September 20, 1904, the league published a set of fifteen proposed laws for the new organization. The *East Liverpool (OH) Evening Review* defended such a top-down approach, writing that "everything in the way of regulations to govern the league has been left to the discretion of the officers, so that the competition will be clean and so far removed from prejudice that the most enthusiastic spectator can have no room for complaint."[101] Several of the laws were basic guidelines designed to insure the league was a seriously run, formal competition. Such measures included rules stating that each team must have a full kit and requiring that the field be properly marked off. Others were aimed at preventing some of the problems that had ruined previous circuits. Rules three and four stated that a player must be registered for thirty days before he could participate in a match and that any team that fielded an ineligible player would forfeit the game. Such a measure was designed to prevent clubs from bringing in ringers for big matches and to stop players from switching teams midseason. Rule five took aim at the issue of clubs not showing up for games or not playing out the rest of their schedule at the end of the season. It declared that any squad that failed to fulfill its obligations would be fined ten dollars for each offense. Finally, to prevent protests and player violence, the laws gave referees the power to remove any player from the field. Reports of such expulsions would be made to the league where a player would likely face a suspension and be unable to play until reinstated. Other notable rules required that each team appoint a representative to the executive committee in charge of naming referees and that said representative be paid by the club.[102] Asking clubs to compensate officers likely was an attempt to end the problems associated with running an all-volunteer organization.

The league was officially constituted during an all-night organizing session at the Seventh Avenue Hotel in Pittsburgh in late October 1904. Although the aim was to have eight to twelve clubs, this new Eastern Ohio and Western Pennsylvania Association Football league began with just six: Braddock, East Liverpool, East Pittsburgh, McDonald, Morgan, and Roscoe. Each club would play the others at home and away for a total of ten league games; the team with the most points at the end of the season would be champions.[103] Casual matches between teams outside the league also continued as coverage of the sport increased in local newspapers. The *Pittsburgh Press* even published a tutorial on the game outlining the basic rules, explaining player roles, and describing its popularity in England.[104] The new organization's first campaign was an unqualified success. Teams only made two protests, both quickly settled with little or no public rancor. Not much is known about average crowd sizes but reported attendances at matches included between three and four thousand on hand to see Roscoe clinch the title on December 26. Amazingly, the weather also proved cooperative, resulting in no breaks, postponements, or missed games.[105]

Despite the success of the Eastern Ohio and Western Pennsylvania Association Football league, the distance and expense of travel made the competition unsustainable after the 1907–8 season. The collapse of the competition illustrates the fact that most of the players worked industrial jobs, often in mines.[106] As a result they had little time and disposable income to support an active playing schedule. It also shows that, during this period, few of the teams seemed to have had the direct support of major firms. Instead, the clubs often took the names of the cities in which they were based, even if the players shared a workplace. Later iterations of the regional competition would feature clubs such as Homestead Steel Works, Edgar Thompson Steel Works, and Westinghouse Air Brake Company.[107] At least some clubs, including Homestead, were formed by athletic organizations affiliated with specific companies. These organizations were often run by and for employees and received some financial support from the firm. Sparse, scattered, and incomplete records preclude determining the degree to which companies supported soccer clubs. Even if they did provide funds, it may not have been enough to cover all of a team's expenses. As a result, the clubs depended on gate receipts and on other measures, such as the dance that East Pittsburgh held to raise money for the team.[108] League rules mandated that teams cover the costs of hosting a game, and the clubs depended on ticket sales to do so.[109] When crowds stayed away, the negative financial impact could impair the squad's ability to remain in the league. In 1910, for example, Ambridge withdrew from the competition, citing a lack of support at home games.[110]

Later that same season, Westland abandoned play due to the suspension of work at the mines. The result of the work stoppage meant that there was "no longer any maintenance for the team," although it is not clear whether the company had stopped providing funds or money was not coming in from spectators and players.[111] As amateur organizations the teams relied on the mostly unpaid labor of staff and players to keep the competitions going. Sometimes work demands had an impact on the success or failure of a particular club. After Tarentum failed to appear for a game against Dunlevy in December 1910, the home team claimed the two points and demanded they be compensated $9.35 for expenses. An investigation by the league discovered that Tarentum's manager had been called out of town on business and his friend who was supposed to handle things could not get the team together in time for the match. In another instance, when the

FIG. 4.3: Team portrait of the 1910–11 Monongahela City squad. Harry Hynds, the team's player-manager stands in a coat and hat on the far left. (Author's collection)

Dunlevy squad did not show it was because the players had misread the train schedule and did not reach the playing field in time for kickoff.[112] Finally, personal circumstances could also impact what did or did not take place on the field. In January 1911, the *Pittsburgh Press* reported that a scheduled match between Monongahela City and Tarentum was not played due to the deaths of players James Hynds and Harry Hynds. A few days later the paper corrected itself: it was the players' father who had died. Nonetheless, no replacements could be found and the game had to be postponed. In an eerie coincidence, two years later Harry Hynds, who served as player-manager of the Monongahela side, perished with ninety-five others in the Cincinnati Mine explosion.[113]

PITTSBURGH AND SOCCER IN THE UNITED STATES

Aside from the visits of Chicago and Toronto in 1892, there was very little interaction or competition with teams outside of the broader Pittsburgh area. The lack of an organized league or association may be one reason for this, compounded by the distance and expense of travel between the region and other soccer-playing centers. Although regular league play restarted in 1904, detailed reports on the region did not appear in the *Spalding Guides* until the 1909–10 edition. This despite the fact that Spalding had a sporting goods store in Pittsburgh by 1905, when the first guide appeared. In the fall of that year there was talk of forming a "Western Socker [*sic*]" league with teams in Chicago, Cincinnati, Detroit, Pittsburgh, and St. Louis. Plans were reportedly made for "an interchange of games" in 1906, but no such matches took place in Pittsburgh.[114] Newspapers in the city reported on visits to North America by English clubs such as the Corinthians and Pilgrims, but they never came to Pittsburgh even though they regularly appeared in Philadelphia. In his review of the state of soccer in the United States published in the 1911–12 edition of the *Spalding Guide*, Thomas Cahill makes no mention of Pittsburgh. He traces developments in historic soccer playing centers, including New York, Philadelphia, Chicago, and St. Louis and also mentions smaller, less-established locations such as Salt Lake City, Denver, and San Francisco.[115]

The formation of the Pittsburgh Press League and especially the Western Pennsylvania State Foot Ball Association helped end the region's relative isolation from national developments. The creation of a formal and

FIG. 4.4: East Pittsburgh Football Club after a game in October 1919. Soccer in the area took a few years to recover from the effects of World War I, but by 1921 more teams were competing than at any other time in the region's history. (Author's collection)

more-or-less permanent administrative structure mirrored developments taking place across the United States. The formation of first the American Amateur Foot Ball Association (AAFBA) in 1911 and the United States Football Association (USFA) two years later helped to launch a truly national soccer community in the United States. Supporters of the sport in Pittsburgh enthusiastically backed the new group, and the Press League became one of the first nine organizations to affiliate with the AAFBA.[116] When the USFA formed in April 1913, the Western Pennsylvania State Foot Ball Association was again a charter member, with secretary David C. Adamson serving on the organization's national and international games committee.[117] The USFA's decision to hold the 1918 annual meeting in the city shows Pittsburgh's growing importance to the national organization. During the gathering, USFA delegates toured the region, attended an athletic meet sponsored by the *Pittsburgh Press* and were guests of honor at a banquet presided over by Western Pennsylvania State Foot Ball Association officials. Near the close of the conference, the secretary-treasurer of the Press League, William S. Haddock was unanimously elected USFA treasurer. Haddock's work at the association while he held the position seems to have been appreciated by USFA authorities, who gave him an ovation after he was reelected in 1921. During his time in the post he presided over the financial expansion of the organization, growing the year-end balance from $1,326.21 in 1917 to $16,266.09 in 1923.[118] Much of that increase likely reflects the general expansion of soccer in the postwar period. The number of clubs and competitions grew across the country and the National Challenge Cup attracted more entries than ever.

5

SOCCER GOES PRO

Many people in Pittsburgh and other communities felt that paying soccer players was both financially and morally questionable. Nevertheless, clubs had long been giving jobs or other sorts of inducements to athletes almost as soon as organized competitions began. Because of its controversial nature and the secrecy surrounding the practice, our knowledge of how this system worked is incomplete. English soccer legalized professionalism in 1888, and Scottish football did so five years later. The United States had a longer tradition of professional team sports, as baseball teams began paying players in 1869. Ultimately, the traditional resistance within soccer communities to professionalism meant that it was baseball owners who created the American League of Professional Football (ALPF) in 1894. The ALPF, however, did not have an uncontested field when it came to professional soccer in the United States. A rival league called the American Association of Professional Football (AAPF) began operations at the same time.

Why did these professional leagues emerge in 1894? The baseball owners launched a soccer league because they wished to maintain control over professional team sports and because they viewed the competition as an additional revenue stream that would eventually allow them to make money year-round. In a bid to keep travel expenses low, not all of the National

League franchises took part in the soccer competition. Six clubs centered on existing baseball teams in Boston, Brooklyn, New York, Philadelphia, Baltimore, and Washington, DC, made up the league. The AAPF was even more concentrated geographically and included only four teams separated by about one hundred miles—Philadelphia, Trenton, Newark, and Paterson, New Jersey. Although it was organized by people with plenty of experience running soccer competitions, the AAPF was not linked to existing professional sports teams. The motivations for launching the AAPF are unclear as is its relationship with the American Football Association (AFA). Formed in 1884, the AFA was the first attempt to create a central organizing body for soccer in the United States. Despite its national claims, the association's influence was mostly limited to southern New England and the Mid-Atlantic states. In 1885 the group launched the American Cup, which soon became the most prestigious soccer tournament in the country as well as a de-facto national championship. Although it had cordial relations with the English Football Association, the AFA maintained a strict position against professionalism. While there is no evidence that the AFA had any official connection to the AAPF, it did seem to prefer that organization to its rival, the ALPF. Ultimately, both professional circuits were miserable failures, shutting down after only a few weeks with just twenty-five games played across the two organizations. The leagues flopped for three main reasons: poor organization, low attendance, and higher than expected costs.[1] The surprising announcement of a possible new rival baseball circuit also gave owners little incentive to try to ride out the soccer league's economic challenges. The failed experiments of 1894 meant that although from time to time there would be discussions about forming another competition, a major, fully professional soccer league would not return to the United States until 1921.[2]

THE ORIGINS OF PROFESSIONAL FOOTBALL

In 1892 William "Pudge" Heffelfinger became the earliest known professional football player when he accepted $500 to suit up for the Alleghany Athletic Club of Pittsburgh. Born in Minnesota, Hefflefinger played the intercollegiate game while a student at Yale.[3] His payday did not lead to the formation of professional teams or leagues. Around the same time, however, newspapers began running stories about the possible formation of a pro football league. In October 1892, the *Pittsburgh Dispatch* reported that an organization could be up and running by the end of the year and that baseball magnates supported the idea. Although the notion purportedly originated with athletes connected to the University of Chicago, it was soon taken up by others in Boston and New York. The aim was to play games in existing baseball stadiums during the winter, although the venues would need modifications such as the installation of heating and glass-fronted stands. The story did not explain what football code would be used, noting that amateur intercollegiate players opposed the idea and that the "scores" of English and Scottish professionals in the United States knew only the association game.[4]

Less than a week later, the same paper wrote that pro football was bound to happen but also pointed out that it faced many challenges. The empty baseball stadiums provided ready-made facilities but did not eliminate the difficult work that would have to be done to create the teams and organize the competition. The league under discussion planned to follow rugby rules but since all the best players of the game were amateur it was unlikely they would turn professional. The article referenced the rugby code but during this period the term was sometimes also used to describe the intercollegiate game.[5] By the end of the month, progress on the plan had stalled because professional soccer players from the United Kingdom refused to give up the association game in favor of rugby. The story gave the impression that a soccer league was not yet deemed feasible and that a professional rugby or intercollegiate football competition would not attract enough quality players.[6]

A year later in 1893 the idea resurfaced publicly when reporters asked John M. Ward, manager of the New York Giants baseball team, about the topic after he attended an intercollegiate football game between Princeton and Cornell in New York. Ward expressed doubts that professional gridiron football could succeed, declaring that "there is a certain romantic halo hovering over the college football players" that would vanish if they were professionals. He also felt the game was too difficult for spectators to follow and that "there is too much massing of the forces, and the forming of human pyramids." He pointed out that while on a baseball tour around the world in 1889 he observed many different versions of football. Ward believed that the Australian rules were the most suitable for a pro league but felt that the association code could also be successful.[7] Ward's comments indicate that talks about a professional football league had already begun circulating within baseball circles during the fall of 1893. A month later, the *New York Tribune* reported that baseball players were uninterested in playing professional football because the game was too rough.[8] The players' attitude may explain why the league eventually opted for the association rules. The owners believed that soccer was easier to learn and would be less physically demanding for the athletes. Despite the decision to use the association code, most baseball players balked at the idea of risking their livelihoods playing an unfamiliar sport. A *Washington Post* story introducing the city's professional soccer club confirmed the idea, saying that the team had no baseball players on the roster due to worries over possible injuries.[9] An earlier article in the *New York Tribune* voiced another concern about soccer declaring that while the association code was not as violent as the intercollegiate game, questions remained about whether it could become as popular.[10]

Within a few months, baseball magnates made the decision to form a pro circuit using the association rules. Few baseball players took part and instead teams tried to sign the best soccer players in the United States and Great Britain.[11] Representatives of the six clubs came together in New York as part of baseball's annual National League meetings and founded the ALPF on February 27, 1894.[12] The group announced its intention to form a professional football league on the East Coast in order to capitalize on existing rivalries among the baseball clubs and to minimize transportation costs.[13] Despite the popularity of the sport in places like Fall River, Massachusetts, and Pawtucket, Rhode Island, the league rejected these cities as too small.[14] When asked about player salaries, Arthur Irwin, manager of the Philadelphia team, told reporters they would be set as high as fan interest and attendance would provide for.[15]

During the next few months, the league gradually took shape. The season would run from October 1 to January 1 and feature a ten-game schedule as each team played the others at home and away. Basic admission to matches would be just twenty-five cents, lower than most intercollegiate football and professional baseball games. The association rules governed match play, although unlike in England substitutions were allowed.[16] The league's bylaws were modeled after the National League's constitution first promulgated in 1880. Although it is unknown what changes may have been made to the document, it likely contained provisions such as limiting teams to cities with a population of at least seventy-five thousand and granting owners exclusive rights to a professional franchise in their geographic area. The terms also may have retained a rule that all clubs use the same player contracts, and it is likely these agreements included the reserve clause limiting player movement. A letter from "special correspondent" and Brooklyn Captain Dennis Shea to the *Fall River (MA) Globe* reported that a couple of players from Fall River were on the "reserve list" for next season. Each athlete would sign for the three months from September 15 to December 15.[17] The document established a championship of the United States and explained that the club that won the most games would be declared the winner.[18] Despite this method of deciding a champion, Baltimore claimed the first ALPF title not because they had won the most games—Brooklyn had five victories, Boston four, and Baltimore three—but because they did not lose any.[19]

Although the ALPF had been organized by experienced and largely successful sporting entrepreneurs, it nevertheless faced challenges, including a skeptical press. A story on the new circuit in *Sporting Life* pointed out that soccer had been played in the United States for a number of years but mostly by immigrants. Overall, the paper remained unconvinced the league would be successful but conceded that "it is possible . . . that professional football will fill a certain want in the sporting world."[20] The *New York Tribune* acknowledged that soccer was not as violent as gridiron football but argued that it was also not as popular and explained that the ability of the league to increase the profile of the sport would determine the success of the ALPF.[21] Another New York paper, the *Evening World* was more pessimistic, writing that "it will probably be a failure, as the college teams are playing at that season of the year, and Association football no more compares with the college game than beanbag does with baseball."[22] The ALPF also faced the ire of the AFA because the new competition was organizing teams in its region and because the league's championship undermined the American Cup. When it was clear that the professional league was going forward, the AFA adopted a rule to "prevent effectually the national baseball league from encroaching on its territory." The association banned any player who signed with the league from playing in any AFA-sanctioned match.[23]

MOTIVATIONS AND MONEY

Why did baseball magnates who seemingly had little previous knowledge or interest in the game decide to form a professional soccer league? These owners controlled the largest and most lucrative professional team sport, and the periodic discussions of a possible football league may have encouraged them to seize the initiative to form a winter competition in order to retain their virtual monopoly over pro team sports. It would have enabled them to prevent the development of a competitor for spectator dollars while also generating profits throughout the entire year, not just during the baseball season.

If this was their reasoning, it was likely influenced by the fact that they had been constantly battling over control of professional baseball since the formation of the National League in 1876. It was only in 1890–91 that the league outlasted challenges from the American Association and the Players' League to restore its exclusive control of top-level baseball. Indeed, the demise of these rival organizations might have encouraged the owners to invest in a professional soccer league. The American Association had been a thorn in the side of National League clubs since 1882 because it threatened the controls that ensured baseball teams' profitability. The two most important of these controls were territorial monopolies that made the league the only game in town and the reserve clause that limited player movement and suppressed salaries. After the other two leagues disappeared, average National League player salaries dropped from $2,400 to $1,700 in one season. During the struggle with the Players' League in 1890, all but one of the National League teams lost money, resulting in a collective debt of $234,000.[24] As part of the reconciliation that restored the National League's monopoly, club owners spent $130,000 for the assets of the teams that were shut down. In order to eliminate these debts, clubs agreed to pay a percentage of gate receipts originally set at 10 percent but later rising to 16 percent until the balance was paid off in 1893.[25] As a result of these developments, the National League owners ended the 1893 season in an economically strong position—the territorial monopoly was in place, wages were down, and excessive debt had been eliminated. Such conditions made them willing to chance forming a professional soccer league even if, as the clubs themselves admitted, it might lose money in the first season.[26]

As businessmen, the baseball magnates must have also been motivated by the possibility of financial gain. The owners knew large crowds attended college football games and, thanks to reports in US newspapers, were likely aware that soccer teams in Great Britain often played to packed houses. The popularity of amateur soccer had also grown in the United States since the late 1880s, especially in the Philadelphia, Boston, and New York City metropolitan areas. It is no surprise that the majority of ALPF franchises were located in these cities. One article published in February 1894 outlined a more ambitious proposal for the organization that involved importing English players to participate in a ten- or twelve-team league. The plan was meant to be temporary because once baseball players learned the game they would play soccer for six months of the year and baseball for the other six. This arrangement allowed owners to fully utilize stadiums and also provided a steady source of income year-round. Baseball owners believed they could offer fans a professional sporting experience when there were few alternatives for consumers. In many cities, baseball facilities already hosted an array of events during the off-season, including college football games.[27] The formation of the soccer league was not designed to substitute

FIG. 5.1: Charley Abbey in his Washington Senators baseball uniform circa 1894. Abbey, along with Sam Thompson and Charlie Reilly (both with Philadelphia), were the only baseball players to compete in the ALPF. (Library of Congress, Prints and Photographs Division, LC-DIG-bellcm-07126)

for profits generated from Saturday college football games but instead to supplement such revenue by expanding the number of events held in the facilities. Hosting soccer games on weekday evenings while the theaters were closed generated revenue when stadiums would otherwise sit empty. The soccer league would also face less competition once the intercollegiate football season ended after the turn of the New Year. By having the stadiums filled on as many days as possible, the baseball magnates increased the facilities' profit-making potential. Initially, at least, the owners were willing to be patient with the new competition and they acknowledged that the inaugural season would be an educational experience designed to win over fans.[28] Finally, because there was talk that the popularity of baseball was declining, the owners might have been looking for another sport to provide income should the national pastime cease to attract crowds the way it had been.[29]

THE AMERICAN ASSOCIATION OF PROFESSIONAL FOOTBALL CLUBS

As it happened, the baseball owners soon found themselves in another struggle for control over professional sport when the American Association of Professional Football (AAPF) announced its existence in August 1894. In an extraordinary article published in the *Philadelphia Public Ledger*, the organization portrayed itself as the exact opposite of the ALPF and even the name of the group—the American Association—seemed like a direct challenge to National League baseball owners.[30] In fact, the *Fall River Globe* reported that "moneyed men" from Philadelphia, Trenton, Newark, and Brooklyn organized the second circuit to "run in opposition" to the ALPF.[31] The main force behind the AAPF was Clement Beecroft, who had long been active in Philadelphia soccer circles and has been described as "the father of league football" in the city. Beecroft was born in England around 1860 and came to the United States sometime in the 1880s. An avid cricket player, he eventually operated a sporting goods store that served as an organizational hub for Philadelphia's nascent soccer community. When the Pennsylvania Football Union formed in 1889, Beecroft was elected its first president. Under his leadership, regular league play began along with intercity matches against teams from Trenton, New York, and other cities.[32]

Shortly after the announcement by baseball owners of the formation of the ALPF in early 1894, Beecroft began writing to friends in different cities declaring that "the time had arrived to play foot ball professionally in this country." In addition to Beecroft, who represented Philadelphia, delegates from Brooklyn, New York, Trenton, Newark, and Paterson met to found the AAPF. Despite plans for a six-team league, not coincidentally the same size as the ALPF, the AAPF ultimately included just four clubs: Philadelphia, Trenton, Paterson, and Newark. The team usually referred to in newspapers as Newark, however, was actually the Union Athletic Association team from Kearny, New Jersey. Newspaper reports indicated that a field had been rented and players had been signed by teams in Brooklyn and New York, but those clubs never joined the organization. As late as October 13, 1894, the league may have still expected a team from New York to compete, because an AAPF league table appearing in the *Public Ledger* included the Cosmopolitans from New York but showed they had not played any games. If the teams from New York had joined, it would have meant that the two soccer organizations directly competed with each other in half of their markets.[33] Eventually the AAPF planned to challenge the baseball league by placing a team in Boston and by adding a club in Fall River. Having a franchise in the Spindle City might put pressure on ALPF rosters since many of the players came from the area. The association planned to play a fall season from September to January and a spring campaign from March to June.

The story in the *Public Ledger* compared the ways that the AAPF ran its organization with the league headed by baseball owners. Like the ALPF, Beecroft's group felt that having a geographically limited league, at least in the first season, would keep transportation costs low. Unlike its rival, however, the AAPF only scheduled games on Saturdays and holidays. Such a calendar mirrored not only intercollegiate football but also the format of England's First Division. The decision was in part a cost-saving measure because teams would not pay lodging fees at away matches. Further, it kept wages under control because players could continue working other jobs during the week. The story reasoned that because players in the AAPF would not need to quit their existing positions, they did not need to be paid as much by their teams. The article suggested that even if some clubs, presumably those in the ALPF, paid an athlete one hundred dollars a month to play soccer exclusively, it would not attract the best workers.[34] The qualities that made them successful on the field also meant that they had well-paying careers off the field. Such an attitude reflects the fact that many of the British immigrants who played soccer in the United States during this period generally held higher-skilled and thus higher-paid jobs. The story took a number of other jabs at the organization and plans of the ALPF, especially the idea of playing on weekdays: "those people who are talking about playing four games per week evidently know nothing about this sport." Soccer was not yet popular enough to attract paying fans on weekdays, the story continued, especially once the weather turned cold. The article concluded that having so many games per week would also be hard on the players and ultimately meant that payroll costs would grow as squad sizes had to be expanded to twenty-five or thirty-five players per team.[35] The article may have been correct that the baseball magnates' lack of familiarity with soccer caused them to underestimate the physical impact of playing multiple games per week. Since baseball team rosters were generally set at around thirteen, the larger numbers needed for soccer would have undercut the financial rationale for having baseball players play soccer games.

In some ways, the decision to form a second professional soccer league was a strange one. Beecroft began the process immediately after the ALPF announced it was creating a league. As with the new rival baseball league proposed in the fall of 1894, talks leading to the formation of the AAPF were conducted in secret and only revealed to the public six months later, just a few weeks before the ALPF was scheduled to kick off. Given the timing of the process and some of the other factors discussed below, it does seem apparent that the formation of the AAPF was part of a determined effort to undermine the baseball owners' league. One explanation for the *Public Ledger*'s attacks on the ALPF is that although the article does not have a byline, Horace Fogel was a sportswriter at the paper. He was actively involved in the formation of the AAPF and eventually served as president of the Philadelphia club.[36] Strangely, Fogel also had a connection to National League baseball, as he had been manager of the Indianapolis Hoosiers in 1887 when the club was owned by John T. Brush. After the Indiana club went under, Brush was given a stake in the New York Giants franchise and by 1894 was reportedly trying to buy the club outright.[37]

Another open question is the relationship between the AFA and the AAPF. Although Beecroft and Fogel came from Philadelphia, the meeting announcing the formation of the AAPF took place in Newark, one of the AFA's headquarters since its founding.[38] After his years of being involved in Philadelphia soccer and especially in organizing intercity clashes,

Beecroft had established relationships with members of the AFA.[39] Other officials from AAPF clubs, such as William Turner, Arthur Goldthorpe, and William Guthrie, had been or would later be closely involved in AFA business, with both Turner and Goldthorpe serving as president of the organization.[40] It seems unlikely that Beecroft and the others decided to organize a professional league in the heart of AFA territory without consulting the association. Since the AFA revered amateurism, it is hard to reconcile such an attitude with even an indirect support of professionalism. Not all of the teams in the AAPF, however, were composed of professional players. Philadelphia, Paterson, and Trenton were likely paid squads, while the Newark side remained amateur and was allowed to continue playing in the American Cup even as the AFA announced it was banning professionals. The case of Hugh McGhee illustrates the AFA's inconsistent attitude toward professionalism. McGhee reportedly signed a contract with the New York team before the AAPF season began. Because that club never materialized, McGhee went back to his old team, the Unions (i.e., Newark). Since he competed in American Cup matches during the AAPF season, he must have avoided an AFA ban.[41] After losing to the Kearny Unions 15–0, amateur side Centerville filed a claim with the AFA, alleging that some of the opposing players were professionals, but the AFA dismissed the protest.[42] Allowing an amateur squad to compete in a professional league at the same time it remained in the American Cup shows that the AFA did not object to the AAPF in the same way it did the baseball owners' league.[43]

The notices announcing the AFA's ban of ALPF players emphasized that the rule was enacted because the league was encroaching on its territory and enticing its athletes to turn professional.[44] In the eyes of the AFA, the baseball owners were doing to them what rival leagues had done to the National League for years—challenging their territorial monopoly and poaching their players. Nearly the entire Brooklyn team came from well-established Fall River clubs such as East Ends, Olympics, and Rovers, all of which had won the American Cup in previous seasons. Several Washington players had been signed from Trenton, home to one of the AAPF's franchises.[45] After the two professional leagues dissolved, the AFA reinstated the amateur status of players who had signed professional contracts with teams from both organizations. The notice was made directly to the newly formed Manz FC, a team composed almost entirely of players

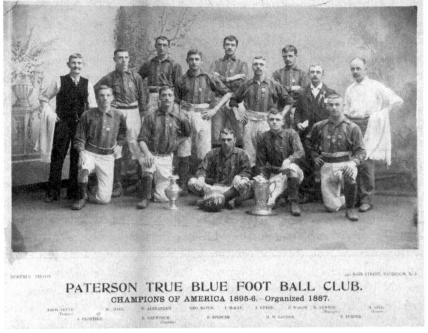

PATERSON TRUE BLUE FOOT BALL CLUB.
CHAMPIONS OF AMERICA 1895-6. Organized 1887.

FIG. 5.2: Paterson True Blues, winners of the American Cup in 1896. As many as six players from the team competed as professionals in 1894: George Eaton, Ralph Hall, James Oldfield, Robert Spencer, and Thomas Turner played for Paterson in the AAPF; Robert Wason lined up for Philadelphia's AAPF squad. (Author's collection)

from Philadelphia's AAPF side. The club went on to become the first team from the city to win the American Cup in 1897.[46]

BUILDING A SQUAD

Most of the AAPF sides recruited players from existing local teams. As already noted, the Newark team was really just a rebranding of an existing squad, but clubs from Paterson and Philadelphia were newly created teams.[47] The ALPF clubs signed experienced soccer players from league cities like Philadelphia and New York, but a good number also came from Fall River, Pawtucket, and other communities in New England where the sport was popular. Brooklyn's squad, for example, included many well-known players from Massachusetts headlined by Dennis Shea, perhaps the country's best goalkeeper and a member of the Canadian-US team that had toured Great

Britain in 1891. Boston also recruited a number of players from Fall River, including John Sunderland and Thomas Kenney of the Rovers, along with James Irving and Arthur Puleston from the Olympics.[48] Reported wages of sixty-five dollars a month, however, were insufficient to tempt all players to leave the area. Fred Gregory of the Pawtucket Wanderers refused an offer to sign a professional contract, declaring that the money was not enough due to the risk of injury.[49] Ultimately, Charlie Reilly and Sam Thompson of Philadelphia along with Charley Abbey from Washington were the only professional baseball players to appear in the soccer league.[50]

Baltimore reportedly got off to a slow start landing players but claimed to have spent the most money. Later the team complained that the other owners decided to end the league because the Orioles were too good.[51] Ned Hanlon, the ostensible manager of the side, used his connections in Detroit to enlist veteran player A. W. Stewart to assemble the squad, play goalkeeper, and captain the team.[52] To help build the roster, Stewart brought experienced players with him from Michigan, most notably three

THE DETROIT ASSOCIATION FOOT BALL TEAM.

J. D. KING.	WM. KAY.	M'PHERSON.	FLEMING.	JOHN M'KENDRICK.	J. S. M'KAY.	A. P. YOUNG.
	CORBETT.	COLLIE.	MASCOT.	M'MILLAN.	STEWART.	JAS. M'KENDRICK.
		RAMSEY.		HENDERSON.	W. M'KENDRICK.	

FIG. 5.3: Detroit Association Football Club, 1891. A. W. Stewart played goal and assembled the Baltimore squad of the ALPF. In addition to the players who came from England, Stewart arranged for three McKendrick brothers—William, John, and James—to join him from Detroit. (*Detroit Free Press*, November 21, 1891)

of the McKendrick brothers.[53] A story in *Sporting Life* claimed that, because Baltimore had won the baseball pennant and was competing in a newly created postseason series called the Temple Cup, they had been late to sign players. As a result, the club's owner, Harry Von der Horst, asked a well-known former baseball player and manager named Ted Sullivan to go to Great Britain to find established professionals. According to the article, Sullivan sailed from the United States on September 3, 1894, and visited Glasgow, then Liverpool and Manchester. After a bit of chicanery that supposedly involved the Irish-born Sullivan faking a Scottish accent, he convinced several clubs to release players by claiming that they would be participating in a series of friendlies in Scotland. Once the arrangements had been settled, the men traveled to Liverpool and on to the United States.[54] The club caused some controversy by signing five British players—Mitchell Calvey, Archibald Ferguson, Thomas Little, Alexander Wallace, and Fred Davis. Four of the players had been under contract with Manchester City; the exception, Little, had played for City the previous season but was now with Sheffield United.[55] Newspapers later reported that Baltimore was being investigated for violating federal law prohibiting employers from offering contracts to workers before they entered the United States. Stewart denied that the players had signed before they left Britain, and the investigation seems to have been dropped once the league ceased operations.[56]

The circumstances surrounding the signing of foreign players remain murky, and there are reasons to believe that the versions reported in the press do not tell the complete story. The players had all played for a Manchester club, traveled together on the SS *Teutonic*, and except for Davis are listed consecutively on the ship's passenger manifest. Davis is listed next to Alex Ireland, who also seems to have played for the Orioles.[57] Stewart denied any premeditation in signing the men, claiming instead that he had gone to New York to meet a friend who was arriving on the same ship, only to find that three other professional footballers had landed at the same time.[58] Despite Stewart's explanation and the story in *Sporting Life*, not all of the reported facts add up. Sullivan's name, for instance, does not appear on the *Teutonic*'s manifest, indicating that he did not return to the United States with the players. Another account claimed that Sullivan brought seven players with him; Calvey, Davis, Little, Ferguson, and Wallace are five, while counting Ireland only makes six who arrived on the *Teutonic*.[59] The final member of the squad, a forward, is known only by his surname, Barkey, and likely came from Canada and not England. In July 1894 the Toronto Scots defeated a select team from the local league playing in Buffalo, New York. In addition to a forward named Barkey who scored a goal, the visitor's lineup included a McKendrick, probably John, at half back. During their time in Detroit, the McKendrick brothers and A. W. Stewart regularly competed against Canadian teams, including those from Toronto. It is likely that one or more of them knew Barkey either from those contests or from playing together in the summer of 1894.[60]

Evidence suggests that other teams also signed, or tried to sign, players from abroad. After the first league match was held in the city, the *Philadelphia Inquirer* wrote that some of the players "have been imported especially to play in the new league."[61] James McKay, New York's goalkeeper, arrived from Liverpool just a day before the club played a warm-up friendly against a team from Brooklyn. McKay claimed to have been an established keeper in England having played for "Bootles and Evertons" of Liverpool.[62] Other members of the squad had reportedly lined up for Preston North End reserves in England, although many of them had relocated to the United States before the announcement of the new league. Brooklyn captain Dennis Shea's comment that he had seen players he faced while touring England in 1891 now playing for ALPF squads prompts a question about the timing of their arrival.[63] Washington also signed a player named Parr, who one newspaper report praised as "the English crack" although it is unclear if he came to Washington directly from Europe.[64] Several articles reported that Boston had contracted a pair of brothers from Manchester, one of whom had been captain of a youth team called the Swifts.[65]

A TALE OF TWO SEASONS

The AAPF got the ball rolling, playing the first explicitly professional soccer league matches in the United States on September 29, 1894. Taking place in Philadelphia and Newark, the games featured a lot of goals, twenty-three in total, including Philadelphia winning 11–1 over Trenton. Such lopsided scores were not uncommon in both leagues, suggesting a lack of competitive balance. Philadelphia proved to be the class of the AAPF, winning three and drawing one while scoring an average of six goals per game. Attendance numbers were only reported for the Quaker City match; a figure of around one thousand boded well for the upstart association.[66] A week later the crowd was even larger, as up to five thousand fans packed Cosmopolitan Park in Kearny to see the home side lose a squeaker to Philadelphia 1–2.[67] The weather was a factor in at least two of the match weeks, as rain led to the cancellation of games on October 13 and November 3.[68] Without concrete figures, it is hard to draw conclusions, but it may be that the lack of competitiveness combined with winter weather suppressed crowd totals.

Another factor may have been the seemingly inconsistent scheduling. An announcement in the *Newark Sunday Call* on September 23 stated that the home squad would play the following fixtures: September 29 at Paterson; October 6 vs. Philadelphia; October 13 at Philadelphia; October 20 vs. Caledonians; October 27 at Trenton.[69] As it turned out, the September 29 match was actually held at Newark, the October 20 contest was not a league match, and there is no record that the game at Trenton ever took place. Overall the association managed to complete only seven games in what was presumably meant to be a twenty-four-game season. Two of the matches were set to go ahead but were canceled while others may have been called off once it became clear that Philadelphia was likely to win the title. In other competitions in cities around the country, such inconsistency was often viewed as stifling both the popularity and the growth potential of the sport. No official announcement was made ending the league, although the Philadelphia team would go on to challenge the city's ALPF side and play a friendly versus Princeton Theological Seminary before transforming into the Manz squad.[70]

The ALPF kicked off its campaign a week after the AAPF with two games on October 6, 1894. After dropping the opening day match to Boston 3–2, Brooklyn would not lose again and ended the season with five wins, tops in the league. On the same day, Philadelphia lost to New York 5–0, prefiguring the Quaker City squad's lack of success—they played eight games, the most of any team, and lost six, also leading the league in futility. Perhaps because of the British professionals, Baltimore won all three games the team played, including a 10–1 rout of Washington on October 16. All told, just seventeen games took place before the owners decided to shut down the league.

Both competitions suffered from some of the same issues that plagued amateur soccer organizations during this period, including overly rough play, problems with officials, a lack of planning, and poor weather. During the season opener at Boston, Arthur Puleston of the home side and Robert Pickup of the visitors got tangled up, and, after Puleston fell to the ground, his opponent kicked him several times. Pickup was soon taken off and, lacking the proper kit, his replacement played in "long trousers and street shoes." Later in the same match, two players came to blows and spent several minutes pummeling each other.[71] Some days later, the ALPF failed to name a referee for a game between Boston and New York, and the one who finally started the match made so many bad decisions that he was substituted at halftime.[72] The man in charge of creating the schedule for the league was Brooklyn owner Charles Byrne, who initially planned for each team to play the others five times. Whatever the intent, the result was a chaotic format that left the teams playing an uneven number of games. Other problems included the fact that Philadelphia had completed six games and New York and Brooklyn five before Baltimore had played even a single match. The excuse of an extended postseason baseball schedule does not seem to hold water, as the Orioles' opponent in the Temple Cup was New York, which nevertheless ended the soccer season playing twice as many league matches as Baltimore. The Orioles may have been waiting for the British players to arrive before starting the season.[73] The weather also interfered with planning, as matches scheduled to be played on Sunday, October 14, had to be postposed to the next day because of a poor field in Brooklyn and rain in Philadelphia.[74] Moving the games to a weekday likely did not improve attendance, although the baseball clubs regularly played weekday games. During the 1894 baseball season, for example, Brooklyn drew three thousand people to a contest with Boston on Monday, April 23. Other weekday baseball games played against cities that also had soccer clubs regularly drew similar or greater numbers.[75]

Numerous pronouncements both during and after the season indicated that the ALPF did not necessarily expect to turn a profit in the first year. Nevertheless, ownership must have been shocked at the dismal attendance figures. During the 1894 baseball season, the clubs averaged around 1,500 spectators per game over a 132-game schedule.[76] The numbers for the football league are by no means complete, but it seems that most games drew only a few hundred fans, with only one or two attracting more than one thousand. At times the crowds were almost comically small. Even after promoting the match as "Ladies Day," only eighteen paying customers (four of them ladies) saw Brooklyn beat visiting Philadelphia on October 18. Across town on the same day, around fifty people watched New York play Boston at the Polo Grounds (capacity of 16,000).[77]

On October 18, the baseball magnates voted to suspend the league, effective after the October 20 matches. The reason stated in the *Baltimore Sun* was that losses had already climbed to $2,000, in part because total gate receipts had not topped $25.[78] It is unclear from the article, but the figure of $2,000 must have been per team, because with little or no gate revenue salary costs and other expenses would have meant that each team was in the red by at least that amount. The low attendance figures clearly played an important role in the decision but were not the only reason for shutting down the circuit. One key to the profitability of baseball teams was the development of additional revenue streams beyond gate receipts. Player fines and suspensions became a way to recover salary costs, but the soccer league had not played enough games to make this a meaningful factor in reducing costs. Other factors in baseball's success were the sale of concessions, telegraphing rights, and other products.[79] Harry Von der Horst, the owner of the Baltimore franchise, for example, was a brewer who used the team as an outlet for selling beer.[80] Low attendance combined with colder weather may have reduced income from concessions at all stadiums. In general, newspaper coverage of the league was not as comprehensive as for baseball, making it likely that the value of any sort of telegraphing rights would have been substantially lower if they could be sold at all. Finally, given the novelty of the league and its low level of popularity relative to baseball and intercollegiate football, the market for ancillary products was probably nonexistent. As a result of these factors, the clubs became even more dependent on the income generated from disappointingly low ticket sales.

The AAPF also relied on gate receipts to pay player salaries. A story published October 14 in the *Philadelphia Times* claimed that the home team's players were angry with the club because they had not been paid. The article stated that when Beecroft arrived for a scheduled match he "saw that the gate would amount to nothing" and canceled the game. Even after the referee had awarded the match to the visitors, the angry players decided to go ahead with the game anyway and afterward demanded to be paid.[81] The next day, however, the *Public Ledger* published a rebuttal to the story, describing Philadelphia's team officers as "indignant" over the story in the *Times*. The article noted that, despite the fact there had been no gate, the players had still been paid. On October 16, the *Philadelphia Times* printed a retraction to the original story, writing that it had been "misinformed" about the incident. The story highlights how dependent on gate receipts the team was to pay the players. Even the *Public Ledger* maintained that the team had covered the salaries even though they had made no money on the game. Such a statement implies that the usual practice was to pay the salaries out of the revenue generated from ticket sales.[82]

Although National League baseball seemed to be on sounder financial footings than in previous years, the margins of profitability remained narrow and lower revenues combined with unexpected costs could wreck the bottom line. Indeed, such disasters happened during the 1894 baseball season, as first Boston and then Philadelphia had stadium fires. The blaze at South End Park in Massachusetts caused an estimated $75,000 of damage to the facility, not all of which was covered by insurance. The total losses for the fire in Philadelphia, including surrounding homes and businesses, was around $250,000.[83] The price of rebuilding the facilities was not trivial: Boston's East End grounds had cost $75,000 when it was constructed in 1888, and the price tag for Philadelphia's new stadium built in in 1895 eventually totaled $101,000.[84] Despite the fire, Boston realized a net profit of $35,000 for the 1894 baseball season, in part by keeping spending low, a decision that caused angry fans to complain about "the close way the club was run."[85] Even if as reports indicated Boston had gone into the soccer season prepared to lose $5,000, the way things were going it was likely that the overall total would be much higher. While such amounts may not seem excessively large, it is important to note that, for the most part, the baseball magnates were small-business owners and professionals, not wealthy industrialists or robber barons. They were lawyers, brewers, and meat packers who were used to operating the clubs on small margins, so the decision to end the league may have represented their recognition that it would be a long and difficult challenge to make professional football profitable.[86]

The way that ALPF owners dealt with player salaries following the dissolution of the league reveals how ruthless they were about containing costs. Although the players signed three-month contracts for the season, the clubs announced that they would only pay wages up to November 1, 1894. Such an offer allowed them to save money but represented a setback for the players, especially those who had relocated in order to compete. Not surprisingly, the *Boston Daily Globe* reported that the players felt they were entitled to the full amount whether the league continued or not.[87] Eventually, a group originally from Fall River headed by Arthur Puleston retained the law firm of Swift and Grime in order to recoup lost wages. Comparing the money they received as professional footballers to what they may have made in their regular jobs explains why the players fought so hard for their money. In 1894 wage earners in manufacturing industries took home on average thirty-two dollars a month. The top wage in the ALPF was set at sixty-five dollars a month—over twice that earned by manufacturing workers.[88] Although negotiations took more than a year, the club eventually paid the players.[89] Newspapers in England also reported that not only had Baltimore refused to pay the full salaries of the foreign players on the team, but it was also reluctant to pay their return passage to England. The intervention of the British Consul resolved the matter, although the players were given steerage-class tickets rather than the second-class ones that brought them to the United States.[90]

Baltimore's decision to import so many foreign players may have led other owners to fear that the competition for and the cost of signing top talent would only increase over time. These concerns were not unanticipated, and when the league had only begun to organize in early 1894 they had considered requiring that teams only sign players based in the same city or state. Such a measure was designed to prevent the kind of excessive competition for players that drove up salaries. The rule was never enforced, but the fact that it was floated as a possibility indicates how keen ownership was to keep player costs as low as possible.[91] Although they were accustomed to searching out baseball players from throughout the United States, the nature of competitive soccer now meant that they would have to look even farther afield. The price of finding, recruiting, and relocating players from overseas was undoubtedly higher than signing them from Pawtucket and Fall River. The success of the Orioles in limited league play may have signaled to the other owners that if they wanted to remain competitive they would need to at least consider recruiting talent from abroad. It may also explain some of the announcements in the press that a few clubs had not wanted to end the competition but had been convinced or overruled by those that did.[92]

Although the virtually empty ballparks and the potential of increasing salary costs may have made some owners nervous, the formation of another rival baseball league killed any desire they might have had to continue with a money-losing soccer competition. At the very moment the ALPF began play, the baseball owners looked to be facing another potentially costly battle over control of their primary sport. The threat was serious and, according to *Sporting Life*, "the first announcement of the proposed Association fell like a bombshell into the base ball camp."[93] The thought of a renewed challenge enraged the owners. They immediately called a secret meeting to deal with the crisis and sent agents around the country threatening to ban anyone who signed with the new organization. They also authorized the creation of a committee that would find and punish any National League figures who aided the new association.[94] Unlike the smaller and less established AAPF who challenged them on the soccer field, the new baseball circuit had a number of advantages. The organization planned franchises in Brooklyn, Philadelphia, New York, Washington, Pittsburgh, Milwaukee, Detroit, and Chicago. Reports praised the new league's experienced leadership and noted that they had solid financial resources behind them. The group proposed lower ticket prices and refused to honor the reserve system, meaning they would compete with National League clubs to sign out-of-contract players. Overall, *Sporting Life* felt this was a serious operation that "stands upon the winning platform of fair competition and popular prices."[95] The formation of the new association once again threatened the two pillars of National League profitability: territorial monopoly and control over players. Ultimately, the new baseball league never materialized, but by the time that was clear the owners had already voted to end their dalliance with professional soccer.[96] It would take a number of years before self-described professional football returned to the United States. It is likely, though, that players continued to receive covert payments along with other benefits for playing the sport. One notable example came a year after Pudge Heffelfinger became the first male professional football player, when a group of women in San Francisco were paid to play association football games. In contrast to Heffelfinger's five hundred dollar payday, the female soccer players received just two dollars a match.[97]

COLLEEN BAWNS AND BONNIE LASSIES

Early attitudes in the United States toward women playing football tended to see such games if not as a joke then at least something to be approached with bemused curiosity often combined with voyeuristic sexism. Despite these views, many of the first female players took on the new pastime determined to show they could excel at the sport. Nevertheless, throughout the late nineteenth century the media depicted most women's football games, including those played outside the United States as unusual spectacles and not as serious sporting contests. While the development of commercialized mass sport for men accelerated in the second half of the nineteenth century, team competitions for women remained limited. Nevertheless, some individual sports and noncompetitive athletic activities became increasingly available to women.[1] Historian Susan Cahn argues that gendered attitudes toward athletics during this period created a distinction between "manly sport" and "female exercise."[2] Medical science supported this notion by classifying menstruation as an "eternal wound" that weakened women's physical constitution and disqualified them from engaging in vigorous exercise. Doctors increasingly viewed moderate activities like walking as useful in strengthening women's bodies without overtaxing them.[3] In addition, many physicians advocated exercise as a solution to the supposed problem of excessive mental strain suffered by young women who were attending colleges in increasing numbers. By the 1890s, a cadre of female physical education instructors coached these students in a variety of sports, including field hockey and basketball.[4] Many of these educators felt that intercollegiate competition would negatively impact the development of women's sports. As a result, much of the activity remained limited to intramural contests, often organized around competitions between classes.[5] As cultural norms shifted and women began to take part in more team-centered recreational activities, soccer emerged as one of a series of sports deemed appropriate for female participation.

The limited opportunities for recreational activity and the economic investment needed to compete in "respectable" sports—cycling, croquet, golf, tennis, and the various games played on campus—led some women to seek alternative pastimes. These activities included less socially acceptable types of competitions, especially those increasingly seen as exclusively male, like baseball and boxing.[6] By the 1870s, even as events such as bike races became more commercialized, there remained a stigma attached to professionalism, especially for women.[7] Competing for money not only threatened women's physical well-being but, as historian Jean Williams notes, "implied both dubious character and questionable moral choice."[8] Nevertheless, people began to organize women's games and even team tours as novel sporting spectacles aimed at generating profitable returns. By the late 1860s, women were "performing" baseball as part of the growth in popularity of burlesque shows. The first women's professional teams emerged from these types of spectacles.[9]

In Great Britain, the earliest known association football game played by women in 1881 was the start of what became an eight-game tour. About one thousand spectators gathered at Easter Road in Edinburgh to watch teams of young women compete as Scotland versus England. According to one newspaper, the overall quality of play was lacking, although some participants displayed a fair amount of skill. Despite positive early notices, disruptive crowds, field invasions, and hostile press reports plagued other matches.[10] In 1890, two male entrepreneurs formed the Original English Lady Cricketers who played each other as the Blues and Reds. The women were paid one shilling per day, competed using pseudonyms; like all previous attempts at organizing a sustained women's competition, the effort lasted only about a year.[11]

Press in the United States paid some attention to Netty Honeyball and British Ladies FC when they began play in 1895.[12] The coverage included cartoons of women playing football like the one used to promote a medicine designed to cure "female weakness." The copy acknowledged that, although many women rode bicycles, they were not strong enough to compete in more vigorous sports such as football or tennis. Rather than suggest that athletic activity might help strengthen women's bodies, the story promoted a medicinal cure called Dr. Pierce's Favorite Prescription. Another drawing appeared in a humor section called "Let us All Laugh" and joked that although women played football they were still afraid of mice.[13] Both images repeated long-standing beliefs surrounding women and sport. The first image reinforced the idea that women were inherently weak, making certain types of sports unsuitable for them. The second cartoon used humor to reassure readers that even as women began to participate in athletics they nonetheless retained typically feminine characteristics.

THE EARLY WOMEN'S GAME

Indigenous women and girls participated in various types of kicking games, but evidence of European-American women playing any version of football before 1893 are scarce. One of the earliest depictions appeared in the August 28, 1869, issue of *Harper's Bazaar*. The picture was part of a set of four illustrations on the page, all beginning with the caption "The Girls of the Period." The pictures show young women engaged in different leisure activities, including bathing, rowing, fishing, and "playing ball." The set is not linked to any article or story in the volume and is presented without additional comment as a standalone tableau. With the exception of the bathers, the scenes depict women enjoying typically male pastimes in traditional male settings. In three of the images, including the bathing view, women are smoking cigarettes. While some members of the fishing group hold poles, others are enjoying a meal and one is drinking from a bottle. The rowers are cheered on by a group of young women on the shore, who seem to be devoted followers of the sport, much like the schoolboys who formed Oneida FC. In the background of the football scene, women are participating in the types of recreational activities often held at ethnic

THE GIRLS OF THE PERIOD—PLAYING BALL.

FIG. 6.1: Women kicking a football as other games and activities take place behind them. Such events recall the sort of games that took place on holidays or at ethnic festivals. (*Harper's Bazaar*, August 28, 1869, 557)

and other sporting festivals, including climbing a pole, playing cricket, and running races.[14] Taken together, the images serve as commentary on the shifting mores of young people but also reflect slowly changing attitudes about women and physical activity. The pictures also reinforce the notion that football was largely viewed as sport for young men.

In 1874 the *Detroit Free Press* announced that women at Vassar College were allowed to play football, adding "it is an inspiring sight to see one of them miss the ball and land on her head in the grass."[15] A telling early example of the way the press approached the women's game appeared in the *National Police Gazette* on July 27, 1878. The notice includes a full-page illustration of three women dressed in full skirts; one of the women looks to have just kicked the ball into the air. The activity takes place at Prospect Park in Brooklyn, a relatively rural location lacking the crowds of other metropolitan spaces, including Manhattan's Central Park. The accompanying text explains this "opportunity for blooming city beauties with a taste for active sport and a romp untrammelled by conventionalities to give vent to their healthful animal spirits in a manner that they would not dare indulge in under the gaze of the multitude of profane eyes in less favored localities."[16] The description highlights the voyeuristic nature of the spectacle by placing the reader in the position of a presumably male viewer who might chance on the bucolic sight while walking in the park. The scene and the language call to mind images of nymphs caught at bathing, a popular subject in Western art since classical times. The eroticized language describing the players as unconventional women indulging their "animal spirits" emphasizes the notion that the picture was not really about athletics but instead served as a titillating tableau for the paper's largely male readership.

Several years later, the *Fort Wayne Sentinel* provided a different account of women's football in a pair of notices published in the spring of 1882. The first story told of a surprise party thrown for Mrs. Judge Lowry by the "Ladies' Football Club." The piece noted that the partygoers did not actually play football during the event, but they did dance. A few weeks later, another article in the same paper announced that West End Ladies' FC was to be reorganized and soon the group would again be kicking a "rubber ball" on the lawns of Berry and Wayne Streets.[17] Census records indicate that Robert Lowry was a federal judge living in Fort Wayne, Indiana, with his wife Charlotte and three children, all girls. The oldest, Anna, was born in 1849 and was listed as Robert's daughter, likely from a previous marriage. The younger daughters were Lida (b. 1865) and Lotta (b. 1872). The family lived on West Main Street very near to the streets listed in the article.[18] The specific mention of kicking the ball across yards lends credence to the notion that the group actually did meet to play some type of football and was not simply a cheeky name for a social organization. The lack of detail makes it impossible to determine what type of football may have been played, but such activities were usually not organized according to a strict adherence to a particular set of rules and instead resembled an informal type of kick-about. The fact that the household consisted of girls of various ages may be further evidence that it was a type of pastime or recreation and not an organized contest.

Other early press reports of women playing football come from advertisements promoting burlesque and vaudeville shows. In most cases the football played was probably meant to mimic the intercollegiate rules as they became increasingly popular at the nation's universities during the

1880s and 1890s. In 1894, the "Yale and Princeton lady football players" were set to appear as part of a show at Epstein's Dime Museum in Chicago. The notice declares that "the girls play to win, and the customary thumps, bumps, and bruises of this amiable sport are incidents of nearly every game."[19] Such language, combined with the fact that the sides took the names of well-known colleges, shows that they were at least inspired by the gridiron code. A similar, albeit less specific, ad gave notice that "the Lady Football Team" was included as part of the Harry Morris Burlesques and Vaudeville Company scheduled to play a matinee performance in Cincinnati.[20] Such activities were similar to the first women's baseball clubs that initially began playing as part of burlesque shows. Eventually women's baseball teams separated from the traveling vaudeville troupes and tried to make money as singular attractions.[21] By the fall of 1894, at least one team of women had been organized, presumably with a goal of making money by playing competitive football. A report in the *Los Angeles Herald* declared that a women's gridiron football team from Denver had been in touch with an all-American team based on the West Coast. Supposedly a game between the teams had already been scheduled, but there was no report on the result of the contest.[22] A few weeks after the original story, the *Philadelphia Times* added more detail on the event, noting that the players wore regular football uniforms, including padded trousers. Other details in the story suggest that the rules used may have been a hybrid that combined aspects of the rugby, association, and gridiron games. According to the report, the contest was not as rough as gridiron football and the team captains were familiar with both English codes. The clubs played indoors, giving some indication that it was designed less as a sporting contest and more as a form of entertainment. Nevertheless, the fact that the winning team earned a fifty-dollar prize may have ensured that the matches were seriously contested.[23]

THE EARLIEST WOMEN'S SOCCER GAME

On December 3, 1893, at San Francisco's Central Park, the Colleen Bawns defeated the Bonnie Lassies 2–0 in the earliest documented women's soccer game played in the United States. While women in the United States had been playing various types of football since before the country was founded, the 1893 contest was the first known match using association rules. Despite the fact that the same teams met again on December 10, the two matches did not lead to the development of stable women's clubs or the establishment of a regular playing schedule.[24] The contests had been organized as a novel and attractive sporting spectacle designed to make money, rather than as a serious attempt at encouraging female participation in athletic competition. Nevertheless, the games symbolized broader cultural changes regarding the value of athletics for women in the United States and illustrated the continued development of commercialized mass leisure industries, including soccer, in San Francisco during the late nineteenth century. The sparse information about individual players from the Bawns and Lassies shows that some of the women approached the games with a genuine competitive spirit along with a desire to make the contests more than just curiosities aimed at amusing the crowd.

The promoter who sponsored the game between the Bawns and Lassies was a Canadian named Daniel Roderick McNeill. He was born on Prince Edward Island in 1848, and his father likely came from Scotland. McNeill immigrated to the United States around 1868 to settle in Lynn, Massachusetts. By 1876 he had relocated to San Francisco and become a naturalized citizen.[25] McNeill was heavily enmeshed in the city's social and cultural networks, especially recreational life. Among other groups, he was active with the Canadian Association, the Scottish Hall Association, and the Pacific Coast Lacrosse Association.[26] In 1884 the *Daily Alta California* announced the formation of the Central Park Association, whose aims were to "purchase, sell and lease real estate, erect buildings, let halls, gardens, rinks, parks, etc., hold bazars and give concerts and theatrical, athletic and other entertainments." McNeill was one of eight initial investors who planned to build a "sporting park" at Eighth and Market Streets in San Francisco.[27]

For the next several decades, McNeill served as superintendent of the complex and president of the association, and seems to have been the driving force behind the group's operations. Within a few weeks, a baseball diamond was nearly ready and plans were made for the construction of more facilities, including a track and other grounds.[28] The official opening of the park on Thanksgiving Day 1884 featured a diverse program of recreations, including amateur and professional baseball games, German turnverein exhibitions, and athletic competitions featuring strongman and wrestler Duncan C. Ross.[29] As revealed by the range of sporting activities offered, Central Park was not simply a baseball stadium but, true to the charter of the original association, presented a variety of entertainments. By 1887 the complex was also home to a saloon, restaurant, barbershop, cigar store, and candy shop.[30]

Although Central Park hosted a number of diverse events, the popularity of baseball in the city meant that the sport quickly became an important component of the association's plans. Baseball had been played in San Francisco since at least the Gold Rush days (1848–55), but its popularity exploded in the decades after the Civil War. By 1878 the Pacific Baseball League had become the area's first professional organization, while another competition called the California League began play the following year. Despite its popularity, baseball struggled against the perception that its players were undisciplined, rowdy drunks both on and off the diamond. Eventually the Pacific League collapsed, while its rival faced a number of challenges, including a game-fixing scandal that helped scuttle the 1883 season.[31] Notwithstanding such tribulations, California League president John J. Mone worked hard to increase spectator interest by imposing player discipline and improving the quality of play.[32] Such methods proved generally successful, and by the time Central Park opened, games routinely attracted crowds of five thousand. The interests of the league and those of Central Park, however, did not necessarily align, as tensions grew between the two entities. The final break occurred in 1886 when McNeill canceled a scheduled league game in favor of hosting an exhibition of women's baseball teams. The incensed Mone declared that hereafter no California League games would be played at Central Park; McNeill responded by quickly organizing a new rival circuit called the California State League.[33]

The incident reveals how lucrative commercialized mass leisure, especially sporting events, had become within the city. Despite the break with McNeill, Mone predicted that the California League would clear a profit of at least $30,000 in 1886 ($856,539 in 2020).[34] A year later the group constructed a new stadium in San Francisco called the Haight Street Grounds with an initial capacity of ten thousand.[35] Although it is unclear if McNeill set out to deliberately alienate the California League, he certainly did not delay in forming a competing association and play began in the California State League just over a month after the separation. McNeill was on the board of directors of the new organization and was soon elected its president. Although the league initially had only four teams, McNeill was determined to make it profitable using a variety of promotions. He introduced to the

West Coast the idea of Ladies Day, "when ladies can come unattended and see or hear nothing that can at all be deemed improper," and admission to most league games, at least that first summer, was free for women.[36]

The focus on increasing female attendance to baseball games and to the Central Park complex likely had several motivations. As a means of countering the sport's still somewhat dubious reputation, club owners had been trying to improve baseball's public image. Efforts to raise the number of women attending games and the construction of private boxes for wealthier fans aimed at making baseball more respectable.[37] Marketing the sport to women also made sound economic sense because by the 1890s almost half the city's population was female. The stress on attracting women to the games also anticipated broader changes in San Francisco's social and cultural landscape as public spaces became more gender mixed. Leisure pastimes such as attending the theater or participating in parades and public celebrations emerged as common reasons for women to appear in urban spaces.[38]

The increasing number of sporting events in the second half of the nineteenth century also gave women the opportunity to compete in public competitions. The change in women's roles from passive spectators to active participants can be shown in the ways clothing was marketed. In 1884, the pages of one newspaper explained how women's fashion emulated the "natty lawn tennis suits for young men," but by 1890 there were advertisements for tennis dresses designed specifically for women and girls.[39] The city's St. Andrew's Society along with the Caledonian and Scottish Thistle Clubs hosted annual festivals that often included athletic competitions for women and girls. By the 1890s Thistle Club games awarded a total of $4,000 in prizes (not all for women) and attracted at least five thousand spectators.[40] A Scottish games festival in 1877 included women's foot races in ladies', young ladies', and girls' categories, and the winners of each category received awards. McNeill would have known of such events because he served as a judge at the 1877 games and less than a decade later was a trustee of the Caledonian Club.[41]

McNeill's position as superintendent of Central Park meant he was constantly seeking original and interesting programming that would attract crowds to his facility. Such happenings included staples like baseball and wrestling, but tug-of-war competitions and more unique events such as "The World's International Candle Contest and Baby Show" were also on the schedule. The latter spectacle featured large candles representing different nations and states of the United States along with a young woman who stood by clad in a "typical" costume from that locale. Visitors could win prizes by guessing how long each candle would burn.[42] Such a willingness to experiment with different types of unconventional amusements may help explain why McNeill was receptive to the idea of women's baseball and soccer games. Not only was he a prominent entertainment impresario, McNeill was also well connected within the city's social and political worlds. In 1882, he was named to the lucrative post of city license collector, and two years later was a delegate at the Democratic Party's state convention.[43] In addition to his links with various sporting and ethnic clubs, he also participated in broader civic organizations, including serving as head of the city's Fourth of July Parade Committee in 1887. The next year he was selected to be the event's grand marshal.[44] Because of his prominent status McNeill may have had the clout to promote athletic events featuring women competing publicly in ways that previously would have been unacceptable. It also reflected how attitudes toward women's participation in sport had begun to change.

By the 1890s, women were increasingly involved in recreational events, including athletic competitions, but still faced resistance from men who questioned their abilities. Nevertheless, many women grasped the opportunity to compete and strove to do their best. In October 1893, for example, the Schuetzen Club, a group organized by the city's German community, held a shooting contest for members' wives and daughters. The *San Francisco Call* reported that many in the club previously believed that a women's competition would be nothing more than a "humorous fiasco." The participants, however, took the event seriously, and soon the shooting range was crowded with women practicing for the competition. On the day of the contest, the newspaper described the women as competitive, enthusiastic, and confident in their handling of the rifles. It was reported that male members of the club found their marksmanship to be "astonishing," their skills "surprising to their better halves, who were around expecting to jest their wives, but when they saw the good scores made they began to act as if the laugh was on them."[45]

Women's public recreation as an entertaining spectacle led to all-female acts like acrobats and minstrel troupes.[46] Such attractions appeared at Central Park and, given McNeill's penchant for hosting a wide variety of amusements, it was perhaps not surprising that he was open to the idea of having women's baseball clubs play at the park. Held on Valentine's Day 1886, the first game featured two teams called the Chicago Red Stockings and the San Francisco Blue Stockings. Although it took place at Central Park, the game was actually organized by a grifter named Victor Gutmann.[47] McNeill clearly had reservations about the idea—whether it was the nature of the contest or Gutmann's dubious reputation is unknown—but he did place a notice in the newspaper declaring that the playing field had been rented and that "the Park Association will not be responsible for anything in connection with the exhibition."[48] Overall, the game, along with another played a week later in Sacramento, drew a mixed response. The *Daily Alta California* wrote that a crowd of several thousand attended the first game, which followed a contest between two male squads. The paper admitted that nobody viewed it as a serious athletic competition and instead most thought of it as a curiosity. Despite a lack of skill among the players, the article deemed it successful because "an immense amount of amusement was furnished to those present."[49] The poor quality of play contrasted with advertisements produced before the game that hailed the contest as a "Champion Female Base Ball Game" to be played by "18 Expert Players on the Diamond."[50] The brief notice recounting the game also mocked the players in specifically gendered terms, noting "there was the usual women's method of pitching, and every member showed an impulsive disposition to catch the ball in their aprons, but first they opened wide their arms as if they intended to fling them about a man."[51] Such barbs diminished the challenge of women's public participation in athletics by associating the manner of play to traditional roles as homemakers and spouses, that is, defined by their relation to men rather than as individuals.

The critical reception of the next game played in Sacramento on February 21, 1886, may have altered plans for a longer tour and influenced how McNeill later approached hosting the women's soccer matches. A reported crowd of 1,200 paid to see the game but left disappointed by the result because it began thirty minutes late, featured only fourteen players, and ended after just six innings. The article maintained that, like the crowd in San Francisco, the fans had not come expecting great athletic skill but were nevertheless appalled by the lack of quality. The *Sacramento Daily Union* criticized the athletes for not playing a more masculine game, writing "the whole band appeared afraid to bring their limbs together, man-fashion, to stop the ball." The article noted that the most amusing part was when a stray dog joined in but was removed from the field because he played the game too well. In addition to criticizing the women's athletic abilities, the paper also insulted their "costume" and declared that the women were "not so remarkably handsome and graceful themselves as to compensate for it." Finally, the paper quoted one man as saying that he had rarely seen worse entertainment and that afterward the crowd seemed embarrassed to have been there.[52]

The different reactions to the women's shooting competition and baseball game reflect the distinction between acceptable and unacceptable types of female recreation. Generally, sporting activities held mostly in private, such as tennis, golf, or shooting, were deemed more appropriate for women, while public spectator sports like baseball were seen as less so.[53] In the shooting contest, the women's skills reflected the seriousness with which they approached the competition and by extension validated the social meanings of the club and its activities. While it may have been temporarily amusing to see women fail to demonstrate skill playing a "manly sport" like baseball, it could also be seen as making a mockery of a game that already had obtained a level of cultural significance when played by men. The newspaper account of embarrassed fans may reflect this feeling of discomfort. The male patrons of the shooting club initially treated their wives and daughters with patronizing bemusement, but the women's determination and skill earned the men's respect. The anonymous and likely working-class women who played baseball, already a sport with disreputable connotations, were judged much more harshly. Indeed, one newspaper later noted the women's "toughened and weazened faces" and referred to them as "Morton Street alleged ball-tossers," after one of the city's most notorious red-light districts.[54] The women may also have been paid for playing, which further distinguished them from the women shooters as well as those who competed in the various athletic events organized by the Scottish associations.[55]

One reason McNeill may have decided to stage a women's soccer game at Central Park despite the baseball debacle was the growing popularity of soccer in the Bay Area and the establishment of a men's league in 1892. Games using football codes of various sorts had been documented in the city as early as the 1860s, but the earliest confirmed soccer match took place in 1888.[56] Four years later, a group of men formed the Pacific Coast Football Association (PCFA) and league play began in October featuring a handful of teams: Alert Athletic Club, Oakland Athletic Club, Pacific Wanderers, and Scottish Thistle.[57] After several matches, the new competition attracted the attention of the press and the *Call* enthusiastically covered this "strange and astonishing game."[58] By the turn of the New Year, the paper had declared a "football craze" in the city that saw large crowds of both men and women attending matches. New teams rapidly formed, and these clubs may have included industrial sides (e.g., Levi-Strauss), neighborhood squads (e.g., one from Richmond), and occupational teams (e.g., granite cutters). The PCFA even organized a youth league and attempted to schedule an interstate clash with a team from Washington. The articles in the *Call* suggested a more than passing familiarity with the game, as match reports offered detailed analysis of tactics and the performances of individual players.[59] By mid-January 1893, three new clubs had appeared—Richmond FC, Rovers Association FC, and the American Eagles. Richmond represented the city neighborhood of the same name, while the Rovers included at least three Levi-Strauss employees, although it's not known if it was officially connected to the company. In addition, wine and liquor merchants the Hilbert Brothers, described as former players and "strong admirers of the game," donated a $100 loving cup to be given to the winner of the PCFA competition, henceforth to be called the Hilbert Trophy.[60] In less than six months, the organization, now renamed the Pacific Association Football League (PAFL), had grown to include six junior squads and nine senior teams, although not all of them played regularly or competed for the Hilbert Trophy.[61]

As indicated by some of the club names, Scottish immigrants played a key role in San Francisco's early soccer organizations. The Thistles dominated the first few years of the competition, and league meetings often took place at Scottish Hall.[62] Scots had a long presence in San Francisco and as in other locations formed a variety of social organizations. A St. Andrews society first organized in the city in 1863, the Caledonian Club followed three years later, and the Scottish Thistle Club appeared in 1882.[63] From the start, all of these organizations sponsored athletic competitions of one sort or the other, so it was in keeping with the traditions of Scottish societies for many of the members to become involved in soccer. Archibald MacKillop, David Ferguson, David Pollock, and other Scottish-born men founded or were early leaders of the PCFA. MacKillop was especially active in promoting the game and after being confirmed as league secretary in 1893 gave talks on the history of the sport and published a pamphlet explaining its rules and tactics.[64]

The game quickly grew in popularity, and by early 1893 the *Call* proclaimed that "the football fever shows no abatement and has now assumed the proportions of an epidemic."[65] The league sought to extend the game beyond San Francisco and Oakland by publishing the association code and distributing it free to anyone who asked. They sent players and other representatives to nearby communities in order to develop the game and encourage the formation of clubs. Aficionados believed that intercity matches would increase the popularity of the sport across the region.[66] In addition to reporting on games, one newspaper promoted soccer by printing short biographies, sixteen in all, of prominent PAFL players and administrators. Eight of these subjects had been born in Scotland, and most reportedly had some previous experience playing the game, usually at a junior or scholastic level. A few claimed to have suited up for some of the most prominent Scottish sides of the era, including Renton FC and Hibernian. The other men profiled were from England, Australia, Canada, New Zealand, and the United States.[67] As was common for the time, match reports usually listed the players only by position and surname. Examining the lists reinforces the notion that most soccer players had surnames of Scottish or English origin, though whether or not they were immigrants or US-born is unknown. These demographics served to differentiate soccer from baseball, where most of the players had Irish or German roots. In addition, some baseball clubs were formed by or included African Americans and Latinos, something that, based on the names at least, was not the case for soccer.[68] The only Spanish name mentioned in early newspaper reports was a halfback called Fernandez. An anecdote from the newspaper story announcing his arrival sheds light on the racial climate of the sport. Fernandez had arrived in San Francisco from Honolulu, where he had lived for some time; likely due to his darker complexion, the "irreverent spectator" commonly referred to him using a racial slur.[69]

Newspaper coverage of soccer highlighted the growing interest women took in the game. The appearance of female spectators contributed to the notion that for the male players it was an opportunity to demonstrate a type of appropriate athletic masculinity. During the league's first season, the *Call* trumpeted the virtues of the association game, stating that, in contrast to intercollegiate football, soccer could be understood and followed by "a pretty girl in the stand."[70] Another story emphasized the performative nature of the sport and suggested that it played a role in advertising the male players' availability. After a tilt between Thistles and Wanderers, the match report noted that women in the crowd judged Wanderers' halfback Franklin "Bauldy" Bowring to be "the loveliest of all the players."[71]

The growing popularity of the game in the city and the size of the crowds, including many female spectators, soon attracted the attention of promoter McNeill. While limited evidence links him directly to the soccer associations or any of the clubs, he likely knew many of the participants through his involvement with the various Scottish organizations. Declaring that the "Association rules are the best for attracting public interest," McNeill praised the game's continuous action, speed and combativeness. A newspaper report indicated that he was also considering organizing an international soccer tournament. Although there is no record of such an event being played, other matches did take place at Central Park.[72] At the same time that soccer's popularity skyrocketed, baseball was experiencing something of a crisis. McNeill's California State League collapsed in 1887, while the California League limped along until August 1893.[73]

Despite previous events featuring all-female performers and players, the *Call* declared the notion of a women's soccer game a "startling innovation." McNeill even cited the success of female soccer in England as motivation for the idea. Recruitment for the game began in early November, and one report indicated that he had "readily secured a number of women who were anxious to develop their latent kicking proclivities."[74] A newspaper advertisement appeared on November 12, 1893, and ran for three consecutive days: "Wanted—A Number of Active Young Ladies at Central Park, 1189 Market st.; call from 9:30 to 11 a.m. and from 2 to 3 p.m., Tuesday, Nov. 14. Inquire for Capt. Wilson."[75] The women had already begun practice games with Captain John Wilson and Dan Hughes serving as coaches. Both men had been involved in the city's nascent soccer community while playing for a military team called the Fort Masons. These reports indicated that more practices were being planned and that the women, including some with "a good deal of skill," were excited about playing.[76] Such preparations may have indicated a desire on the part of soccer enthusiasts like Wilson and Hughes to ensure the game would not be seen as a joke.

Although the popularity of soccer had rapidly increased since the founding of the men's organization the year before, it had not yet become an established part of the city's sporting landscape. Along with the Scottish-tinged names chosen for the women's teams, the participation of Wilson and Hughes showed that the men's association must have been closely connected to the event. For his part, McNeill might have wished to avoid the bad publicity that followed the disastrous hosting of women's baseball teams by making sure that participants had at least basic playing skills. It may also be true that the women themselves were, as the *Call* noted, enthusiastic about the match and eager to have the opportunity to compete publicly. The same newspaper reported that the teams arrived at Central Park on the day they were scheduled to play only to find out that the game had been canceled due to poor weather. After being informed that the game would not go on, the women expressed disappointment the rain had "spoiled the opportunity of their lives to demonstrate to the San Francisco public that when it comes to 'kicking,' even at a pigskin filled with leather, the women can knock the stern sex into a cocked hat."[77] We'll never know whether the speaker misspoke or the reporter misquoted about the leather filling.

Newspaper reports of the first game on December 3, 1893, were generally positive and described a festive atmosphere complete with "flaming posters" and plenty of noise-making fish-horns. A subheadline in the *Call* declared the contest "A Healthy Pastime on a Healthy Day, in which Femininity Displays Power of Endurance."[78] The *Call*'s coverage of soccer had generally been positive, and the headline may be seen as a continuation of efforts to promote the sport and to contrast it with the violence of other football codes as well as the unsavoriness of baseball. McNeill had earlier indicated that he thought gridiron football and rugby were too rough for women to play.[79] The article reporting on the match claimed the women showed how soccer could be "an artistic as well as athletic exercise" while revealing some unspecified "new features of the game." Overall, the reporter felt the contest would help increase the popularity of the sport on the West Coast.[80] The story also featured patronizing language regarding the women, and it devoted several lines to describing their appearance. The analysis of the match in the *Call* differed from its usual treatment of men's games in that detailed reports about league matches often included a discussion of individual play and team tactics.[81] Comment on the physical appearance of the players was almost nonexistent, and discussion of clothing was limited to a brief mention of team colors, if mentioned at all. In contrast, the newspaper's account of the women's game reversed the ratio, featuring a more detailed focus on the looks and dress of the athletes and only brief commentary on game play.

As the starting time for the match approached, the paper reported "a couple dozen fairy-like creatures tripped lightly upon the sward." They were clad in outfits that recalled cycling clothing, including jerseys, knickerbockers, sashes, and small caps. Most wore tennis shoes, although the article noted that some arrived in high heels. Such attire connected the women to previous forms of female recreation practiced in the city. The article paid special attention to the hairstyles of the players, whether they wore it short and tied in a knot or left it "streaming around their shoulders." This emphasis revealed that although the women were there to play, they were also treated as sexualized objects by the reporters and by the largely male gaze of the crowd. The description of the various hair treatments acknowledged that one purpose of the game was to appeal to male spectators, noting that "the various tastes of the assembled multitude were gratified."[82] In this case, the women's appearance complemented the sporting display unlike the women's baseball game, where the physical attractiveness and charm of the participants proved, at least in the eyes of the press, unable to make up for the inconsistent play.

The paper reported that the crowd of several thousand cheered at kickoff and shouted encouragement and praise to the players during the first half. The article described an uneven level of play, writing that the women ran "hither and thither," missed kicks, and sometimes fell down while attempting to strike the ball. Still, the *Call* declared that "some astonishingly good plays were made" and explained how the time spent practicing had helped develop their skills. The author of the article singled out individual players for praise, noting the defensive prowess of Catherine Howard and writing that "it would take volumes to describe how that Florence Montmorency aimed an excellent shot at the goal, which was just frustrated by the timely interposition of the hands of the enemy's goal-keeper." The story also singled out Adie Beaufort along with Josie Koster and Katie Koster as the stars of the match. Josie Koster and Beaufort scored goals, while Katie Koster provided "yeoman service" and "the pluck of a Roman warrior." The author peppered the story with martial imagery, perhaps with the intention of poking fun at the athletes, but it may also have been an attempt to capture how seriously the women took the game and how much genuine effort they made to win. After the match, the women changed out of their playing clothes and sat in the stands in order to pick up pointers by watching a men's game that followed their own. Despite the overall positive tone of the story, it ended by asking, "is football a game in which girls should be encouraged to exhibit their prowess?"[83]

Another report on the match published in the *San Francisco Chronicle* began condescendingly but was also generally supportive of the event, declaring that "if any scoffing man went to Central Park hoping to see the girls make a show of themselves, he was sadly mistaken." The article led by portraying Lulu Woods, the Lassies' captain, as a petulant young woman who was upset about losing the match because she felt her team had too many older players. Nevertheless, the article made clear that she was determined to improve her team's play so that they might win the next contest. Although the story admitted that a few of the participants lacked skill, it also remarked that "some truly phenomenal players have been developed." Like the previous match report, the *Chronicle*'s version praised the skill of specific players, including Katie Gray, Josie Carter, and Ada Beaufort, the last of whom supposedly had a football at home and practiced with it daily. The article admired her speed and technical ability while also stating she had "a large crop of football brains under her red hair." It also claimed that Carter, who scored a goal, had wagered twenty-two beers with Coach Jimmy Tobin that her team would win the game. After the match, Carter was reportedly incensed because Tobin canceled the bet, claiming that the Lassies had been hard done by the referee.[84] Since activities such as gambling and drinking were already associated with some sporting events, the inclusion of the anecdote helped to normalize the presence of female athletes who participated in sporting contests in the same ways as their male counterparts.

In contrast to the attention given to the first game, the second match between the teams on December 10, 1893, was largely ignored by the press. The *Chronicle* did not publish a story on the game, and the *Call*'s treatment was far less detailed than the first match. The brief article stated that most of the 2,500-person crowd had come simply because of the novelty of the game.

According to the paper, the quality of play, outside of a few participants, was not high and in sporting terms "there was nothing noteworthy about the game."[85]

Information about the players themselves is scarce, although unlike the baseball game played earlier, newspaper accounts did include rosters and listed individual names. One reason for the lack of biographical detail is the general absence of documentation for female lives in the late nineteenth century. Edith Sparks noted in her study of female proprietors in San Francisco during this period that sources can be hard to come by and those that do exist tend to highlight the failure of women-owned small businesses. She also observed that women's appearances in the city directory could be erratic and inconsistent.[86] The situation for the female soccer players in San Francisco is similar to that of nineteenth-century England in that most of the information we have comes from newspapers.[87] Women, especially young women, were less likely to appear in the newspaper unless they were socially prominent or had gained some notoriety due to either positive or negative action. In addition, the team rosters listed in the city's newspapers often changed from day to day, contained multiple spelling variations, including nicknames, or provided only a first initial and surname. Some of the women used their real names; it is possible that others competed under pseudonyms, although none of the newspaper accounts implies this was the case. Finally, the lists included many common names that generally prevent even a reasonable attempt at identification. For example, one of the players listed on the roster of the Colleen Bawns on November 26 was Annie Johnson; the 1894 city directory lists three widows, three domestics, a weaver, a teacher, a nurse, and a married woman under that name.[88]

The match reports make it clear that the players were of various ages and there was at least one pair of sisters (Kotter, Koster, or Carter) and one mother-daughter combination (Beaufort). An article published before the match declared that "two Algerian dancing girls" from Chicago were scheduled to participate, but the published player names seem to contradict the claim.[89] Another story reported that two of the women had learned the game in England and in Canada where they had been born.[90] The 1900 US Census recorded that Jennie S. Beaford was living in San Francisco along with her daughter Adela B. Beaford. By that time a widow, Jennie Beauford had been born in England and came to the United States in 1887, but her daughter had been born in Canada. The ages are also a good fit indicating that Jennie (b. 1861) was around thirty-two when the soccer game was played, while her daughter Adela (b. 1879) would have been fourteen. By the turn of the century, the senior Beauford's occupation was a landlady, while her daughter was a stenographer.[91] People in such occupations would have appreciated the extra money; McNeill reportedly paid two dollars per game.[92] The same is true for most of the women whose names can be reasonably matched to those in the city directory. For example, the only Ella Anderson listed was a dressmaker, while the lone Catherine Howard was a widow. The directory recorded Bessie Mills and Daisy Perry as actresses and the sole Lizzie Smith as a clerk for the American Press Association.[93] Other participants may have been attracted to the game not simply because of the money but also for the opportunity to compete. One of the players consistently included in all of the published rosters was Bessie Gardner. Later newspaper reports indicate that a Bessie Gardner was involved in both equestrian and tennis competitions in the area.[94]

CONCLUSION

Even as the men's PAFL celebrated the end of the 1893–94 season, plans were being made for the next one. Although early reports were optimistic, there were also troubling signs regarding the competition's future. Initial reports stated that the 1894–95 season would be played in two rounds, with the first running from November to January and the second from January to March. The number of clubs also seemed to be on the rise, with five teams listed as committed to playing and another handful as possibilities. The league had a new trophy to award to the winning side, donated and named for City and County Assessor John D. Siebe. Finally, contact had been made with soccer teams in Utah and Colorado about the possibility of arranging matches, and there was even talk about the possibility of forming a national organization that would consolidate the various leagues from around the country and even in Canada.[95]

Despite enthusiastic reports on these developments, the season quickly began to fall apart. One long-standing issue had been the lack of suitable playing fields, but the most significant problem facing the league was the inability or unwillingness of clubs to turn up for matches. Such absences had the potential to alienate current and potential spectators, either because the games had to be canceled or because the quality of play suffered. When not enough Thistle players suited up for a game to determine which league side would meet a visiting squad from British Columbia, the teams were forced to compete with just ten players each. An article about the match warned that disappointing the crowd in such a way was not helping to grow the game.[96] By the fall of 1894, the problems only grew worse. When the first round of games was scheduled to be played on November 11, the league's dominant side Thistle did not appear for their match against Presidio. This prompted the *Call* to angrily declare that such actions "showed a total disregard of sportsmanlike spirit, which will tend to bring association football into contempt."[97] The last match report for the original PAFL appeared in February and described a game between Oakland and Wanderers in which two Oakland players lined up for their opponents who otherwise would not have been able to field a complete team. To make matters worse, one of the Oakland players assigned to Wanderers performed "listlessly" according to the crowd and even scored an own goal for the home side.[98] After that farcical display, the league and its clubs seem to have evaporated. The economic recession that hit the country beginning in 1893 also contributed to the demise of the first organized soccer league in San Francisco. Edgar Pomeroy, writing later about the history of the sport in the city, declared "the panic so disturbed men in California that the league broke up for want of clubs." The Oakland clubs continued to play the occasional game against British sailors, but such matches were sporadic as organized soccer in the city entered a hiatus.[99]

In contrast to the failure of the men's soccer league, physical education and athletic opportunities for women boomed in the years after 1893. William Greer Harrison, president of the Olympic Club, oversaw the construction of a women's gymnasium and declared his "thorough faith, not only in the value and advantage of athletic training for women but in women themselves."[100] A few years later the *Call* published a long article detailing the rise of women's physical culture in the city. In addition to recognizing the Olympic Club's facilities, where fencing and swimming were the most popular pastimes, the article noted that the YMCA women's club had over one hundred members. There was also a Women's Club for Physical Culture in the city and the local turnverein had classes for women of various ages.[101]

FIG. 6.2: Female football player as depicted in the *San Francisco Call*, December 21, 1897. (California Digital Newspaper Collection, Center for Bibliographic Studies and Research, University of California, Riverside, http://cdnc.ucr.edu)

Such forms of exercise were largely conducted outside of public view in gender-segregated spaces, but women also began to participate in more visible expressions of recreation. One of the most noteworthy, at least as far as the city's press was concerned, was bicycling. The Alpha Cycling Club became the first such women's organization in the city when it formed in June 1895. Over the next year, the club became a regular part of the local cycling scene, even prominently marching in a massive protest aimed at improving the streets of San Francisco.[102]

Although public recreational opportunities increased for women in the years after 1893, there is no evidence that more soccer games were played. Even after new men's clubs formed around the turn of the century and renewed league play began in 1902, formal women's soccer did not reappear in San Francisco. In December 1897, however, newspaper advertisements appeared promising "a novelty in Football."[103] Two entrepreneurs had decided to sponsor a women's football game using a modified version of the rugby rules. Initially two games would be played between the San Francisco Grays and the Oakland Browns, but future plans called for teams from all the major cities of the state to compete in the Pacific Ladies Football Association.[104] The motivations for sponsoring a women's football game and the coverage it drew in the papers was similar to that surrounding the soccer game. Once again, the goal of the promoters was not about supporting women's sports but rather to put on an interesting spectacle designed to make money. Newspaper reports of the games described a fairly rudimentary level of play while acknowledging that some of the players had the potential to become good athletes.

Coverage of the two matches also revealed some important differences in the way the media described the game play. While the articles on the soccer match tended to fixate on the women's clothing and physical appearance, the stories on the rugby game highlighted the expectations of the male crowd and emphasized the titillating nature of the spectacle. Almost every article leading up to and following the first game on Christmas Day 1897 included some reference to hair pulling. On December 21 the *Call* noted that the women had been practicing and "already the players have learned that hair-pulling is not one of the essential points of the game."[105] A match report printed the day after the game described how the crowd observed play with "a delightful, placid indifference as to which side was to win and a mild desire to see some hair-pulling and, incidentally, a slight spilling of feminine gore." It continued by noting that the level of violence in the game was low and the lack of hair-pulling disappointed the crowd.[106] The *Chronicle* featured much of the same language, commenting on the absence of hair pulling while acknowledging that many in the crowd were there not to view an athletic event but rather to ogle women in public: "the crowd was not over-refined in its audible comments on figures and bloomers."[107] The slightly dubious nature of the event can also be seen in that the promoters

BALLET DESERTS THE STAGE FOR THE GRIDIRON.

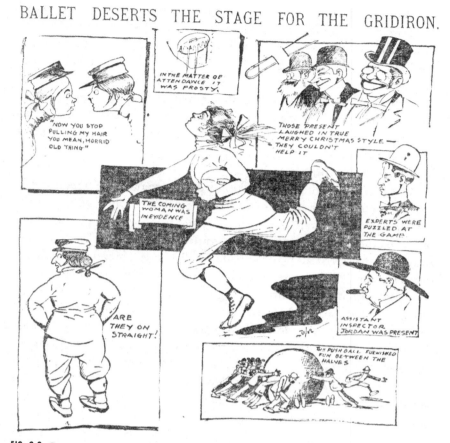

FIG. 6.3: Cartoon mocking the women's football games played in 1897. Note the hairpin in the top right panel. *San Francisco Call*, December 26, 1897. (California Digital Newspaper Collection, Center for Bibliographic Studies and Research, University of California, Riverside, http://cdnc.ucr.edu)

went to great lengths to assure the public that all of the players were "of irreproachable character."[108] The paper also noted that at least three of the athletes—apparently all sisters—played under a pseudonym borrowed from an army officer based at the Presidio.[109]

Despite the best efforts of the promoters to sell the notion that this was an unusual event, the fact that women were playing what was generally considered a men's game was not all that new, and the low turnout indicates that San Franciscans did not think so either. Reports estimated the crowd as between two hundred and three hundred, significantly fewer than turned out for the baseball and soccer games. The *Call* reported declining interest in the event, noting that "there was none of the wild enthusiasm one learns to expect in contests of this kind."[110] The increasing presence of women in public spaces not only as athletes but also as consumers may have lessened the novelty of the event.[111] If the tone of the coverage reflected its true atmosphere, the match became something less than an athletic or entertainment event and more an almost voyeuristic spectacle, as evidenced by the obsession with hair pulling.

At least some of the players continued to seize on these opportunities to perform in public as athletes. In fact, one quoted in the *Call* saw this as a chance to demonstrate that women should be allowed to play any kind of sport, even those considered to be overly violent: "yes, we will show the men folks that girls can play football as well as ride a bicycle, ride a horse or play tennis."[112] The increasing availability of recreational opportunities combined with high-visibility sporting events for women may have inspired others to become active. A week after the final game between the Grays and the Browns, a newspaper article demonstrated the impact of the two games. A sixteen-year-old girl from Oakland named Nora Sullivan was arrested and charged with vagrancy after she ran away from home. Eventually she was spotted in Golden Gate Park "kicking the pigskin" and wearing "an unconventional costume." It seems that she had left home in an attempt to join the "San Francisco Browns [*sic*]" football team.[113]

WOMEN AND SOCCER IN THE EARLY TWENTIETH CENTURY

The 1893 games in San Francisco did not result in a widespread boom in the number of women playing soccer. No ongoing clubs or competitions formed and for at least the next ten years there were no documented women's games played outside of schools in the United States. As cultural norms continued to shift, larger numbers of college women took part in recreational activities. While the gridiron rules became established as the nation's dominant football code for men, soccer was often put forth as a less physically taxing and safer version of the sport. By the first two decades of the twentieth century, girls and young women across the country were playing soccer at playgrounds, high schools, and colleges. A few even began to participate as administrators, coaches, and referees. In addition to school- and playground-centered activities, evidence suggests that some corporations and ethnic societies endorsed the sport by sponsoring teams for their female employees and members. Eventually soccer became an established and accepted part of physical education programs for women and professional fitness organizations actively promoted the sport.

Many educators felt, however, that intercollegiate competition would have a negative impact on the development of women's sports. As a result, much of the activity on campus focused on intramural contests between

FIG. 7.1: A staged photograph showing young women from the Washington, DC, area playing soccer circa 1918–20. (Library of Congress, Prints and Photographs Division, LC-DIG-npcc-00423)

class teams.[1] The formation of the women's division of the National Amateur Athletic Federation in 1923 solidified such attitudes. The professional educators who controlled collegiate athletics aimed to use sport to develop "womanly qualities," preserve reproductive health, and provide recreational opportunities for all students. Historian Ronald Smith argues that the leadership also wished to retain female control over women's sport.[2]

One challenge to researchers on the women's game is that because there was neither an established league structure nor intercollegiate contests, many of the teams seem to have played intra-squad games and rarely had the opportunity to compete against outside clubs. As a result, matches between different teams were relatively rare and media coverage often claimed that a specific match represented the first time such a game had been played in a given area. In other words, there was no continuity in play or social memory of women's soccer games. Like much of the history of men's soccer in the United States, the women's game remained a local phenomenon, rarely garnering attention outside of a particular area. Future research that investigates Philadelphia, New York, Los Angeles, Seattle, Boston, and other locations may prove fruitful in uncovering the true extent of women's soccer in the first half of the twentieth century.

Because our knowledge of the history of women's soccer in the United States is undeveloped, it is important to document all the ways that women participated in the sport. In general, the existing research has focused on women playing soccer, and little is known about the other ways that women contributed to the game over time. Historians have concentrated on players, teams, and matches, often at the expense of administrators, managers, and, the most reviled of all, referees. Part of this chapter is devoted to close this gap by looking at two women pioneers who broke barriers, not as players but rather in their roles as referees, administrators, and coaches. The two women lived on opposite sides of the country and were unrelated although they shared a surname: Doris Clark and Helen Clark. The careers of the two women illustrate broader points about the history of soccer in the United States. The sport boomed in the period after World War I in places like Northern California and New England, and each woman played a role in the development of the game in these areas. The work of the two Clarks also demonstrate broader changes in attitudes toward women in sports, leading to more women and girls participating in soccer, especially in high schools and colleges.

SOCCER IN THE SCHOOLS

As women began to attend college in greater numbers during the late nineteenth century, they had more opportunities to participate in athletics, including soccer. The women's colleges, especially the Seven Sisters—Vassar, Smith, Wellesley, Bryn Mawr, Mount Holyoke, Barnard, and Radcliffe—helped normalize women's participation in sport. The institutions and the women who ran their physical education programs proved enormously influential in the expansion of women's sports, especially basketball, field hockey. and soccer. Founded between 1865 and 1893, the Seven Sisters provide some of the earliest documentation of female student athletes during the crucial period of development at the end of the nineteenth century.[3] As historian Jean Williams cautions, however, the relatively privileged status

FIG. 7.2: Smith College students at soccer practice. Intra-class games were common on campus during the 1920s. (Author's collection)

of the institutions and students meant that sources on their sporting activities have been more likely to survive. Meanwhile, information on the participation of athletes of color or from lower economic positions may not have been preserved.[4] Despite the importance of the Seven Sisters for the emergence of women's athletics, evidence of organized soccer at these schools emerges relatively late. Some of the earliest notices include a 1915 story in the *Philadelphia Inquirer* reporting on the results of a soccer game between residence hall teams at Bryn Mawr, a diary entry from Radcliffe in 1918, and the publication of the *Smith Book of Soccer* in 1924—one of the first sources to document widespread intramural and interclass soccer contests.[5]

The digitization of newspapers over the past decade has allowed researchers to expand our understanding of the way women's soccer emerged in schools across the country. New evidence validates Williams's caution about an overreliance on information from elite institutions. It turns out that soccer began to be widely played in the 1910s and 1920s at state colleges, especially normal schools for educating teachers, in many different parts of the United States. Sometimes the emergence of soccer at these institutions can be linked to the private women's colleges through alumnae who took jobs as physical-education teachers. In other cases, female instructors arrived from less well-known physical education schools, and at times the organization of women's soccer was led by men. A few of these non-elite schools hoped to encourage the development of intercollegiate competition, and there is evidence that at least one soccer game between teams from different schools took place in 1910. Apart from that single match, there is no evidence that other intercollegiate soccer matches took place before the 1950s. Games between school sides and independent teams without any educational affiliation, however, have been documented.

The earliest mention of women's soccer teams at public universities and a report of an intercollegiate match comes from 1910. Less than thirty years after its founding in 1863, the Kansas State Normal School enrolled 1,404 students, both male and female. The school began offering a bachelor of arts degree in 1906 and essentially transitioned into a liberal arts school. As part of this process, the college increased its commitment to sports education by building a new physical education hall at a cost of $75,000. In addition to opening the new structure in 1910, the institution also constructed a soccer field and began forming women's teams.[6] Within a few weeks plans were made for an interclass tournament to determine a school champion.[7] The final game of the season took place on December 2, 1910, and featured a contest between the school and the nearby College of Emporia. The article described the match between squads called Normal 1s and the College 1s, with the former winning 1–0. A previous article on the organization of the tournament explained that the Normal School teams were organized by classes and were referred to as N1, N2, N3, and N4. The story on the conclusion of the competition notes that the Normal 1s were first-year students, likely the N1 from the previous article. In other newspaper stories, the Kansas State Normal School was often abbreviated as "The Normal," while the College of Emporia was called "The College." The language of the article states clearly that the win "gives the championship of the schools to the Normal is."[8]

Other early notices of female students playing soccer include several newspapers reporting in 1915 that the University of California would form a team for the first time in the school's history. The university hired Mary Blanchard, "an experienced soccer player of Mount Holyoke College," as coach.[9] The report indicates that soccer had been played at Mount Holyoke before this date, although we do not have records of any organized competitions at the school. The women's soccer program at the University of Missouri was launched in 1917 by faculty member Dr. Walter E. Meanwell, originally from England. The newspaper claimed that the team was only the second women's squad organized at a school west of the Appalachian Mountains, the only other western school being Downer College in Milwaukee, Wisconsin.[10] The year 1920 brought news of women's teams forming at colleges in many parts of the country. The author of a somewhat disparaging article on women's teams at Michigan Agricultural College (now Michigan State University) wrote that seeing female students take to the field made him feel as though he had "strayed into the territories of some modern Amazonian tribe." Several different class teams were being organized and plans were made for an interclass championship. Such competitions also took place around this time between classes at the University of Nebraska.[11]

OUTSIDE THE SCHOOLS

Examples of women trying to form soccer teams outside of the schools cropped up only after 1900. In 1905 the *Seattle Star* reported that Dorthea Kingston, formally of England but now resident in the city, wished to organize a women's football club. A "soccer enthusiast," Kingston noted that if women could play baseball they could also play football. She aimed to compete against men's teams and wished to start a squad because "I want to show the people that a woman can play foot-ball as well as a great, big strong man."[12] Less than a week later, the same newspaper reported that Kingston's plan was moving forward, having been contacted by many interested players. Although the article claimed the team's first practice had been scheduled, no further information on the club has been found.[13] Such fleeting mentions of soccer clubs independent of schools or colleges sporadically appeared in newspapers during these years. In 1908 the *Milwaukee Journal* reported that two "girls' soccer football teams" called the White Diamonds and the Red Diamonds had played a match on April 29. The article offered no additional information except that the Whites prevailed 2–0.[14] Although not indicated in the original report, the teams may have been connected with an existing ethnic club. Milwaukee was home to a number of such organizations, many linked to Eastern European immigrants, a fact that might explain the red and white colors.

Perhaps the best documented women's football match of the period occurred in New York City on Christmas Day 1913. The original plan was for the St. George's Club to compete against another side, but one could not be located so they split into two squads known in reports as A and B, or the Blue and Whites versus the Blues. The *New York Times* called the match "the first game ever played by women in New York," and the *New York Tribune* also noted that it was "said to be the first game of its kind in this locality."[15] The match featured only eight players a side and followed a

FIG. 7.3: The Blues, also called Team A, took part in a soccer match on Christmas Day 1913. They are wearing proper soccer jerseys from the Sons of St. George, and none appear to be in hobble skirts. Sarah Tennant, at center in the white shirt, played in goal for the team. (Library of Congress, Prints and Photographs Division, LC-DIG-ggbain-15057)

modified version of the association rules where the teams played fifteen-minute halves on a shortened and narrowed field with "an abbreviated goals space." The *Times* reported that although the quality of play was not high it was an entertaining event: "scientific soccer was not the result of play yesterday, but as a novel exhibition the game was a merry one from start to finish, and yielded more genuine enjoyment than a host of cup matches."[16]

As did the stories on the 1893 games in San Francisco, some of the coverage focused less on the women's play and more on their appearance. The *New York Herald* declared that, although the game finished 1–1, more goals could have been scored if the players had not worn "pointed shoes," "long skirts," and at least one hobble skirt that severely restricted the ability to run. The article recorded the scorers as Mrs. Sedgwick who opened for Team A and Mrs. Molineax who equalized on a penalty.[17] The Tennant family featured prominently in the games, with five members participating: William as referee, his wife, Sarah, and their daughters Jane, Isabel, and Margaret as players. William Tennant and his children had been born in Scotland before the family immigrated to the United States in 1906.[18]

FIG. 7.4: Isabel Tennant played outside left for the Blue and Whites on December 25, 1913. She was around seventeen years old at the time. (Library of Congress, Prints and Photographs Division, LC-DIG-ggbain-15058)

The women's teams formed in Europe during World War I received more press in the United States. Often, however, newspapers included only brief reports or photographs and linked the playing of sports to the jobs that women had taken as a result of the conflict. On June 3, 1918, the *Ogden (UT) Standard* printed a photo of a women's soccer match, captioned "French girls, doing men's work now, play men's games."[19] Another photograph contrasted how US athletes aided the war effort by knitting things for the Red Cross with an English munitions worker who was "making a good save" in a soccer match. The headline declared "Women War Workers are Taking Lead in All Masculine Sports."[20] It's unclear how much of an impact the foreign women's teams had on soccer in the United States. The trend for women and girls to play at school had already begun by the time war broke out in 1914.[21]

ETHNIC AND INDUSTRIAL TEAMS

Like evidence for games outside the schools, the efforts of ethnic organizations to form women's teams occasionally appear in the press. In 1928 the girls' team of the Hungarian Athletic Club of Milwaukee presented a floral horseshoe to the organization's men's side at an end-of-the-season awards ceremony.[22] A newspaper article from the same year announced the formation of a women's team by the Maccabee Sport Club of Brooklyn, New York. The organization had been chartered the year before and already fielded men's sides. The story listed Miriam Schneid as manager and indicated that the team was interested in playing other women's clubs if they existed. The paper indirectly acknowledged the lack of other female teams by stating that the Maccabee squad "is probably the first soccer team of its kind affiliated with any sport club in the United States."[23] Such a quote also demonstrates the lack of memory and history surrounding women's teams—the St. George's Club of New York had organized a women's team fifteen years earlier. As in Wisconsin, Hungarian immigrants were active in promoting early women's soccer in California. In the fall of 1931, the Pasadena Athletic Club's women's team played at least two matches against a club called the Magyars. Although the sides appeared to have first met in September, the *Los Angeles Times* called their November match the first-ever women's game played at Loyola Field and noted that it "drew a big hand." The same two teams were scheduled to play again on Thanksgiving Day as part of a benefit sponsored by the Sons of St. George.[24]

A few years later, in 1932, Adolph Stroinski of First German AC in Philadelphia was determined to form a women's soccer team. Although just seven volunteers began practicing, Stroinski felt confident that his team would soon be playing intercity matches against German societies of New York that already had established female sides.[25] Once again, the lack of sources beyond occasional newspaper references makes it impossible to determine whether such a statement was true and, if it was, how long these teams had existed and who they played against. In Chicago, when the first women's clubs appeared in the 1910s and 1920s, some had links to various ethnic associations. The earliest documented women's club in the city was a playground or school team called LaGrange that formed in 1914. One of the earliest sides was affiliated with the Czech group Sparta, while later teams were sponsored by the Olympia and Suburban Trans soccer clubs.[26] Although not explicitly linked to an ethnic organization, all of the players on the Southtown (Chicago) Girl's Soccer team were either first- or second-generation Swedes. One notice declared that they had scheduled a contest against a more experienced men's team, although no further information on the match or the team appeared.[27] In what was perhaps a one-time event, women's teams played a benefit match between Chicago's German all-stars and Hungarian Americans in 1935.[28]

Both before and after World War I, some US companies supported recreational activities for their female employees. The Western Electric Company of Chicago launched one of the largest athletic organizations for women. According to the *Chicago Tribune* the firm's Hawthorne Athletic Club had seven thousand participating resident athletes, about a third of them women. The 2,400 active female plant workers included 540 bowlers, 300 tennis players, and enough baseball players to field ten complete teams. By 1922 the organization decided to form a soccer team, and fifty-six women responded to the initial call, with another fifty recruited shortly afterward. The baseball teams tended to play among themselves while also fielding an all-star team to complete against outside clubs. Likely, a similar arrangement could have been made with the soccer clubs.[29] Because no match reports have survived, other industrial teams, such as the Pullman Free School of Manual Training, are known mainly from photographs.[30]

In general, our knowledge of women playing soccer outside of the schools is limited because there seem to have been very few clubs, and those that did organize often could not find other teams to complete against. A few locations—Connecticut, California, Illinois, Maryland, and Massachusetts—provide instances where women's teams played matches where the main goal was competition rather than entertainment. Generally, these scant examples were different for several reasons. First, there was often a committed individual who wanted to invest time to support the game for women. Second, these areas usually had more than one team and so there was at least the possibility of sustained competition. Third, local sporting organizations supported the development of the women's games and integrated them into existing institutional structures.

TWO EARLY PIONEERS

Doris Keziah Clark was born in Volga, Iowa, on January 31, 1888, but at some point her family relocated to Montana.[31] From a young age she showed a level of academic achievement, something that would eventually lead her to college in California. At age sixteen she earned a gold medal from the Montana State Department of Education for the best student essay written on the theme "Pioneer Days." The *Anaconda (MT) Standard* published the article, along with a picture of Clark on January 1, 1905.[32] Notice of the award also appeared in several other papers in the state and was even mentioned in the pages of the *Evening Times-Republican* from Marshalltown, Iowa, a city about 120 miles from her birthplace.[33] In 1909, Clark enrolled at the University of California. Women's athletics were fairly established at the school, and as early as 1898 the school's basketball team scheduled an intercollegiate game against a team from Nevada.[34] The Pastimes club formed by 1901 with the goal of providing women various recreational opportunities, including tennis, boating, and archery. The Women's Field Club also planned to organize a series of "tramps" or hikes.[35] Female athletes became most visible during the school's annual Woman's Day celebration. Students and alumnae competed in events such as rowing and basketball and produced special issues of various campus periodicals. An edition of the *California Occident* magazine from 1909 noted the prominent role of sports in the celebration: "the fact that athletics were deemed by the women of sufficient importance to occupy the whole of Woman's Day shows more clearly than anything else, perhaps the place they have won in college."[36]

Woman's Day was not simply about having fun and taking a turn to produce a magazine, it could also be an opportunity for larger political statements. In 1910 for example, an editorial by Marguerite Ogen in the *Daily Californian* argued that women be allowed to serve as elected representatives on the university's executive committee, which oversaw student activities. She demanded that they be given equal status and be judged solely on their abilities and qualifications and not on the basis of good looks and charm.[37] A few years earlier, women had attained a measure of athletic equality when the school decided that basketball players who achieved success in intercollegiate competitions would be awarded gold letters, as did their male counterparts.[38]

Doris Clark took part in the Woman's Day celebrations while on campus. In 1910 she helped produce a special edition of a student humor magazine, the *California Pelican*, and she rowed for her class crew boat all four years.[39] Despite her participation as a rower and her later career as a park supervisor, there is little evidence that Clark was especially engaged with athletics while in college. It may be better said, however, that her participation in musical performances attracted more attention from the press than any of her sporting activities. Clark was part of both the Glee and Treble Clef Clubs and sang soprano in a variety of performances.[40] In 1913 she once again had her picture in the paper thanks to an incident that took place during rehearsal for a show called *The Mischief Makers.* The *Oakland Tribune* reported that after a mouse ran across the stage, many of the women in the chorus "ran shrieking toward every possible exit." The newspaper noted that Clark's reaction was different from the others, as she "directed one look of scorn in their direction, another of interest at the cowering rodent and deliberately crossed the stage in the direction of the latter."[41] The *San Francisco Examiner* quoted her on the incident as saying, "I thought that the poor little thing was hurt . . . and anyway, it wasn't anything that I would consider brave. I'm from Montana and I didn't do anything more than I would expect any girl from Montana to do."[42] The portrait of Clark that emerged from this scant evidence revealed her to be an intelligent young person who involved herself in a variety of activities, including sports, and who was unafraid to do things that may have been viewed as unusual for a woman.

After graduating from the University of California with a degree in economics, Clark was appointed assistant supervisor of playgrounds in Sacramento. She was chosen over two other candidates, including the sister of the woman who had previously held the position. Although nothing in her academic background seemed to qualify her for the job, one newspaper report indicated that a previous connection to an Oakland playground may have been decisive.[43] The monthly salary, determined by the number of hours she put in, ranged from $45 to $60, and she was initially based at Oak Park.[44] As part of her duties Clark organized hikes, Easter egg hunts, and once managed to convince a group of local merchants to provide uniforms for the boys' baseball team.[45] Eventually she moved to McKinley Park, where she performed similar duties.

Clark made a special effort to encourage young women and girls to participate in athletics. In 1917 she founded the Lotus Athletic Club, an organization whose aim was to improve the physical training and recreation of girls aged twelve to fifteen. Planned activities included rowing, tennis, hiking, and basketball.[46] Many of these sports had long been practiced by women and girls, but Clark had no qualms about her charges learning games that were often seen as less appropriate, such as baseball. Early in her tenure at Oak Park, she formed a baseball team for girls that went undefeated that season. The following year she organized two clubs, although they were often forced to face boys teams because they could not find enough opponents who were willing to play using traditional rules. The girls of Oak Park refused to play indoor baseball, a version of the sport they disparaged as "tame" and "baby play."[47] Although Clark seemed especially interested in developing recreational activities for girls, she also catered to other populations. During her time at the facility, McKinley Park received over one hundred thousand visitors per year of all ages and genders.[48] Initiatives for these populations could be as diverse as writing a set of rules to prevent "Court hogs" from monopolizing the tennis facilities, or installing checkerboards for use by elderly gentlemen who frequented the park with their grandchildren.[49]

The community appreciated Clark's efforts at the park and she earned the trust of recreational organizations who appointed her to important positions. The Federated Trade Council announced in 1918 its support for the construction of a municipal park for working people. The organization praised Clark and other staff, declaring that "their children have been given more attention by playground officials this year than any year in the history of the Sacramento playground department."[50] When the *Sacramento Bee* organized a basketball league, Clark was not only placed on the committee tasked with writing the organization's constitution but was also named its chair.[51] She was the only woman appointed to a city soccer league committee charged with adjudicating a dispute between the Rovers and Acorn clubs.[52] In 1919 the California Football Association named her, along with two men, to be commissioners for the Superior California and Sacramento Region. The duties included organizing the local cup competition, handling disputes, and ruling on protests. Clark never took up the position, however, because she had resigned from the parks department several weeks earlier.[53]

Although she encouraged the participation of women and girls in sports, Clark was also active in promoting activities for boys, including soccer. It is unknown whether she had much experience playing the sport, but she may have been exposed to it at college. Just two years after Clark graduated, the University of California became one of the first public universities in the country to sponsor a women's soccer team.[54] In 1917 the *Sacramento Bee* called her the main organizing force behind a school soccer league for boys. The league featured nineteen teams playing in two divisions based on the players' weights. At the same time, she founded and served as coach for the McKinley Park side.[55] Sportswriter John R. Young called her squad "the baby team of the league" but noted that she was a good coach who earned the respect of her players.[56] She excelled at club management and shaped the side into a successful unit despite their youth and inexperience. Clark was determined to show "what purely local talent raised and fostered on our own playgrounds is capable of doing."[57] The work she did improving the team and taking them to the semifinal of the city's cup competition prompted one newspaper to exclaim: "The fact that the McKinley Park club entered the final play of this city is certainly a credit to the younger set of players in bucking older and more experienced opposition. Miss Doris Clark, Playground Supervisor, deserves much credit for the manner in which her players have battled all competitors of the league."[58]

Not only did Clark improve the team, she also displayed a competitive streak and seemed determined to win. Less than six months after calling McKinley Park a baby team, the *Sacramento Bee* observed that three of the players were as good as anyone in the league at their positions.[59] Before a match against Grass Valley in early 1919, Clark expressed confidence in her players, telling the *Sacramento Union* that her side "expects to carry home the honors."[60]

Although the team won the league in the 1918–19 season, Clark resigned from her position in July, likely to take a job as a reporter for the *San Francisco Daily News*.[61] Despite leaving coaching and moving away from

FIG. 7.5: This syndicated photograph of Helen Clark from 1919 was published in newspapers around the country after she became known as the Queen of the Whistle. (Author's collection)

Sacramento, she continued to support soccer in the city. On at least two occasions she returned to the city in order to watch soccer games.[62] In the short term, the park team had some difficulties adjusting to the loss of their coach, and some of the best players left for other squads.[63] A few years after Clark left her position, however, the McKinley Park soccer team won both the state championship and the Northern California Challenge Cup. Several of the players on "Sacramento's wonder team" had been introduced to the game and first coached by Clark.[64]

Even as Doris Clark ended her coaching days in California, across the country Helen Clark (no relation) helped launch women's soccer in Connecticut. From 1919 to 1921, teams in Bridgeport, Hartford, and elsewhere competed for city championships and attempts were made to organize a state competition, although those plans never came to fruition. Some of these clubs, especially in Bridgeport, were high school teams while others were linked to ethnic groups or societies. Clark was born in 1898, the daughter of furniture store owner George B. Clark.[65] She attended Northfield Seminary in Massachusetts before continuing her education at the New Haven School of Gymnastics. Founded in 1886, the institution's stated purpose was "to fit persons of suitable age, personality and general education to teach physical training in all kinds of educational institutions . . . in Christian associations, social settlement and private clubs; to become playground directors in swimming and other outdoor sports."[66] At the school Clark learned a variety of outdoor games including baseball, tennis and soccer. After graduating in 1918, she returned to Bridgeport and took charge of the Old Mill Playground. Later that summer she became a member of the Executive Public School Soccer League and had already served as an official at Public School league games.[67] A few months later the *Bridgeport (CT) Evening Farmer* called Clark the "Queen of the whistle" and declared her the first woman to referee a soccer game in the United States.[68] As with many of the claims of "firsts," it is virtually impossible to confirm or deny such assertions. A few years later *Spalding's Official Soccer Foot Ball Guide* claimed there were six female referees in the city and they officiated nearly all of the Bridgeport Public School Soccer League matches.[69]

By June 1919 Clark was elected third vice president of the city's public-school soccer league, becoming the first woman to hold such an office. The newspaper declared that soccer was growing in popularity and soon would be as accepted among women in the United States as it was in England. In addition to refereeing thirty-one soccer matches during the previous year, Clark managed the Barnum School boys' team that won a schools' knockout tournament and finished second in the league.[70] Within a few months, Clark was coaching the high school women's soccer team and preparing them for a match against a team called the Swedish Ladies. The *Evening Farmer* noted that both teams had joined the Connecticut State Football Association and claimed they were the first female sides in the country to be affiliated with the United States Football Association. The headline called the match the "First Women's Soccer Game Played," but it is unclear if that meant in the city, state, or even the country. There is no evidence, however, to dispute the claim that the two teams were the first to be connected to an official state association.[71]

FIG. 7.6: A cartoon mocking Helen Clark's role as a referee. (*Riverside Daily Press*, February 20, 1919)

The next report of a women's soccer team in Bridgeport appeared in late spring 1920. The May 1 notice announced that Bridgeport City FC was to play the Swedish Ladies Soccer Club for both the city and the national championship.[72] The two clubs had met in November 1919 and the City side won 2–1. A good number of people had turned out for the match despite poor weather. Although the teams had already played at least one match, the 1920 article still referred to the contest as "this novelty game" and noted that the teams would play thirty-minute halves and were allowed up to four substitutions. Organizers expected a large crowd, and the president of the state association would be on hand to kick off the contest.[73] The games continued into the winter of 1920; in December the high school team and the Swedes were preparing to meet again, with a prize called the Esling shield set to be awarded to the winning side.[74]

Just as women's soccer had begun in Bridgeport, a similar movement took place sixty miles away in Hartford. In February 1920, a newspaper wrote that the women's clubs had developed a "fierce rivalry." Perhaps with tongue in check the author claimed that it might become necessary to bring referees in from out of town because "a man who takes in these games takes his life in his own hands as the women are great fighters."[75] A few weeks later the same paper wrote that a women's soccer league for the state was being considered with teams in Hartford, Bridgeport, and New Haven.[76] The first report of an actual match played in the state capital came in April 1920 when the newspaper described a scheduled contest between Hartford City and Hartford United. The match was set to take place at Charter Oak Park, and, despite earlier reports about a possible women's league, the *Hartford Courant* still claimed it would be "the first girls' soccer game ever played in this state."[77] Such inconsistency demonstrates the continued lack of information and memory about the women's game even within the pages of a single newspaper over the course of a few months. A few weeks later, a story appeared noting that the Olympians from South Manchester would soon face Hartford City at the Cooper Street ground. The article reported that the teams were trying to arrange games against the Bridgeport teams in order to determine a state champion, but there is no indication that such a tournament ever took place.[78] The *Courant* also reported that other organizations including the Hartford Hebrew Association and the Travelers Girls' Club were considering organizing soccer teams. These groups may have already sponsored women's basketball teams, and the paper directed any hoops teams who wished to form soccer clubs to contact the league secretary.[79] By the fall of 1920, the newspaper reported that the Hartford City team was preparing for a new season with an upcoming match against a squad from a nearby suburb called the New Britain Swedes. The story boasted that the Hartford club had played four games last season and won them all.[80]

The early development of women's soccer in Bridgeport and in other communities around the state lasted only about two years. In the fall of 1921, the high school team began practice and was preparing for the first game of the season. By December, news about the team and its competitions was not good. The *Evening Farmer* announced that efforts to arrange games against clubs from other cities had failed and instead the team was organizing intra-squad games.[81] A brief notice in the school's yearbook confirmed the report and lamented that the team had not managed to play a single game all year. In her summary, Captain Genevieve Stone wrote that games against sides in other cities had been canceled, previous rivals the "Swedish Maidens" had disbanded and poor weather prevented them from playing a senior–junior game. Despite the lost season, Stone concluded on a positive note: "The girls' soccer team is awaiting a chance to play rivals next fall. It is hoped more schools will enter teams next year."[82] Unfortunately, by the following year the lack of opposing teams combined with changes to state educational requirements meant that Helen Clark no longer had the time to coach the team, and it was forced to disband.[83]

CONCLUSION

After leaving her job at McKinley Park, Doris Clark began working as a reporter for the *San Francisco Daily News*. It may be that Clark had long wished to write for a newspaper, given her early success at composition. In 1914 an article called "Just How Old is the Corset?" was published in the *San Francisco Chronicle* with a byline by Doris Clark. Although mainly a lighthearted history of the garment, the article nonetheless showed its author to be fairly progressive in her attitudes toward women's clothing. Clark argued that, historically, a woman often chose to wear an ornate corset "despite its repressing and torturing effect" because it made her look more elegant. Later she recalled the damage caused by garments worn in her grandmother's era, including "the tragedies of sterility, or of death in childbirth of young mothers who had deformed themselves." She didn't outright condemn corsets but rather concluded that modern versions such as the tango model were more in keeping with her generation's sensibilities "Does it not savor more of the century of suffragettes, if you please, of child labor laws, of social welfare, of college education for women than does the iron corset?"[84] Few issues of the *Daily News* during Clark's tenure at the paper survive, so it is difficult to know what sort of stories she wrote although her participation in various public events implies that so-called women's issues were a mainstay.[85] In addition, she wrote for a time as "Cynthia Grey," whose advice column received forty letters a day from "wives who can't hold their husbands, husbands who can't hold their wives, or who can and do not wish the honor, lovelorn or stage struck girls, unhappy boys who want to run away from home, and so on and so forth."[86] She was also involved in more serious reporting, such as the Argonaut Mine disaster that killed forty-seven workers in 1922.[87]

Eventually Clark became an editor at the *Daily News* but seems to have left the position by 1924.[88] It was likely through her newspaper work that she met Brelsford William Hellings, a veteran of World War I who worked as a photographer for various agencies and eventually at the *San Francisco Chronicle*. The two married in 1923, and within a few years Clark no longer worked outside the home.[89] The two never had children, and she virtually disappeared from the public record until her death in December 1975.[90] Helen Clark did not marry or have children and continued working at Bridgeport High School until she died in 1945.[91] Although they had relatively short careers in soccer, both Doris Clark and Helen Clark nonetheless showed that women could not only play the game but successfully take on other important roles in the sport.

8

SOCCER GOES TO WAR

In September 1918, the U.S. Army's Eighty-Sixth Infantry Division set sail for England. One soldier making the trip was a young man from Illinois named Joseph Cunat. The journey across the Atlantic was uneventful, if not particularly comfortable, because only some of the ships had bunks installed while others contained simple hammocks. All of them were so tightly packed that at times it became difficult to breathe. After landing, the soldiers were immediately confronted with English autumn weather—drenching rain—along with long marches through mud-choked lanes. The unit lost a number of men to the Spanish flu. They crossed the channel at night, landed at La Havre, France, and continued on by rail southwest to the Medoc region. Cunat billeted at Saint Loubès, a few miles northwest of Bordeaux. As a sergeant, he was probably one of the noncommissioned officers sent to "finishing schools" and not one of the nine thousand men transferred to other units as replacements. By November 8, the division was ordered to Le Mans, where they would prepare for combat. The signing of the armistice on November 11 canceled these plans, and the next day the unit broke up and most of its members soon returned home. Cunat, however, remained in France and was assigned to the American Expeditionary Forces Departure Center, duty that some disparaged as being akin to hotel keepers.[1] Cunat arrived back in the United States by the end of summer 1919.

A few weeks after Cunat's unit sailed for Europe, elements of the US Seventh Field Artillery Regiment were positioned near Exermont, France. The unit, part of the famed Big Red One, the First Infantry Division, was taking part in the Meuse-Argonne offensive, a decisive action that eventually helped end the war. Among the soldiers likely present was twenty-something Private Maurice Hudson. Born in England, he arrived in the United States in 1907 and enlisted in the army ten years later. By the summer of 1918, he had become a US citizen and soon traveled with his unit to Europe.[2] Hudson survived the conflict and almost fifty years after the war was elected to the National Soccer Hall of Fame as a builder. He was largely recognized for his role as secretary of the California Football Association and the San Francisco Soccer League from the 1930s to the 1960s.

Both Cunat's and Hudson's playing careers spanned an important transitional period in the history of soccer in the United States. Even before the nation entered the conflict, the demands of war had led many foreign-born players to return home. Once the United States became an active belligerent, the impact grew as teams disbanded and entire leagues ceased to function. Initially, the conflict slowed the development of the game in the United States, but overall the experience of war helped transform soccer from a relatively marginalized pastime into an established part of the sporting landscape. No less a figure than US Football Association (USFA) president Thomas W. Cahill declared the immediate postwar years as "the most important period in the life of the game in this country." He saw this time as an opportunity to increase soccer's popularity among all Americans.[3] By several measures the sport took full advantage of the opportunity noted by Cahill, ushering in what historian Colin Jose has called US soccer's golden years during the 1920s.[4] Local soccer competitions expanded in many areas of the country, the fully professional American Soccer League (ASL) launched in 1921, and the USFA's National Challenge Cup saw substantial growth.[5]

This chapter considers how the war contributed to the progress of soccer in the United States. Cunat's and Hudson's stories illustrate two main developments: First, a foundation of soccer clubs, leagues, and players already existed in many communities, including areas around Chicago and San Francisco, where the two men competed. Since the formation of the USFA in 1913, the sport had witnessed steady growth in many parts of the country, a trend that only accelerated after the war. Second, the government along with the Young Men's Christian Association (YMCA) and other organizations devoted enormous resources aimed at encouraging soldiers to both play and watch soccer. Such investments introduced the game to hundreds of thousands of men and provided a new cohort of potential players and spectators who fortified the leagues and other competitions that had emerged over the past decade or more. Cunat and Hudson played soccer both during the war and after the end of hostilities became teammates on the US squad during the Inter-Allied Games held in Paris.

THE FOUNDATIONS OF POSTWAR GROWTH

The two men's experiences serve as examples of the kind of soccer communities that had emerged in many parts of the United States during the second decade of the twentieth century. Their stories also show how both native-born and foreign players participated in the game's development. Joseph Cunat was born in Braidwood, Illinois, on March 13, 1895. His parents came from what was then called Bohemia, in what became part of Czechoslovakia after World War I.[6] Coal had been discovered in Braidwood in 1864 and, like many immigrant men, Cunat's father worked in the mines. Joe Cunat spent his childhood in typical boyhood pursuits: hunting mushrooms, swimming, fishing, camping, and roughhousing with friends. By the time he was in his early twenties he had moved to Chicago to work as a printer. The midwestern metropolis was a mixture of various ethnic groups and Czech-Americans like Cunat, and his friends settled in neighborhoods like Pilsen, South Lawndale, Cicero, and Berwyn. Many of these pals joined him in playing for the Rangers Athletic Club baseball team.

By 1913 soccer was booming in the Czech areas in and around the city, and Cunat lined up for clubs such as the Hungarian-Bohemians and the American-Bohemian club. Within a few years a number of other teams sprouted, including Atlas, Olympia, Union, and Sparta. Participating in these activities helped connect second-generation immigrants like Cunat to older, mostly foreign-born members of the community. Negative attitudes toward Czechs from some corners of the city, however, led to tensions that sometimes played out on the field. After a series of controversial decisions and even some on field violence, most of the Czech teams decided to organize themselves as the fourth division of the Chicago and District

FIG. 8.1: Joe Cunat in his Rangers uniform circa 1918. (Hantak Family Photo Collection)

Association Football League. Formed in 1915, the league brought together a number of the city's soccer competitions into one association. Initially, thirty-two clubs were organized into four divisions, each contending for a trophy sponsored by a local business.[7] Cunat's side Rangers claimed the John A. Gauger Cup as fourth division winners in 1916–17, when they managed to score one hundred goals while conceding just one, and even that single tally was an own goal.[8]

While conflict raged in Europe, normal life continued for Cunat as he worked as a printmaker and played soccer. In the 1917–18 season, his Rangers squad completed a local double, winning the Chicago league's third-division crown with a 12–1–1 record and capturing the third-division cup. The squad also reached the semifinal of the Peel Challenge Cup, Illinois's most prestigious statewide competition. After losing a closely contested match to the Bricklayers and Masons 2–1, all fifteen Rangers enlisted.[9] Eventually Cunat reported for training to Camp Grant at Rockford, Illinois.

Officially he was a sergeant with Company E, 343rd Infantry Regiment, 172nd Infantry Brigade, Eighty-Sixth Infantry Division—also called the Blackhawk Division. Even while stationed in Rockford, he continued to turn out for various camp teams as well as for Rangers.[10]

Maurice John Hudson was born in London, England, on October 24, 1890, and emigrated to the United States in November 1907. After landing in New York he eventually made his way to San Francisco. He held a variety of jobs, and on the eve of the US entry into the war Hudson worked as a clerk for dry goods wholesaler Heller Klein and Company.[11] Organized soccer in the city began in 1892, but economic recession along with other problems led to the league's demise after only a few seasons. Five years later teams again formed and began playing friendlies with clubs from different communities as well as visiting British sailors. The game was closely associated with the British immigrant community in the city and one report from early 1898 called soccer "English football."[12] A new competition known as the California Association Football League kicked off in 1902, and a year later the California Association Football Union organized. The California State Cup competition began in 1903, and teams from the San Francisco Bay Area dominated the tournament until 1921–22, when a team from Sacramento claimed the trophy.[13] All of these developments meant that, by the time Hudson arrived in San Francisco, soccer had a solid organizational and administrative foundation, not just in the Bay Area but across California.

FIG. 8.2: Maurice Hudson with the Barbarian team 1915–16. Hudson is marked 12, seated in the front center row just behind the boy mascot. (*Spalding's Official "Soccer" Foot Ball Guide*, 1916–17. Courtesy of the Library of Congress)

According to one newspaper report, Hudson made his debut for the local club, the Barbarians, in 1911.[14] The Barbs, as they were known, began as a rugby club that competed with local colleges, but around 1910 they absorbed a soccer team called the Hornets and began to play both sports.[15] The Hornets had links to one of the oldest association football clubs in the region—Oakland FC. Edgar Pomeroy, former captain of the side, wrote that the club had originally been a rugby team but was playing soccer as early as 1891. Oakland FC declined to participate in the Bay area's first league because "nearly all" of the players on other squads had learned the game in England or Scotland, while "the Oakland boys were only picking it up." After the league's demise, Oakland continued to play the odd friendly versus local sides or teams from visiting British ships. After briefly disbanding around the turn of the twentieth century, the club reformed in 1903, adding Hornets to the name in order to distinguish themselves from a local baseball team. The club also adopted distinctive orange-and-black striped kits inspired by the coloring of actual hornets.[16] The team participated in regional competitions, and Hornet's center forward H. R. Elliot captained a league select team that visited British Columbia in 1909.[17] By the next season the club had merged with the rugby-playing Barbarians.

The fact that the Barbs also played rugby made them less competitive at soccer. The reasons for this included the challenge of having the same players competing in different sports on consecutive weekend days. As a result of such hardship, the club experienced a great deal of turnover and in the 1910–11 season thirty-eight individuals made an appearance for the club. Such change limited the ability of the squad to perform consistently, and although they were generally viewed as a talented side, they struggled to rise above mid-table.[18] The five-foot-nine-inch Hudson quickly showed his quality, earning a spot as center forward in the squad and helping the Barb's five-a-side team win the city championship in 1912.[19] Two years later, Hudson was made captain of the first team and soon earned a reputation as the city's best striker. A *San Francisco Chronicle* article in the spring of 1916 marveled at his abilities, exclaiming "one thing is certain, whenever Hudson starts something he makes his presence felt."[20] The Barbs continued to finish in the middle of the pack in the league, although they won the California Football Association Cup in 1914–15. Hudson featured prominently in the final, scoring a goal and setting up two more.[21] After joining the army in 1917, Hudson trained at Camp Kearney near San Diego, but when he could he returned to San Francisco to play for the Barbarians.

SUPPORTING SOCCER IN THE MILITARY

Camps Grant and Kearney were among the many training centers established by the US military in 1917. The army quickly developed athletic programs at the facilities as a means of improving physical fitness and to provide activities and entertainment for the soldiers.[22] All camps had an athletic director who organized competitions in a variety of sports, including soccer.[23] In August 1917, the *Camp Sherman News* reported that the war commission had ordered 7,000 soccer balls, enough to outfit 1,750 companies or 125 regiments.[24] As a result, organized soccer games took place in many parts of the country, some of which had an established history with the sport while others did not. Documented competitions took place in New Jersey, Ohio, South Carolina, and Pennsylvania, but such events likely were common in other camps as well. At the newly constructed Camp Meade in Maryland, for example, one soldier from Bristol, Pennsylvania, reported that the soldiers enjoyed playing soccer.[25] Soccer teams of eleven starters plus three substitutes formed on a regimental level and sometimes trophies or cups were awarded to the winning squad.[26] These competitions also took place when US units were in Europe. The Fifty-Fourth Pioneer Infantry Division held a tournament while stationed in Germany, recruiting a British officer to referee the final.[27] In addition to matches among the units organized at US training facilities, military clubs sometimes ventured beyond the base to challenge civilian teams.[28]

Although most of the documented matches used the association rules, some matches recalled previous versions of mob-style football. When the newly appointed director of the Division of Health Hygiene and Athletics, Dr. James H. McCurdy, arrived in France in 1917, he immediately organized large-scale "company soccer" matches among the troops. Part of an effort to live up to the YMCA's motto of "Every Man in the Game," the activity involved as many as 175 men on a side with four balls in action at the same time. Although later described as an innovation, the activity closely resembled traditional nineteenth-century mob-football games, especially those played during the Civil War. Having been born in 1866, McCurdy may have experienced such matches during his childhood before association football became more widespread.[29] Company soccer also took place on US soil; one report from Camp Sherman in Ohio for example, described hundreds of competitors with multiple balls on the field at the same time.[30]

Various nongovernmental organizations helped the army raise interest and knowledge about soccer and also provided equipment to the camps.[31] At times the assistance was small and local, as when the Hudson Valley chapter of the Knights of Columbus delivered twenty soccer balls to Fort Dix. Other examples included Philadelphia teams playing an exhibition match at the fort and the Bethlehem Steel team lining up against a handpicked side from Camp Crane.[32] Local football associations also sponsored benefit matches, such as the one held at Shibe Field in Philadelphia on November 16, 1918. Organized by the Football Association of Eastern Pennsylvania and District, the proceeds of the game were divided between the Soldiers' and Sailors' Tobacco Fund and the British Patriotic Society.[33]

Fund-raising and other initiatives also occurred at the national level as the USFA spearheaded a number of programs to support the war effort. In May 1917, the federation launched the Soccer Football Chain Letter Fund as a way to raise funds to purchase sporting equipment for the troops. The results were disappointing as the appeal raised just $597.54 despite mailing out ten thousand letters. Still, the fund provided enough money to send material to military bases in traditional soccer hotbeds, including Pennsylvania, New York, and Massachusetts, and also to states with less-established playing traditions, such as Oklahoma, Texas, Georgia, and Alabama.[34] In addition to the chain letter, an appeal to various regional associations raised nearly ten thousand dollars for the United War Work Fund.[35]

By far the military's biggest partner was the YMCA. The organization helped by assigning personnel to arrange competitions and also by providing equipment. Ultimately nearly thirteen thousand men and women from the YMCA served the American Expeditionary Forces (AEF) during the war. The commander of US troops, General John J. Pershing, delegated control over military canteens and morale in Europe because it freed up his men for training and fighting.[36] Once the United States formally entered the conflict, the YMCA quickly organized the National War Work Council on April 10, 1917. The group's self-described mission was "to assist in maintaining and promoting morale," and it soon launched a drive to construct hundreds of service centers at various military installations across the country and eventually in Europe. The sponsored activities included such diverse things as providing writing paper and stamps, screening movies, and hosting educational lectures. Athletics quickly emerged as one of the most significant elements of the YMCA program, as the organization itself boasted after the war "more Americans at one time undoubtedly learned to play more new games than in any previous sporting season in the history of the country."[37] A month after the government announced a plan to spend $250,000 on athletic supplies, the National War Work Council spent double that amount on equipment. The order included 14,000 soccer balls worth a total of $70,000 or around $1.3 million in 2020 dollars.[38] Overall, between July 1918 and March 1919, the organization spent a total of $104,470 ($1.8 million in 2020) procuring soccer balls for the troops, a sum exceeded only by the amount used to buy baseballs.[39]

THE MILITARY AND POLITICAL BENEFITS OF SOCCER

The imperial expansion of the United States around the turn of the twentieth century led to a growth in the military along with a reconsideration of its role and preparedness. Officials developed formal sports programs in part for entertainment but also for more practical reasons: "to actively promote the value of athletic training as an adjunct to drill and as a means of instilling the values of teamwork and cooperation in the troops." Since foreign-born white men were overrepresented in US ranks during World War I, the government prioritized the playing of US games such as intercollegiate football and baseball to speed their assimilation. The military also believed that by competing in these sports the men would learn a specific type of masculinity centered on toughness.[40] Despite such desires, officials recognized that many soldiers, including both US-born citizens like Joe Cunat or immigrants such as Maurice Hudson, had grown up playing soccer. The sport fit the general athletic program adopted by the military and also had several advantages over gridiron football and baseball. To begin with, soccer required little in the way of specialized equipment. Once US troops were stationed in Europe, bats, gloves, helmets, and padding could be lost when units moved positions or the enemy sank transport ships. By contrast, soccer balls were easy to carry and were not as difficult to replace. Another advantage was that company soccer games allowed more men to take part than did traditional versions of baseball and intercollegiate football. Along with its positive contributions to exercise and entertainment, soccer also had specific military benefits. Finally, because soccer was popular internationally, it provided a unique opportunity for friendly cooperation and competition between Allied nations.

FIG. 8.3: The US Army Forty-Second Division soccer team at a match versus the Canadian Second Division on January 18, 1919, at Bonn, Germany. (Library of Congress, Prints and Photographs Division, LC-DIG-ggbain-28804)

During World War I, the US military believed that athletics should have a direct relation to combat.[41] An article in the military newspaper *Going Over* argued that soccer was not only an enjoyable pastime but also helped prepare men for the experience of war: "The inspirational value of playing needs little exposition, but the parallel between playing and fighting may be illustrated in a number of ways. While playing soccer a man must be ready constantly to strike at the ball with either foot. In this way he naturally acquires a short gait and balance that will serve him in good stead in traversing the churned and furrowed surface of No-Man's-Land. Soccer is a highly exhilarating game, combining the maximum of exercise and recreation with a training that will be exceedingly useful when there is an enemy to be reckoned with."[42]

In addition to helping soldiers prepare for combat, soccer could also assist in their recovery from the harmful effects of fighting, according to the USFA. As proof, the organization cited "competent army officers" who declared the sport "one of the greatest aids possible to restore the nerves of the soldiers, shattered by the crash of tremendous guns, half asphyxiated by poisonous gases, depressed by the sight of shattered comrades."[43] In a story for *Going Over*, sportswriter Thomas S. Rice concluded that soccer had several practical advantages over popular sports such as baseball. A simpler set of rules made it far easier for an "innocent bysitter" to follow a match and for people to learn the sport more quickly. Association football required less equipment and less space than other games and could be played on fields of varying quality. Rice also noted that soccer had overtaken rugby in popularity and that the army had begun discouraging the latter game because of the number of injuries sustained. He argued that soccer also facilitated matches across nationalities and predicted that after the war the sport would become popular in the United States: "When peace is declared the world will be filled with wanderers from the Entente armies, adventuring in the far corners of the earth, and they will carry with them soccer as well as baseball. It is most certain that upon the return of peace soccer will experience an enormous boom in the United States. The returned soldiers and sailors will spread the game, precisely as the returned men of the Civil War spread baseball by furnishing the players and also the nucleus for the present generation of baseball fans."[44]

The ease with which basic rules could be learned, combined with the opportunity presented through official encouragement and the availability of equipment, meant that large numbers of US soldiers played soccer during the war. Undoubtedly some of the more accomplished teams, including the finalists of the AEF Championships, were made up of semipro college players or foreign-born athletes like Hudson.[45] Nevertheless the sheer number of participants and spectators reveals that a broader diffusion of the game took place. An April 1919 report stated that more AEF soldiers participated in soccer than any other major sport except gridiron football. Commenting on these numbers, the authors of the *Official Almanac of the American Expeditionary Forces* wrote that "readers of American sporting news may be astonished to know that soccer was ranked high in popularity if the participation figures are to be taken as any indication."[46] Such a comment illustrates that although soccer was not generally thought of as a popularly played sport back home, the experience of war exposed more people to the game as both participants and spectators. Along with the 527,495 who played soccer between August and December 1918 another 578,819 watched matches. Perhaps reflecting Rice's comments on its accessibility, soccer was one of the only major sports where the number of players and spectators was nearly the same.[47] More complete data published in 1919 showed that 1,557,927 US soldiers in Europe played soccer during the first five months of the year. While baseball remained by far and away the most popular sport to watch and play, more soldiers took part in a soccer match than a traditional baseball game in January 1919 (557,244 to 105,350). Although the numbers of soccer players declined over time, the figures still show that the game had been consistently popular as both an activity and as entertainment.[48] It is noteworthy that the numbers produced only tallied members of the AEF in Europe and not those who took part in or watched a soccer match before they left the United States. Although baseball remained king and sports like intercollegiate football, basketball and boxing were also popular, the experience of war led to more people playing or watching soccer than perhaps at any other time in the nation's history to that point.

The popularity of soccer within the US military mirrored broader trends among the Allied armies. Although sport had long been an informal part

FIG. 8.4: Still from a film showing a match between the US Army's Twenty-Eighth and Thirty-Fifth Divisions at Le Mans France on March 29, 1919. (*Activities at the Le Mans Embarkation Center, December 22, 1918 to April 1, 1919*; motion picture 111-H-1469 [historical film 1469]; Records of the Office of the Chief Signal Officer, record group 111; National Archives at College Park, College Park, MD)

of British military life, such activities became compulsory during the Great War. By 1915 organized soccer competitions had begun and the YMCA played a key role in forming leagues. For British commanders, soccer served the same role as baseball did for the US military: it gave the men a shared cultural language, helped to solidify a sense of esprit de corps, and improved morale.[49] As soon as they arrived in France, other Allied troops began organizing competitions, which often included squads made up of locals from communities where the soldiers were stationed. Matches between nations proved especially popular and regularly attracted large crowds. Such trends continued throughout the remainder of the war and even afterward; between March 1917 and May 1919 international matches between soldiers from France and New Zealand never drew fewer than fifteen thousand supporters.[50]

Once the United States joined the war, AEF soldiers began to compete at soccer against people of other nations. Such activities demonstrated Rice's notion that soccer had the ability to foster cross-cultural interactions.[51] Historian Gabe Logan describes a letter from a former Chicago-area player who while stationed in Siberia played in a match that pitted US and Czech teams. Another correspondent serving in Wales with the Canadian army wrote that his main duty was to organize the camp soccer squad and that many of the players were from the United States.[52] In more formal matches, AEF soccer players faced Allied sides with mixed results. In December 1918, a US military team lost 7–0 to an English club from Vendôme while a crowd of 1,200 saw members of the French Le Mans Sportive Association defeat the US Army's Twenty-Sixth Division squad 4–1 in February 1919. A month later a team from the Fifty-First Field Artillery of the US Twenty-Sixth Division beat the champions of the French Fourth Army 4–0.[53] There is also evidence that soldiers sometimes organized informal matches between men of different nationalities. One YMCA service worker reported that at his post they had initially discouraged international competition for fear it might damage relations between the troops. One day, however, he found that US and French soldiers had started playing soccer together and, although he had little knowledge of the game, he agreed to serve as referee.[54]

Due to its popularity among the Allied nations, soccer was one of the most anticipated events at the Inter-Allied Games held in Paris between June 22 and July 6, 1919. The US military and the YMCA jointly organized the games to celebrate interallied cooperation while promoting US values and sporting culture. Of the twenty-eight nations invited to compete, ultimately eighteen sent representatives.[55] For the competition's eight-team soccer tournament, the nations were organized into two groups of four, with only the top team advancing to the final. One group included the United States, Canada, the new nation of Czechoslovakia, and Belgium, while France, Italy, Greece, and Romania made up the other.[56] Ultimately, Czechoslovakia and France met in a closely matched final, with the Czechoslovaks taking home the trophy in a 3–2 win.[57]

In many sports the athletes and teams who represented the United States in the Inter-Allied Games were decided at the AEF Championships conducted between January and June 1919. In preparation for the tournament, the military ordered that for most events teams would be organized at the company or battery level to compete for the division championships. Winners at the division level would play for the corps title, with the victors moving on to the AEF Championship.[58]

FIG. 8.5: The American Embarkation Center Soccer Team, winners of the American Expeditionary Forces Championships 1919. Joe Cunat is standing in the back row at the far right. (Hantak Family Photo Collection)

Intercollegiate football and soccer were among the sports that could not be organized according to this structure. Gridiron football required too much equipment to properly outfit an estimated ten teams per division, and it seems that many units lacked soccer clubs. Nevertheless, the army's expressed desire to encourage the development of soccer combined with a wish to have a team at the Inter-Allied Games meant that a tournament had to be organized. As a result, the championship was contested "among such units as have soccer teams" and the AEF was divided into four sections, with elimination tournaments held to determine representatives in the finals.[59] The four areas and the units representing them in the finals were General Headquarters by 603rd Engineers; Third Army by Sixth Division; the Le Mans American Embarkation Center (AEC) by Eightieth Division; Advance Section by Services of Supply and Intermediate Section by Services of Supply. Generally the level of play was good, but there were some uncompetitive results, including AEC's 10–1 victory over General Headquarters and Third Army's 12–0 shellacking of Advance Section. The final on May 15, 1919, pitted AEC versus Third Army and was called "one of the best games witnessed in France." The evenly matched sides battled to a 1–1 draw after ninety minutes and then played two full overtimes without another goal. Finally, in the third overtime and after more than three hours of soccer, AEC scored from forty yards out and then added a penalty to seal the victory. Ultimately eight players from the championship game went on to represent the United States at the Inter-Allied Games including one of the key defenders from the winning side: Joe Cunat.[60]

The military tasked veteran soccer official Johnny Mackenzie with organizing the US team for the Inter-Allied Games. Mackenzie had refereed all of the matches in the AEF Championship and set about picking a squad and arranging friendlies with other sides. A resident of California, Mackenzie already knew of Maurice Hudson's skill, and perhaps Cunat's performance in the AEF tournament caught Mackenzie's eye as the two men along with thirty-nine others were selected to begin training for the games.[61] The US squad played eight matches in preparation for the Inter-Allied Games: three inter-squad scrimmages, three friendlies against France, and two friendlies against Romania.[62] Ultimately Cunat and Hudson were among the thirty men listed as part of the US squad for the games, but because no lineups for the team's three tournament matches

FIG. 8.6: The United States versus Canada at the Inter-Allied Games in Paris on June 25, 1919. The United States won the match 5–4, with both Joe Cunat and Maurice Hudson likely taking part. (Canada. Dept. of National Defense, Library and Archives Canada, PA-006640)

have surfaced, it is unknown exactly how many games they each may have played. Both men appear in a photo of the eleven-man squad taken on the field during the competition, so it is reasonable to assume they made at least one appearance.[63]

Although now mostly forgotten, US troops remained stationed in portions of the Rhineland for four years after the Armistice as occupation forces. Those who stayed continued to play soccer. During the occupation period, the YMCA carried on its mission of encouraging men to play sports as a means of keeping them both physically prepared and morally wholesome. The organization set up and maintained many of the same types of entertainments that had been offered throughout the conflict. Such pursuits included soccer, and specially designed fields were created in the German towns of Koblenz, Mayen, and Andernach.[64] The American Forces of Germany (AFG) continued the tradition of friendly competition among US units and Allied armies. During the 1920–21 season, the AFG conducted three soccer competitions including a league, a cup, and a unit championship. The league featured six teams playing a schedule of thirty-three matches. The Third Battalion of the Eighth Infantry captured the title with an undefeated record of seven wins and one draw. The same side won the cup while Headquarters troop earned the AFG Championship.[65] A select team of AFG players also took part in the Armies of Occupation Track and Field Championships held at Carnival Island in Koblenz in July 1921. Despite the name, the tournament also featured a soccer competition involving the United States, France, and Great Britain.[66] Although exact match results are not known, the British squad ended up capturing the title, with the French finishing second.[67] In June 1921, the United States won a soccer competition held during an interallied athletic meet at Mainz.[68] During the occupation period, the US teams recovered from a shaky start in which they lost four of their first five matches versus allied nations, finishing with a respectable overall record of eleven wins, six draws, and seven losses.[69]

THE GROWTH OF SOCCER IN THE 1920S

The evidence that World War I helped raise soccer's profile and popularity leading to increased attention and participation in the 1920s is both anecdotal and empirical. One indication of growing popularity is that many in the leadership of the USFA were convinced that the conflict had a positive impact on the development of the sport. Thomas Cahill, in his several postwar editions of *Spalding's Official Soccer Foot Ball Guide*, consistently repeated the message that the war had helped to grow the game. In 1919–20, he declared that the Great War "carried the knowledge of soccer football to sections of the country where it has heretofore been known only by name."[70] In the next published edition of the guide, he proclaimed the 1920–21 season "the greatest year in the history of soccer foot ball."[71] A year later he continued to be positive "soccer in this country is in a far more advanced state than any of its most optimistic advocates dreamed when the national body was incorporated on April 5, 1913."[72] Other officials of the USFA were equally enthusiastic. Peter J. Peel, in his annual presidential report for the 1919 season, declared, "the night is past and the day is here and to-day we stand on the threshold of a new era in sport in which soccer is destined to take a prominent part."[73] In 1923 USFA president George Healey acknowledged that a recent economic downturn had slowed growth but stressed that the maturation of younger players had improved the quality of play.[74] Naturally Cahill, Peel, and Healey had a vested interest in fostering the idea that soccer was on the rise, but because they had an intimate and comprehensive view of the sport and its development, their optimism cannot be completely discounted. Since the sport tended to be regionally based with consistent but limited interactions between different communities, the national federation had the best contemporary picture of the state of the game across the entire country.

The enthusiasm of the USFA leadership is also reflected in quantifiable gains on the field. The launching of the ASL in 1921 gave the United States its first major professional league since 1894 and the first that would last more than a handful of weeks. Within a few years, the ASL had established itself as one of the premier soccer leagues in the world. A willingness to pay high salaries meant that the competition attracted talented players from around the world. By 1926 British authorities had become concerned enough over the loss of skilled players that they took steps to limit their movement.[75] In addition to helping launch the ASL, the USFA saw its own National Challenge Cup experience growth in the years after the conflict. After doubling from the first year (1913–14) to the second, the number of entries remained steady between 1915 and 1917. Following the country's entry into the war, the numbers dipped as players enlisted and clubs dissolved. The 1917–18 edition had 54 entrants and the low point occurred a year later when just 48 teams competed for the trophy.[76] Once peace was restored, the number of entries quickly returned to prewar levels before growing rapidly. The 1921–22 edition featured 118 teams, while the next year a record 132 clubs signed up for the competition. By 1924 the tournament had grown so large that the federation's cup committee recommended capping the number of entries at 128.[77]

The data available for regional competitions show that in most areas steady growth occurred after the war. The numbers compiled from reports published in *Spalding's Official Soccer Foot Ball Guide* show that, in almost every case, local league or cup competitions saw an increase in the number of entries during the 1920s.[78] In some cases the raw figures do not tell the whole story. In Chicago new leagues formed at a rapid clip and the city was soon home to three different professional leagues as well as several semipro or amateur circuits.[79] A similar scenario played out in Cleveland as the historic league saw the formation of a rival International League in the 1923–24 season.[80]

Attendance figures for the National Challenge Cup final confirm an increased level of interest, especially in the second half of the decade. Between 1914 and 1919, championship final matches averaged 9,500 spectators, while the number increased in the decade following the war to 12,904.[81] The final match of the competition was the most anticipated soccer game of the season, as the 1923 championship illustrates. The match set a historical high for attendance at a soccer game played in the United States when fifteen thousand fans witnessed a 2–2 draw between Paterson Silk Sox and Scullin Steel.[82] The record only lasted a few years however, as a reported seventeen thousand saw Boston take home the Lewis Cup in 1925.[83]

Tours by international teams also increased after the war, with fifteen clubs touring the United States between 1921 and 1930 and some—including Glasgow Rangers, Worcestershire, and Hakoah Vienna—appearing more than once.[84] The visit of the Austrian club was especially noteworthy because it drew a crowd of 46,000 to New York's Polo Grounds in 1926, a figure that would not be matched in the United States until almost five decades later.[85] Use of the term "soccer" in a variety of publications increased fairly dramatically during the 1920s, validating George Healey's claim in 1923 that the sport was receiving more publicity than ever before.[86] Finally, the sport of soccer also benefited from broader cultural shifts that helped to promote athletics in the United States. The expansion of sports as part of the educational curriculum at schools and colleges created new generations of athletes and fans. Between 1919 and 1921, seventeen states passed new physical-education measures and such laws helped shift the emphasis from traditional calisthenics toward team sports.[87] After the sport was shifted to a fall schedule for men's games at colleges and universities in 1914, it expanded on many campuses, especially in traditional soccer-playing areas like the Northeast.[88] As seen in the previous chapter, women and girls also began to play soccer in greater numbers during the 1920s and 1930s.

CONCLUSION

After returning to the United States on July 3, 1919, Joe Cunat was honorably discharged August 11.[89] For his military service he earned $8,135 and a train ticket home to Chicago. After returning from Europe, Cunat took up with his old side, playing for Rangers before moving to Sparta Union in 1923.[90] Along the way he met a woman named Emma; the two married on April 21, 1920. It is unclear when he stopped playing soccer, but it may have been when the couple had children—Joseph, who lived for only a day in 1923, followed by Grace in 1925 and Robert four years later. Cunat saw his daughter married in 1945, and Emma passed away in 1947. Eventually he relocated along with Grace's family to a new house in North Riverside, Illinois. All the while he continued to return to his childhood home of Braidwood—to collect black walnuts with his grandchildren, smoke his pipe, and hunt mushrooms like he did as a boy. Cunat died on December 18, 1969, and was buried next to his wife and parents in the Bohemian National Cemetery in Chicago.

After returning to California, Maurice Hudson also continued to play with his prewar team. In 1921 at a banquet the Barbarians presented him with a gold watch to celebrate ten years of service to the club.[91] Two years later Hudson was part of the team crowned state champions after defeating rivals Thistle in the cup final.[92] Soon after the victory, he seems to have retired as a player, but in 1926 he made a comeback. After a decent first match, he struggled in the second, prompting the *San Francisco Chronicle* to note that "the Barbarian warhorse proved that he is 'through.'"[93] Still, Hudson was not deterred and just over two years later he once again returned to the field, this time for the Hornets. According to one newspaper report, the thirty-seven-year-old "did very well at outside left considering his ample waistline."[94] The match with the Hornets seemed to end his playing career, and by 1935 Hudson had been appointed secretary of the California Football Association.[95] He had begun his career as an administrator and as a builder, one that would eventually lead to the National Soccer Hall of Fame.

9

ETHNIC AND INDUSTRIAL SOCCER

The history of football and soccer in western Massachusetts reflects many of the main themes of this book. Long before the arrival of European settlers, Algonkian-speaking peoples made their homes along the banks of the Connecticut River and its tributaries. Although there is no evidence they played football like other groups from the same language family, their life routines may not have differed much. The people lived in small bands of farmers who traveled seasonally from settlement to settlement. They preferred areas along the floodplains and terraces near the water; archaeologists have found other encampments used for larger social gatherings.[1] It is not hard to imagine that they could have played football in the same way Powhatans, Narragansetts, and Mi'kmaqs did. Once Europeans occupied the lands, they brought their sporting traditions with them and soon young men kicked footballs across the fields of Amherst, Easthampton, and Springfield. A few players even organized early club sides perhaps using the game as a winter diversion during baseball's off-season. Women at Smith College in Northampton and Mount Holyoke College in South Hadley also picked up the sport, often competing in class matches or contests between students and faculty. Ethnic organizations, many linked to the British isles, formed soccer clubs just as their countrymen had done in Chicago, Pittsburgh, San Francisco, and other communities.

In addition to its long history, soccer in the Pioneer Valley also highlights characteristics that shaped the development of the sport in the United States during the early twentieth century and beyond. Just as in many locations across the country, soccer teams and competitions emerged in western Massachusetts beginning in the late nineteenth century and continued into the first two decades of the twentieth. The region demonstrates the important role that industry and ethnicity played in the foundation and development of the sport during this period.

With the formation of the ASL in 1921, the country once again had a major professional competition. Unlike previous efforts, the ASL ultimately thrived, becoming an extremely competitive league capable of attracting high-level players from around the world.[2] One of the teams lining up for the inaugural season was a club from western Massachusetts called the Holyoke Falcos. At first glance, Holyoke seemed an unlikely home for a professional soccer club because the town had neither the population of some ASL cities nor a long history of success in top-level competitions, as did other cities. Nevertheless, the appearance of the Falcos in the ASL reveals important points about this era of US soccer history. First, the professional debut of the Falcos was the culmination of a decades long tradition of soccer playing in the region. Second, industrial firms played an important role in supporting, both directly and indirectly, local soccer communities. Finally, growth of the sport was limited outside of particular ethnic communities.

Teams had been competing across western Massachusetts and beyond since the earliest squads organized in the late 1880s. The predecessor to the Falcos was a club named after the textile company where many of its players worked: Farr Alpaca Co. Employees of the firm helped support the soccer team by hiring workers and providing them with a place to play. Later, as part of efforts to suppress labor strife, the company directly sponsored the formation of the Falcos and financially supported their efforts to turn professional. Such arrangements were not unusual in cities and regions around the country. Due to a lack of source material, however, we have little understanding of how they did so. The case of Farr Alpaca and the Falcos highlights some of the challenges in untangling the obscure financial relationships between players, teams, and industries during this period.

Despite the support of the firm, the experiment of playing topflight soccer proved to be a failure both on the field and in the account books. The attempt collapsed mainly due to an inability to draw spectators. In many ways, Holyoke fits the general explanation offered by Andrei Markovits and Steven Hellerman that professional soccer failed to take hold due in part to "the overwhelming self-identification of American soccer with ethnicity."[3] Such a sweeping claim, however, tends to obscure the specific details of local circumstances. In larger cities like Chicago, New York, and Boston, the sport quickly moved beyond its roots in communities from the British Isles and incorporated immigrant groups from a variety of nations as well as native-born Americans.[4] Such growth also took place in western Massachusetts, but not in Holyoke, where the sport proved unable to expand its base of support beyond its original adherents. The cause of this failure was not necessarily because soccer was seen as un-American but rather because it was too closely identified with a single ethnic group—British Protestants.

THE EARLY HISTORY OF SOCCER IN THE PIONEER VALLEY

An industrial community about one hundred miles west of Boston, Holyoke is situated next to an abundant source of electricity—the South Hadley Falls of the Connecticut river. As the city grew, it became known for textile and paper production, earning the nickname the Paper City. The earliest mention of soccer in the region comes from 1889, when squads from Holyoke competed with groups from nearby Springfield. The teams emerged from Scottish and English communities and took names such as Caledonian Football Club, Springfield Scots, and Holyoke Englishmen.[5] The Connecticut Valley Association Foot Ball League formed in August 1889 and included teams from Holyoke, Springfield, Ludlow, and Worcester. The proprietor of the *Worcester Times* newspaper donated a silver cup to award to the league champion. It is not known with certainty who ultimately prevailed in the competition, but a report from November 1889 noted that on defeating the Springfield Scots 7–2, the Holyoke Scotias took possession of eleven gold badges that had been displayed in a local shop window.[6]

One of the most prominent early squads from the region was the Holyoke Rangers. The club organized as early as 1888 and over the years competed against teams in the Pioneer Valley and beyond.[7] In the summer of 1890, the Scottish Athletic Association held a meet in Holyoke, and the centerpiece of the festivities was a match between Rangers and the Renfrews of Adams, Massachusetts. After marching to the field accompanied by the Holyoke

Flute Band and Highland Pipers, the Rangers emerged victorious with a resounding 5–1 win.[8] Although the club's team sheet changed over the years, it contained a number of players with Scottish surnames including Burns, McDonald, and Muirhead.[9] Soon the club was competing in local competitions against other city teams and squads from the nearby town of Ludlow. They also used the newspaper to challenge teams from as far away as Boston.[10] In the fall of 1896 they traveled to Barre, Vermont, to play the local side as part of Labor Day celebrations sponsored by the Granite Cutter's Association. In an upset, the visitors took home the honors with a 2–0 win.[11] Like in other areas of the country, such games were common and allowed folks who shared a similar ethnicity or occupation to gather and socialize. The Rangers also participated in wider contests outside of the region, including the American Cup, which was first awarded in 1885. Early editions mostly included teams from the area around Newark, New Jersey, but the competition soon expanded to New England. The Rangers participated in the 1890–91 competition, winning their first game but losing 6–1 in the next round to Fall River Rovers who had previously captured the trophy in 1888 and 1889.[12]

FIG. 9.1: The Holyoke Rangers squad with an unidentified trophy, circa 1890s. (Author's collection)

In 1904 clubs from Holyoke and neighboring towns organized a new regional competition called the Western Massachusetts Association Football League. The names of Holyoke's two entries, Caledonians and Celtic, confirmed that it was primarily Scots who played and supported the game in the city.[13] Indeed, virtually all the early players who can be identified with some degree of certainty were born in Scotland. Peter Murray, founder and owner of one of Springfield's largest department stores and a native of Scotland, donated a cup to be presented to the league's winning team.[14] A few years later the league grew to include entries from other local communities along with an outfit called Holyoke Rangers; eventually a second club from the city named Clan MacLaren was added.[15] Initially teams played from September to November, but over time the league expanded the length of the season to include games in the winter and spring. In 1911–12, the teams also competed for the Wolohan Cup, a prize donated by a Holyoke pub owner. The competition was held in the

FIG. 9.2: At least seven members of the Clan MacLaren Football Club and team president Robert Munn were born in Scotland. The image shows the influence of Scottish immigrants on the game. (Author's collection)

spring and was governed by "Scottish cup tie rules."[16] For most of its early history, the regional competitions retained a British flavor and in addition to the Holyoke clubs similar organizations from nearby cities sponsored teams, including Clan Murray, the Sons of St. George, Clan McLennan, and Ludlow Thistle.

Farr Alpaca FC began play in 1909 and was linked to the textile mill that employed most of the team's players. George Randall and Herbert Farr founded the company in 1873 after moving operations to Massachusetts from Canada. The Farr, as it was known, specialized in the production of mohair coat linings and between the 1880s and 1920s held a virtual monopoly, claiming up to 80 percent of the overall market.[17] The connection between the sport and the company may have existed from the start. A lack of skilled labor in Holyoke meant that roughly half of the company's initial workforce of two hundred came from Canada or England. Although a minority in the city as a whole, English, English-Canadians, and Scots remained a substantial part of Farr Alpaca's early workforce, and the company was long known in the city as "an English mill."[18]

It may be that these workers brought soccer with them to the city, and because its employees wanted a space to play soccer and rugby the firm leveled a company-owned plot.[19] Such a pattern of development mirrored the emergence of association football elsewhere in the United States and in England. Historian Tony Mason describes how most English clubs emerged from church groups, existing organizations, or places of employment. The men who tended to play football and became the first professionals were skilled workers and clerks who enjoyed regular work, higher salaries, and more leisure time.[20] Most Holyoke clubs followed this model, emerging from Scottish associations like Clan MacLaren and the Caledonian Club. In the case of Holyoke, club and company may have overlapped, as Farr Alpaca employed several of the players on the earliest city sides, like Caledonians, Rangers, and Athletics. Throughout the early twentieth century, however, Farr Alpaca had the only company-sponsored soccer team in the city.[21]

Farr Alpaca FC joined the western Massachusetts league, taking the place of Rangers for the 1909–10 season. The *Holyoke (MA) Daily Transcript* reported that, although Farr Alpaca FC was a new outfit, it was "made up of a large number of the cracks that have shown on other teams in the city in the past." The squad demonstrated its quality from the start by defeating four-time league champions Ludlow in the season's opening match.[22]

Beginning in 1909, the team also played Clan MacLaren for the Chaloux Cup; a Thanksgiving Day game designated as the city championship. The trophy was donated by William Chaloux, who owned a billiards room called the Pleasure Hour Club. The competition seemed quite popular with residents, in 1911 drawing a crowd reported at two thousand.[23] A year later the league, now called the Western New England Soccer Association, had grown to eight teams and Farr Alpaca emerged as the circuit's dominant squad. After finishing second in their initial campaign the club won the championship four years in a row. In 1911–12, the squad won a local treble, capturing the league title as well as the Chaloux and Wolohan cups. The team did not lose a league game for five years and during one season netted an incredible eighty-seven goals while conceding just ten.[24]

Since its foundation, the team seemed determined to field a quality squad, first by signing local talent and later by adding outsiders when the opportunity presented itself. Near the end of the 1909 season, the Farr

FIG. 9.3: Studio portrait of a player from Thompsonville, Connecticut, circa 1912. Located about fifteen miles south of Holyoke, teams from the city competed in Western Massachusetts leagues in the years before World War I. (Author's collection)

Alpaca squad included Harry Campbell, a fullback who played for the New York Amateur Association Select team that had drawn with the visiting English Pilgrims that summer.[25] Although he lined up for the club, it does not appear that Campbell worked at the Farr Alpaca mill. Nevertheless, the company employed many of the squad's players, and five of the eleven players in a photograph of the 1911–12 title winners worked for the Farr that season.[26] In her book on the company, historian Frances Cornwall Hutner references an interview with a Farr Alpaca employee who confirms that people were indeed hired because of their athletic abilities.[27] The side's best players, including Jock McKinstrie and Patty McManus, had previously worked elsewhere but by 1912 were on the Farr's payroll. A year later the local newspaper reported that the club had brought in player Frank Hirst to reinforce the team; the Holyoke *City Directory* lists him as an employee of Farr Alpaca.[28]

The key figure in such actions may have been the president of the soccer club, John P. Arnold. Born in England in 1869, Arnold worked as an overseer at the Farr Alpaca mill. The position carried a great deal of power, including the right to hire workers, set wages, and control working conditions.[29] Bringing reinforcements into the team may have been necessary as the club began to take part in national competitions against better sides. Notice of Hirst's signing appeared only days before Farr Alpaca faced Bethlehem Steel in the second round of the American Cup competition. At the match played in Holyoke, Farr Alpaca actually led 1–0 at half time before losing 1–3.[30] The *Bethlehem Globe* called it "the best exhibition of soccer ever seen at Holyoke" and praised Hirst as one of the hometown side's better players.[31]

Without access to more documentation, it is difficult to know the extent to which the company supported the club financially. Evidence from newspapers can be inaccurate, contradictory, and difficult to interpret. Several years after the club's founding, the *Springfield (MA) Republican* implied that the players organized themselves and took the company's name only because so many of them worked there.[32] Still, the Farr's treasurer, Joseph Metcalf, a native of Yorkshire, served as the club's honorary president and backed the team "because the members of it were a set of gentleman and whom he liked to have in his employment."[33] Apart from giving jobs to talented players, something that could have been done independently by men like John Arnold, the company may not have provided much in the way of direct funding. When Farr Alpaca reached the final of the

Massachusetts state cup in 1915, the team needed to raise a guarantee of several hundred dollars in order to play the match in Holyoke. Instead of securing the money from the company, the club approached the city's Chamber of Commerce, which rejected the request despite the fact that the team's success had "done much to advertise the name of the city." Attempts to convince a group of businessmen in Springfield also failed, and it looked like the game would be played elsewhere. In the end, the team's manager, Charles Burnett, personally put up the money so that the game could be played at the club's home ground.[34]

By 1914 soccer enthusiasts in Holyoke had reason to be optimistic about the development of the sport in the area. Farr Alpaca won the Northern Massachusetts and New Hampshire Cup and reached the final of the Massachusetts state cup. Although the Holyoke eleven lost the final to General Electrics FC, the game reportedly drew a crowd of three thousand, which paid nearly $600 total to see the match.[35] The local league showed signs of increasing competitiveness, and a record twelve teams signed up to challenge for the 1914–15 title.[36] Most of the league's sides reflected the continued dominance of clubs linked to the British Isles and the competition included Caledonians, Ludlow Thistle, Sons of St. George, Clan Murray, and Clan MacLaren.[37] As the circuit entered its eleventh season and more local squads competed for regional and national honors, the sport also seemed to be developing an institutional foundation in the region. In April the Holyoke Water-Power Company announced that it had purchased the city's Berkshire Street grounds and would rent the facilities for a modest fee, thus insuring that Holyoke's soccer clubs would have a place to play. Later that year, the league's officials formed a referees' association. Within two years, plans were made for both a junior circuit in which each league club would field a second squad, and a schoolboy competition designed "to boom soccer" in the area.[38]

Despite such positives, the increasing competitiveness also forced officials to directly confront the thorny issue of professionalism. Although Farr Alpaca had been giving its players jobs with the company, the western New England league remained an amateur competition. In the spring of 1916, one of the league's clubs accused Chicopee Rovers of "professionalizing its players," although an investigation by the state association uncovered no proof to sustain the allegation. At the same time, local and state officials investigated other charges against two players. Samuel Lowe was suspended for receiving $1.50 for work time lost while playing for Ludlow, even though he had no legal contract with the club. The league declared the second man ineligible because he had been a professional who had failed to reregister as an amateur before signing with Chicopee Rovers. Cases such as these created a considerable stir among league members, with many expressing their strong desire to maintain "a clean sport."[39]

Issues of professionalism played a key role in the conflict that ultimately ended with the expulsion of the Western New England League from both the state association and the USFA. The first indication of trouble came when the league met in August 1916 to organize the season's competition. Reports indicated that Farr Alpaca and Chicopee Rovers might not field teams because "the Fisk and Westinghouse shop teams and the Ludlow club of the Western New England association have signed up nearly all the players of the Rovers and Alpacas."[40] Although Rovers managed to find enough players to form a side, Farr Alpaca seems to have dissolved. The dispute centered on the desire of the newly organized Fisk Rubber Company Red Tops to join the league for the 1916–17 season. After consideration of the request, the league twice voted unanimously to reject the club on the grounds that allowing a "shop team" would upset competitive balance and lead to the commercialization of the game.[41] Although the representatives claimed that at present the Fisk squad was not of sufficient quality to compete in the league, members feared that with company money the team could eventually buy up the best talent. They also felt that charging admission to games would give the club an advantage over those sides that did not have enclosed grounds. Furthermore, the officials believed that charging admission would be a deterrent to the growth of the game because "people in this section are not so crazy over the game that they are going to pay an admission fee to see a game which they do not half understand."[42]

The state association disagreed with the local league and asked them to reconsider Fisk's petition. A month after the organization reaffirmed its decision to bar the club from the league, the state association ordered them to accept the Red Tops or face expulsion. The league once again rejected the petition, confident that the USFA would back the decision. Meanwhile, the league's referees sided with the state association and refused to work any games if the clubs were suspended. When the state association's deadline for acceptance passed, the league was officially expelled from the organization. Ultimately the USFA also backed Fisk and ordered the league to allow the side to join the competition.[43] Although the league, now reduced to just four teams, completed its schedule in the spring of 1917, the competition was unable to reorganize for the fall. Instead, newspaper reports indicated that several clubs, including the Red Tops, hoped to form a "shop league" to replace the now-defunct Western New England league.[44] It is unclear if the industrial league proposed in September 1917 ever began play, since newspaper coverage of the sport over the next two years was inconsistent. While the Fisk squad played matches against a variety of local sides, there appeared to be no organized competition in the region.[45]

HOLYOKE IN THE AMERICAN SOCCER LEAGUE

The effects of war in Europe and the local battle over professionalization led to a reorganization of the sport in western Massachusetts. Both Farr Alpaca, arguably the region's most successful club, and the western New England league itself had been casualties of the two conflicts. Despite such setbacks, the established history and institutional foundation of the competition—combined with growing interest among industrial concerns— helped the sport recover somewhat after the end of the war. During or after the conflict, industrial firms including Fisk Rubber, Rolls-Royce, Hendee Manufacturing, and the American Writing Paper Company formed clubs.[46] Such initiatives were part of the general expansion of recreational activities at the companies during this period. Fisk, for example, created a social and athletic association that sponsored teams and organized recreational outings. One such event in September 1916 included soccer and baseball games as well as races (foot, auto, motorcycle, and bicycle), refreshments, and a wrestling match.[47] In 1914 Farr Alpaca Co. employees, backed by company funding, launched a similar organization called the Falco Athletic Association. The group sponsored baseball, basketball and cricket teams and in 1920 formed the Falco Athletic Association Football Club. Other activities included a band, drama club, and the construction of an auditorium and recreation hall in 1921. The increased attention to cultural undertakings coincided with a general rise in welfare initiatives at the company between 1916 and 1921. The activities were motivated by employee requests, changing state laws, and a desire to promote worker happiness and avoid labor strife.[48]

Also in 1920, the Western New England Soccer League reformed and included shop teams from Farr Alpaca, Rolls-Royce and Hendee Manufacturing—the home of Indian Motocycles. The competition also featured Ludlow Portuguese, one of the first non-British ethnic clubs to join the circuit.[49] The presence of the industrial teams indicates that prewar debates over professionalism had been resolved in favor of allowing teams to contract and pay at least some of their players. It is doubtful that the teams were made up entirely of professionals, but newspaper reports make it clear that the clubs were investing money to increase their competitiveness.[50] The Falcos won the league title and also convincingly captured the state championship, defeating the eastern Massachusetts titleholders 8–1.[51] The team also had one of the state's best players: inside left forward James Downie. When the Scottish Third Lanark team arrived in 1921 as part of a tour of the United States and Canada, he was one of only three players assured of a place in the state's starting eleven.[52] Downie played well against the visiting Scots, directly contributing to two goals and setting up his teammates for excellent chances on several other occasions.[53]

In September 1921 the ASL began its inaugural season of play. The first major effort to create a professional league in the United States after the failed try in 1894, the season featured some of the nation's top teams, and included representatives from New York City, Philadelphia and Fall River. When the formation of the ASL was announced in March 1921, there was no indication that league officials were considering the Falcos as one of the eight original teams. Eventually it became clear, however, that the disagreement over gate receipts meant that Bethlehem Steel would not field a club under that name. According to the *Springfield Republican*, ASL officials offered a franchise to the Holyoke team around the first of August. Club officials and members of the athletic association met on August 9 to consider the proposal and to hear from Thomas Cahill, the ASL secretary, also at the meeting. After "discussing the project from every angle," the members voted to accept the invitation.[54] The league soon returned Bethlehem's $500 deposit and within ten days announced that the Falcos would be joining the ASL.[55]

Reports differed as to the quality of the newcomers; one newspaper included them on a list of "first class combinations," but the *Bethlehem Globe* deemed them unworthy replacements for the paper's hometown club.[56] Charles A. Lovett in *Spalding's Official "Soccer" Foot Ball Guide* declared that "the organization is an out-and-out professional one and with but few exceptions the players of the eight clubs are registered with the United States Football Association on professional forms."[57] The *New York Tribune* wrote that all ASL teams had been "strongly reinforced" in anticipation of the upcoming league.[58] The *Holyoke Daily Transcript* announced two new signings for the Falcos: Joseph Coleman, described as a "star player"; and Tom Foster, who came from Accrington in England. Despite his advanced billing, Coleman appears not to have played in any ASL game for the Falcos, while Foster appeared in just eight.[59]

The decision to participate in the ASL represented a substantial expenditure for the company. The league demanded a guarantee of $500 plus a $50 entrance fee from each club and required that they play in up-to-date facilities.[60] The Falcos had such a facility at their Berkshire Street grounds, which the company had purchased in 1920 with the intention of using it for soccer.[61] Several factors, however, make it nearly impossible to determine exactly how much money the company was spending on the club. From its inception, Farr Alpaca Co. had followed a conservative financial policy based on minimizing reported profits and undervaluing assets. The result was the building up of large reserves that the directors believed would allow them to maintain financial equilibrium even during the roughest economic periods while also discouraging competition from rival firms. The company's financial reports included only minimally necessary figures and contained little specific detail. No effort was made for example to precisely define or explain routine financial report categories such as "debts," and it was standard practice for the company to hold large "secret" reserves of funds.[62] Undoubtedly the firm was spending money on the club, including wages, facilities upkeep, and travel, but such expenditures left no trace in the company's account books.[63]

The schedule makers handed the Falcos a tough test for their first topflight game—they had to travel to Fall River, long one of the nation's foremost soccer-playing areas. With goals from Ernest Logan, James Brown, and James Downie, the Falcos managed to upset the much favored home side 3–2. A week later, the two teams met again in Holyoke. Unfortunately for local fans, the success of the opening week vanished, as Fall River shut out the home side 0–2.[64] The loss was the start of a dismal campaign for the Falcos. The team won only one other game in open play during the season, and since it came against Jersey City, the league nullified the result when the

Celtics withdrew from the competition.[65] The squad finished in last place with 2 wins, 17 losses, and 3 draws while being outscored 64–17.[66] On the bright side, the club retained the Massachusetts state title in May, defeating the eastern champions 3–2 in a replay match that went into overtime.[67]

After finishing bottom in its initial campaign, the club did not continue in the ASL for the following season. Obviously, the team did not have the talent to compete effectively in the league, and the company seemed unwilling to invest in recruiting better players. In addition to constant losses on the field, the results were probably no better on the balance sheet. In a pair of articles from the *Boston Daily Globe* in the summer of 1926, George M. Collins reported on attempts made to bring professional soccer to Springfield. He wrote that, previously, the Falcos "had a try at it, but lost a lot of money and gave up." The new club would play its games in Springfield with the hope of drawing fans from surrounding communities, including Holyoke. The region had plenty of fans, although most were immigrants, and Collins could not help asking, "will Springfield rally after deserting the old Falcos?"[68] Perhaps it is unsurprising that the team had struggled financially, especially in a city whose population in 1920 numbered just over 60,000.[69] Despite soccer being far more popular in England, as early as 1911 one club director there believed that no city below 250,000 could support a major professional team, and even a big club would struggle in a town of 150,000.[70] Indeed, the cancellation of the final two games of the season "by mutual consent" was a result of the teams not wanting to pay travel costs for meaningless contests.[71] The *Boston Globe* wrote that the season had been financially challenging for the clubs and that the Falcos players had not been paid.[72] Farr Alpaca may have determined that it did not wish to invest more money, especially considering that the company had just committed to building a new 75,000-spindle mill at a cost of $2.5 million ($38.8 million in 2020 dollars).[73]

Since clubs depended on home gate receipts to pay the bills, the financial problems stemmed from an inability to attract crowds to the Berkshire Street grounds. It is nearly impossible to determine attendance figures for the games, since newspaper reports often failed to give specific numbers. For the fourteen home games played in 1921–22, the local newspapers give only four concrete figures: crowds of 700, 800, and "about 1000" saw ASL matches, while just 250 watched the team's first round match in the National Challenge Cup. For other dates, the papers give vague estimates, such as "one of the largest crowds seen here in many years," "a good-sized crowd," and, alarmingly, "one of the smallest that ever watched a football game here."[74] A few years later, a match between the Falcos and another Holyoke team attracted 1,200 paying customers, a crowd the *Springfield Republican* called the largest ever in the city.[75] If reports from previous years are to be believed, however, soccer in Holyoke had once attracted crowds of 2,000 to 3,000 spectators. Whatever the actual figures, it seems clear that during its time in the ASL the club never attracted more than one thousand fans to any single match and most likely attendance numbers were routinely much lower.[76] Such figures did not compare favorably with other ASL clubs that often drew several thousand supporters to each game. Even in Fall River, an ASL city of comparable size to Holyoke, the games attracted significantly more fans. With admission prices probably set at fifty cents, Holyoke could at best reach a gate of around $500 to $600, a sum that was unlikely to cover the team's expenses.[77]

Holyoke's failure to support the Falcos might be attributed to bad luck, as several home games were played during terrible weather conditions, including rain and snow. In addition, it was against Massachusetts state law to play games on Sunday, the one day of the week that most workers had off. Another issue may have been the declining economic situation of the region following the boom times of World War I. In the first postwar year, even Farr Alpaca Co. experienced one of its least profitable years, spurring treasurer Frank Metcalf to write in his official report that "the year just finished has been a most trying one."[78] Many of the city's firms never fully recovered from the recession of 1921, and by the end of the decade companies had cut their workforces by 18 percent and lowered wages by 27 percent.[79]

A key factor, especially in Holyoke itself, was that interest in soccer never expanded beyond the Scottish and English communities who first played the game in the city. The problem with soccer may not have been that it was seen as a foreign game, as a good percentage of Holyoke's population was born outside the country, but rather that it was seen as a British game. An analysis of the national origins of the players from 1905 to 1922 reveals that most of the players were born in Scotland or were perhaps second-generation Scots born in the United States. People of English and Scottish descent had never been a large segment of the overall population of the city, although the percentage peaked at around 10 percent between 1890 and 1900, near the time when soccer may have been first introduced into Holyoke. In the following decades, the total numbers of British or British Canadian residents remained constant at about three thousand, but the overall percentages declined until by 1920 they composed less than 5 percent of the city.[80] The lack of ethnic diversity among the squad may also have meant that the German and Portuguese residents of Springfield and Ludlow, who had begun to form their own teams, were never really drawn to support Holyoke's professional club.[81]

The bulk of Holyoke's population consisted of Irish and French Canadians, although a smaller number of Germans resided in the city. These residents formed tightly knit communities where "each ethnic group staked out its own territory and attempted to preserve its cultural heritage."[82] One result of these efforts was the development of social and cultural institutions specific for each group. Religion also served to separate the city's ethnic groups, and between Catholics and Protestants there was "no widespread mingling."[83] The French Catholic churches, for example, functioned as community centers where people participated in theater groups, orchestras, and card parties.[84] German immigrants to the city brought their own athletic traditions; the first Turners Hall was constructed in 1873, and it quickly emerged as the center of the community's social life.[85] The distinctions were especially strong in precisely those areas, such as schools and clubs, where shared athletic experiences might be found. By 1890 40 percent of school-age children attended Catholic schools, and popular recreational groups such as the Canoe Club excluded Catholics from the organization and from its tennis courts and ball fields.[86]

Playing and supporting soccer may have performed an important function in maintaining a separate sense of cultural identity for English and Scottish immigrants. Such notions were certainly true a few decades earlier, when the Springfield Scots refused to merge with a city club whose membership was open to all nationalities and ethnicities.[87] Scottish and English immigrants had their own social clubs and historian William Hartford characterized their relations with other ethnic groups as "not amicable."[88] It was precisely these organizations, however, that sponsored the first-known soccer teams and the games between them consistently drew the largest crowds. In addition, the players seem to have socialized with one another off the field, and by 1913 teams of different players were competing against each other in a local bowling league.[89] In Holyoke, distinct ethnic groups also lived in defined geographical spaces. Plotting the location of known soccer-player residences shows that most lived outside the ethnic neighborhoods populated by Irish, French-Canadian, and German residents.

An additional factor may also help explain why soccer never achieved much of a following outside the British community. In the development of the game during the nineteenth century, many of the earliest players emerged from the ranks of skilled workers rather than from the unskilled working class.[90] In Holyoke, quite a few of the players worked at jobs that would designate them as skilled workers, including loom fixer, superintendent, machinist, clerk, and engineer. The presence of several loom fixers over time is especially noteworthy, considering that they were "the most skilled and indispensable workers in [the weaving] departments" of textile mills. Such men often viewed themselves as superior to regular weavers, and an 1899 pamphlet from the National Loom-Fixers Association discouraged them from becoming too friendly with their subordinates.[91]

CONCLUSION

Although they no longer played in the ASL the Holyoke Falcos continued to field a semiprofessional squad in a variety of competitions, including the old western New England league.[92] In 1924 they took part in a statewide competition called the National Soccer League, although, as with the ASL they withdrew after only one season. In citing the decision not to compete the following year, columnist George Collins wrote that playing without the Falcos would save the other clubs an expensive trip to Holyoke.[93] Once again financial considerations may have required that the club withdraw from competition. By the middle of the 1920s, the fortunes of Farr Alpaca Co. and of the city itself seemed to be in decline. Profits, sales, and production at the Farr fell every year after 1923 until the mill was operating at only 15 percent capacity by 1932.[94] In addition to the economic changes, the city also was experiencing demographic shifts. After peaking in 1917, the population began to decline, and the composition of the residents also shifted, until by 1920 only about a third of them were foreign born.[95] The 1925–26 season was perhaps the club's last great accomplishment. Once again they finished at the top of the western New England league table and once again went through the campaign undefeated.[96] By the fall of 1927, the *Springfield Republican* reported that the Falcos would no longer compete in the league because they "found it difficult to assemble a strong team and thought it best to withdraw." Perhaps fittingly, the club that replaced them was a newcomer from Ludlow called Lusitano; founded in 1922, the club still exists as of this writing.[97]

Soccer had remained a vibrant if not a dominant pastime in western Massachusetts throughout the early twentieth century. The same could be said for professional baseball, where in Holyoke, although local teams and leagues thrived, the city's professional team withdrew from competition in 1914.[98] Baseball, however, offered something that soccer did not: a sporting space that all ethnic groups in the city could enjoy. Unlike soccer with its close connection to Protestant Britons, baseball drew fans from across the city's neighborhoods. A 1913 complaint about games being played on Sunday in violation of state law illustrates the broad appeal of the game: "picture the condition there: a crowd of twenty-five hundred people, ten to fifteen different nationalities, men and women from the shops and mills, each a partisan of the nines . . . eight such situations each Sunday demanded by law-abiding, self-controlled crowds and by nine citizens out of ten, and especially by the mothers of boys over fourteen."[99] Perhaps something like this is what soccer's adherents had hoped would happen once the Falcos turned professional. Although it's impossible to know for sure, it seems unlikely that such a diverse crowd ever turned up for a match in Holyoke.

CONCLUSION

For many decades, aficionados of the beautiful game in the United States have repeated the same joke: soccer is forever the sport of the future. Although the jest may have some truth to it, this book demonstrates that soccer has long been a part of the nation's past. Not only does the United States have a rich history with the sport, but it has also been playing soccer longer than any country apart from the United Kingdom. It was home to the first national football association, cup competition, and professional league established beyond the borders of Great Britain. To say that the United States lacks a tradition of soccer playing is to dismiss over a hundred and fifty years of history. One of the goals of *From Football to Soccer* has been to help restore soccer in the United States to its rightful place as one of the country's oldest and richest sporting histories. Football, and later soccer, has been intertwined with key changes in US history throughout the nineteenth and early twentieth centuries. The study of soccer alongside these larger social and cultural movements helps us to better understand the way that sport intersects with larger historical developments.

Extending the history of football back before the establishment of modern codes shows that the sport has been a part of the cultural landscape in North America even before there was a United States. The study of Native American kicking games underscores the rich and diverse cultural traditions of indigenous peoples. Although more attention has been given to lacrosse, the popularity of football indicates the broad scope of indigenous recreational practices. Such knowledge expands our understanding of Native culture even as it reveals severe limitations on that knowledge. The lack of indigenous source material contrasts with the wealth of settler accounts and highlights the impact of colonialism not only on Native sporting practices but also on the ways that we study those activities today. Chapter 1 relies heavily on non-Native source material and as a result, our knowledge of these kicking games is generally only revealed through the lens of colonialism and the subsequent production of academic knowledge. New practices and new approaches may one day shed further light on these types of games.

As Europeans seized Native lands and began the process of building settler culture, they brought traditional games and practices with them. Although on the surface there seemed little time for games, that football was ubiquitous can be seen in the near-universal use of the term as a metaphor. Our source material may not capture all the ways that people, especially young people, played the game. We are left to mine early football's traces in law codes, legal proceedings, and periodic newspaper reports that show only a fraction of the true dimensions of the sport. Once again, our knowledge of the past is shaped by what remains, and the surviving record is heavily weighted toward the experiences of white, largely middle- and upper-class men. As a result, we know little about when women and people of color played football, what it meant to them and the roles it played in their communities. Recent research has uncovered the earliest documented African American soccer players in the United States. Oliver and Fred Watson played on various teams in and around Pawtucket, Rhode Island, in the years between 1894 and 1907. Significant evidence of African American participation in the sport appears only in the early twentieth century. Young black men enrolled at primary and high schools in Chicago, Brooklyn, Kearny (N.J.), and Springfield (Mass.), played in squads with their white classmates.[1]

By the early nineteenth century, as the nation began to grow economically, new efforts were made to try and tame the wild instincts of boys. In some sense, football was like the country itself: a precocious child filled with a sometimes reckless energy. Football became one recommended practice that would, it was hoped, encourage and channel masculine vitality in productive ways. As the prosperity of the country increased, citizens invested in educational institutions and broadened the availability of schooling. The presence of such places, including public colleges, once again meant that football became part of a larger effort aimed mostly at shaping white, largely middle-class men. By the second half of the nineteenth century, educational expansion included opportunities for women, and soccer took hold on campus as the sport was promoted as a game suitable for young women.

The emergence of intercollegiate football contributed to the growing alienation of traditional kicking games from their place on college greens. Yet soccer did not wholly disappear outside of the schools and instead survived and even prospered beyond the campus gates. Three prominent and related developments in the second half of the nineteenth century provided the conditions necessary to develop soccer in the United States—urbanization, industrialization, and immigration. Urbanization led to the dynamic growth of cities, especially in the Northeast and Midwest. The populations of major urban centers such as New York, Chicago, St. Louis, and Philadelphia grew rapidly between 1870 and 1890, precisely at the moment that soccer became established in these areas. Pittsburgh, for example, grew from 262,204 residents in 1870 to 664,778 just twenty years later.[2] While soccer may not have become the dominant sport enjoyed by urban dwellers, it did emerge as an important sporting subculture. This growth provided the foundation for the creation of the United States Soccer Federation, the National Challenge Cup, and the fully professional American Soccer League in the first two decades of the twentieth century. It is important to note, however, that soccer was also played, albeit on a smaller scale, in other regions of the country. Although not as well-known or as well-documented, soccer competitions took place in Atlanta, Birmingham, Denver, Miami, Salt Lake City, and other cities.[3]

The process of industrialization also contributed to the growth of soccer during the 1880s and 1890s. Workers flocked to major metropolitan areas, where they formed soccer clubs and competitions. Industrialization, however, did not just take place in large cities, as smaller mill towns like Kearny, Fall River, Pawtucket, and Holyoke became known as soccer-playing centers. Not only did workers help to grow the sport, but increasingly companies and industrial firms supported the game. Sponsorship could take a number of forms, including donating a cup, as wine and liquor merchants the Hilbert Brothers did in San Francisco in 1893 or distillers Hiram Walker and Sons (makers of Canadian Club) in Detroit in 1895.[4] It might also mean a larger investment, such as building a stadium or directly financing a club. While many corporate directors had a genuine devotion to the game, promoting industrial soccer also served as a tool to prevent labor unrest. Industrialization did not come without a cost, and at times soccer-playing communities paid the price. The often-dangerous labor performed in the factories and mines claimed the lives of soccer players. An unknown number also suffered workplace injuries that may have hindered their ability to play the sport they loved. Economic disruption not only led to a decline in company sponsorship but also slowed the arrival of newcomers who might have fortified existing clubs and competitions. Conflict between management and labor also created unstable and sometimes violent conditions that led to the collapse of sporting communities.

Finally, just as immigration provided the labor to build and run factories, it also stocked the benches and stands for soccer matches. Alongside organizations such as mutual aid societies, churches, and social clubs, immigrant groups formed soccer teams. Initially, it was the Scottish and English who played key roles in founding soccer communities in US cities. A decline in the numbers of British immigrants around 1900 contributed to the collapse of the sport in many areas.[5] As soccer's popularity grew after the turn of the twentieth century, immigrants from around the world brought the sport with them to the United States or took it up once they arrived. In many cities the fields rang out with a variety of languages as Germans, Argentines, Swedes, Czechs, Portuguese, Spaniards, and many others played together or sometimes in their own leagues.[6] In New York, black immigrants from the West Indies began to form soccer teams that competed on equal terms with other ethnic squads. By the late 1920s, the game took hold at historically Black colleges such as Howard University and Hampton Institute.[7]

The number of women playing soccer increased in the first decades of the twentieth century. Colleges around the country encouraged physical activities for their students, and soccer along with basketball and field hockey emerged as some of the most popular games. Outside of educational institutions, women also organized to play the sport. Sometimes such activities emerged from established social or ethnic organizations, and even some corporations sponsored teams for their female employees. At other times, women sought the opportunity to play even without any connection to a men's side, social club, or company squad. Women also took on roles as referees or administrators to help organize and run competitions. Such efforts reveal how soccer reflected broader cultural change, as women increasingly fought for increased political and social freedoms.

If the developments of the nineteenth and early twentieth centuries provided a foundation for soccer's growth in the United States, the experience of World War I helped the game develop into a major part of the nation's sporting landscape. Exposure to the sport both at home and abroad led to an unprecedented increase in the number of people playing and watching soccer. The 1920s emerged as the sport's first golden age and points the way to further study. The American Soccer League thrived, more and more native-born players emerged as leading talents, and the US men's national team grew into one of the world's best sides. Unfortunately, it did not last, as some of soccer's familiar problems led to its demise as a major professional sport. Economic ruin brought on by the Great Depression combined with internal disputes and mismanagement to end the greatest era in the history of US soccer. Nevertheless, the game survived and continued to be a sometimes ignored but constant presence in US sporting culture. Periodical revivals, including the appearance of Pelé in the 1970s, showed how soccer, despite long periods of inattention, could still capture the hearts of fans. As we enter the third decade of the twenty-first century, soccer has once again established itself as an important aspect of recreational culture in the United States. Thanks to the popularity of soccer video games and the accessibility of international competitions, the sport has grown to be an influential part of popular culture. In many ways, though, it has also remained true to its roots as a game played by children and young people.

NOTES

INTRODUCTION

1. "Carroll College," *Waukesha Freeman*, September 18, 1866; Langill, *Carroll College*, 48. Carroll College is now Carroll University.

2. Langill, *Carroll College*, 49, quote on 51.

3. Mary Rankin and Adela Rankin, *Historical Material about Walter Lowrie Rankin, A.M., PhD., President of Carroll College*, 1866–1904, scrapbook, range 4, shelf 2, Rankin Family Collection, Carroll University Archives; McFadden, Van Dyke, and Johnston, *Presbyterian Church*, 18; Presbrey and Moffatt, *Athletics at Princeton*, 271. For details on the game as played at Princeton, see chap. 2.

4. Presbrey and Moffatt, *Athletics at Princeton*, 20, 21. The star booters included C. F. Hall, W. A. Malloy, and C. Higbee. Rankin's younger brother Edward served as president of Princeton's Nassau baseball club in 1863–64 (68). The class of 1860 was the largest to date in Princeton's history, totaling eighty-five students (W. Scott, "Statistics," 455).

5. "Carroll College," *Waukesha Freeman*, September 18, 1866. Although chartered as a college, by the time Rankin took charge Carroll was functioning as a preparatory academy and not a college (Langill, *Carroll College*, 49).

6. "Base Ball," *Waukesha Plaindealer*, June 25, 1867; "Base Ball," *Waukesha Plaindealer*, June 14, 1870.

7. Langill, *Carroll College*, 100. Rankin continued to believe in the value of college athletics even after he stopped playing. In 1901, Rankin defended the presence of intercollegiate football on campus despite its violent nature. He insisted the sport was

"a noble, manly and heroic game cultivating the generous instincts of a young man's nature." He dismissed press reports of serious injuries and deaths as exaggerations and claimed that boating claimed more lives each year than did college football (Langill, *Carroll College*, 101).

8. "Match Game at Foot-Ball," *Waukesha Freeman*, October 16, 1866.

9. "Foot-Ball," *Students Offering*, October 17, 1866, in "Carroll College Literary Society vol. 1," Student Organization Collection (Interest Group Series) Meeting Minutes, vol. 1, 1866–67, Literary Society, folder 2, box 32, Carroll University Archives. At least for a time, the students seem to have kept playing football, as another story in the *Students Offering* joked about how their purchases were keeping ball makers in business. "Since the Students . . .," *Students Offering*, November 9, 1866, in "Carroll College Literary Society vol. 1." See also Runkel, "Peculiar Scene."

10. Harvey C. Olin, "Carroll after the War," *Hinakaga* [Carroll College Yearbook], 1915–16, 84, Carroll Yearbook Collection, https://archives.carrollu.edu/digital/collection/Yearbook/id/1276, accessed October 27, 2020.

11. Anderson, "Waukesha."

12. The first version of association rules published in the United States is Chadwick, *Beadle's dime book of cricket and football*.

13. Both the compromise rules made for the 1869 Princeton versus Rutgers clash, and the first set of published rules of Princeton-style football mandated twenty-five players on each side.

14. Recent articles have cast doubt on claims these matches used soccer rules and have presented more nuanced explanations of the 1869 and 1873 games (Tomlinson, "Birth of Football"; A. Mitchell, "Transatlantic Football Game").

15. T. Collins, "Early Football," 11–12. The so-called origins debate about the early history of British soccer has produced a body of literature too voluminous to cite here. A recent survey is Curry, ed., *Early Development of Football*. My thinking on the issue of "firsts" has been greatly influenced by Tony Collins, "Watching the Clock."

16. Szymanski and Weineck explore the history of the sport's name in *It's Football, not Soccer*.

17. Although Mexico and some Caribbean islands are part of the North American continent, for the sake of brevity throughout this book when I refer to North America, I mean what is now Canada and the United States.

18. In *Offside*, Markovits and Hellerman outline the process by which football was "crowded out" of the country's sporting space, leading to the creation of a "hegemonic sports culture" that effectively precluded soccer from competing as an economic and cultural entity (5). See also Abrams, "Inhibited." Szymanski and Zimbalist emphasize economic developments and choose not to focus on the broader social and cultural meanings of the sport in *National Pastime*. See also Dure, *Why the U.S. Men Will Never Win*.

19. Key books include Allaway, Litterer, and Jose, *Encyclopedia of American Soccer*, and Jose, *American Soccer League*. A number of broad overviews of US soccer history

have been published: Cascio, *Soccer U.S.A.*; S. Foulds and Harris, *America's Soccer Heritage*; Cirino, *U.S. Soccer vs. the World*; Wangerin, *Soccer in a Football World*; and Scholes, *Stateside Soccer*. Much of the data on early football in the United States were reported by retired meteorologist Mel Smith. Although Smith was among the first to systematically examine pre-codification football, his focus has mainly been on compiling mentions of the game and not analyzing and contextualizing his findings. M. Smith, *Evolvements*; Hay, Harvey, and Smith, "Football before Codification." Smith also produced updated lists for the American Soccer History Archives (https://SoccerHistoryUSA/ASHA). Another work examining US soccer in the context of global developments is M. Roberts's two-volume *Same Old Game*.

20. Allaway, *Corner Offices and Corner Kicks*, is a similar study, examining Bethlehem, Pennsylvania, in the 1910s and 1920s and New York City during the era of the Cosmos in the 1970s.

21. Logan, *Early Years of Chicago Soccer*; Apostolov, "Les hauts"; Kioussis, "Exceptions and Exceptionalism." On youth soccer see Tallec Marston, "International Comparative History."

22. Bolsmann and Kioussis, *Soccer Frontiers*.

23. T. McCabe, "Cooper's Block." See, for example, Holroyd, "First Professional Soccer League"; Farnsworth, "Clement Beecroft."

24. Robinson, "History of Soccer"; Lange, *Soccer Made in St. Louis*; Crawford, *History of Soccer*; Hatfield, *History of Soccer*. International scholars have briefly dealt with the United States, although the focus has tended to be on the periodic competition for players offered by upstart US leagues: Taylor, *Leaguers*; Lanfranchi and Taylor, *Moving with the Ball*; T. Collins, *How Football Began*.

25. Jean Williams, *Beautiful Game*; Ladda, "History of Intercollegiate Women's Soccer."

26. For details on how the gridiron game developed, see T. Collins, *How Football Began*, chap. 15.

CHAPTER 1. INDIGENOUS FOOTBALL IN NORTH AMERICA

1. Markham, *Life of John Davis*, 46.

2. John Davis, *Voyages and Works*, 36. On subsequent voyages, British sailors also played football but only among themselves. Chappell, *Narrative of a Voyage*, 123; Parry, *Journal of a Voyage*, 64; Parry, *Journal of a Second Voyage*, 415; Lyon, *Private Journal*, 397.

3. The unique nature of the encounter, especially the fact that the two groups played together can be shown by the fact that the first recorded games of lacrosse between colonists and Native Americans took place in 1840 (Delsahut, "From Baggataway to Lacrosse," 923).

4. Mancall, "Raw and the Cold," 11; DePasquale, "Worth the Noting," 27.

5. It is possible that the Inuit had been directly or indirectly exposed to European style football games, because some had been in contact with French whaling fleets as

early as 1565 (DePasquale, "Worth the Noting," 23). Nevertheless, the early contacts between Europeans and Indigenous peoples were likely too brief and infrequent to result in much cultural exchange (Fossett, *In Order to Live Untroubled*, 216).

6. Berkhofer, *White Man's Indian*, 62–63.

7. For a review of Culin's books and discussion about some of the issues facing scholars who rely on his work, see Paraschak, "Review of Stewart Culin," and Belanger, "Towards an Innovative Understanding," 16–18.

8. Culin, *Games of Skill*, 697. A recent exception is the brief treatment in M. Roberts, *Before Codification*, 62–63. Steven Apostolov discusses Native American football in New England ("Native Americans, Puritans and 'Brahmins,'" 1260). Horse racing is another Native cultural practice that has been understudied (P. Mitchell, "Horse Race Is the Same," 1).

9. Culin, *Games of Chance*, 21.

10. On lacrosse, see Downey, *Creator's Game*; M. Mitchell, *Teiontsikwaeks*; Fisher, *Lacrosse*; Vennum, *American Indian Lacrosse*.

11. Culin, *Games of Chance*, 36.

12. On the challenges of relying on outsider sources when analyzing the physical activities of Native peoples, see Nash, "Antic Deportment."

13. Downey, *Creator's Game*, 3, quote on 27.

14. Downey, *Creator's Game*, exemplifies how history can be written using not just academic but myriad resources.

15. Gleach, "Controlled Speculation," 41–42. Frederic W. Gleach provides four criteria that must be met for employing controlled speculation and they do fit with the study of football (43). First, is there reason to believe that a practice existed in a particular time and place? Second, can other groups with a similar culture provide a source for comparison? Third, has a similar phenomenon been recorded in a similar context? Fourth, does contradictory evidence exist that would invalidate such comparisons?

16. For an overview of indigenous women's sport, see Delsahut and Terret, "First Nations Women."

17. For a brief discussion of gambling's different cultural meanings, see Belanger, "Towards an Innovative Understanding," 22–27.

18. Downey, *Creator's Game*, 27. Delsahut argues that lacrosse played "a pivotal role between a ritual and game," but there is no evidence that this was also the case for football among most indigenous groups ("From Baggataway to Lacrosse," 926).

19. "Background," American Journeys, https://americanjourneys.org/aj-136/summary/index.asp, accessed October 29, 2020.

20. Hume, *Virginia Adventure*, 245.

21. Ibid., 248–49, 293. Eventually, other Europeans felt that Spelman had become too assimilated to Powhatan culture (Fausz, "Middlemen in Peace and War," 42).

22. Struna, *People of Prowess*, 16, 17.

23. Fausz, "Middlemen in Peace and War," 49.

24. Spelman, *Relation of Virginia*, 57–58.

25. Strachey, *Historie of Travelle*, xviii, xix, xx.

26. Hume, *Virginia Adventure*, 261, 282.

27. Rountree, *Powhatan Indians of Virginia*, 4.

28. Fausz, "Abundance of Blood," 12.

29. Hume, *Virginia Adventure*, 257, 289.

30. Rountree, *Powhatan Indians of Virginia*, 4.

31. Strachey, *Historie of Travelle*, 84.

32. Wood, *New England's Prospect*, 4, 11.

33. Ibid., 7, 10.

34. Ibid., 104–5.

35. Rubertone, *Grave Undertakings*, 5, 6, 7, 14.

36. Rubertone, *Grave Undertakings*, 108, quote on 84.

37. R. Williams, *Key into the Language*, 230, quote on 231.

38. Chief Clearwater, "Pasuckquakohowauog."

39. Denton, *Brief Relation of New York*, 6, 7.

40. Brunet, *Notes on the Early Settlement*, 65, 68.

41. Ibid., 69, 70.

42. The various Lenape groups had been in contact with Europeans almost from the moment the first traders and missionaries appeared. Along with other Native American groups, they "actively participated" in various European imperial systems (Hinderaker, *Elusive Empires*, xi).

43. Rementer, "Pahsahëman."

44. Hager [Hagar], "Micmac Customs and Traditions."

45. Conn, *History's Shadow*, 195, quote on 196.

46. Hagar, "Micmac Customs and Traditions," 31, 36, quote on 36.

47. Bartram, *Travels*, 506, 507.

48. Loskiel, *History of the Mission*, 106, 107.

49. Dewey, "Football and the American Indians," 736, 737.

50. Dewey's account comes from one originally published in Morgan, *League of the Ho-dé´-no-sau-nee*, 282–86. Morgan does not use the word "lacrosse," instead simply referring to it as "the Ball game." Nevertheless, he includes in his book an image of a racket, and from the description it is clear that the activity is lacrosse. Although Dewey cites Morgan as the source, he includes it in his essay of football and claims that the game evolved "from an antecedent of soccer" (Dewey, "Football and the American Indians," 737).

51. Culin, *Games of Skill*, 704; R. E. Dunlop to Stewart Culin, September 1, 1901, Indian Corresp. A–G, Culin Archival Collection Series 7: Games, subseries 7.1, North American Indian, Brooklyn Museum.

52. d'Azevedo, "Introduction," 2.

53. Lowie, "Ethnographic Notes," 308.

54. Freed and Freed, "Persistence of Aboriginal Ceremonies," 34; Price, "Washo Prehistory," 77.

55. Lowie, "Ethnographic Notes," 315.

56. Ibid., quote on 315; Price, "Some Aspects," 109.

57. "Inuit Games," quotes on 16, 17, 21.

58. Ibid., 19, 21. A nearly identical account referring to playing soccer on the ice appears in "Sport and Recreation."

59. Boas, *Central Eskimo*, v, 156, 159, 162.

60. Ibid., 195.

61. E. Nelson, *Eskimo*, 335–36, 337.

62. Nuttall, "Arsarnerit," 275.

63. Egede, *Description of Greenland*, 162–63.

64. Nuttall, "Arsarnerit," 278.

65. K. Rasmussen, *Intellectual Culture*, 94, quote 95; Nuttall, "Arsarnerit: Inuit and the Heavenly Game of Football," 280. The source for the walrus story may have come from E. Nelson, *Eskimo*, 336.

66. K. Rasmussen, *Intellectual Culture*, 27.

67. Delsahut and Terret note that the male authors who composed the original sources tended to prioritize the actions and roles of indigenous men ("First Nations Women," 977).

68. Rountree, *Powhatan Indians of Virginia*, 47.

69. Rountree, "World," 30.

70. Rubertone, *Grave Undertakings*, 110.

71. Lockerby, "Ancient Mi'kmaq Customs," 404.

72. Nuttall, "Arsarnerit," 276.

73. Fossett, *In Order to Live Untroubled*, 195, 208.

74. Prins, *Mi'kmaq*, 27. Simmons, *Narragansett*, 22; Rountree, *Powhatan Indians of Virginia*, 58, 60.

75. Kroeber, "Games," 277; Prins, *Mi'kmaq*, 28; W. Wallis and R. Wallis, *Micmac Indians*, 178, 179, 237.

76. S. Hagar to Stewart Culin, January 19, 1907, Indian Corresp. H–Ma, Culin Archival Collection Series 7. In the letter, Hagar spells the name of the football game as *tooadüik*, which differs from the spelling he uses in his 1895 article. The letter also mentions that a lacrosse-style game was played on day three (not described in his 1895 article).

77. Fisher, "Contested Ground," 10, 15.

78. Eisen, "Games and Sporting Diversions," 85.

79. Simmons, *Narragansett*, 23; Prins, *Mi'kmaq*, 34; Oxendine, *American Indian Sports Heritage*, 143.

80. Oxendine, *American Indian Sports Heritage*, xiii, xxii.

81. Cohen, "Mutually Comprehensible World?," 71.

82. Fossett, *In Order to Live Untroubled*, quote on 6.

83. Salter, "Games in Ritual," 276. European observers stressed the relatively peaceful nature of the game perhaps as a result of their belief that indigenous peoples lived in a primitive state of nature (Clements, "Translating Context and Situation," 399).

84. Rountree, "World," 28, 51.

85. Prins, *Mi'kmaq*, 25.

86. Barrett, "Washo Indians," 9, 10; Lowie, "Ethnographic Notes," 308, 315.

87. Although no Washoe balls survive, the description of the ball is based on the composition of footballs made by other tribes, (Culin, *Games of Skill*, 701–3).

CHAPTER 2. THE SCHOOLBOYS' GAME

1. Hay, Harvey, and Smith, "Football before Codification," 158.

2. Dawson, "Miniaturizing of Girlhood," 69. For girls, childhood more closely mirrored the ideals of nineteenth-century womanhood (66).

3. David Block debunks the notion that baseball developed from rounders, instead arguing that it "evolved from a matrix of early English folk games" (*Baseball before We Knew It*, quote 75, 77, 157, 158). See also Szymanski and Zimbalist, *National Pastime*, 12–34.

4. Thorn, *Baseball*, quote xv, 35, 63, 65; Schiff, *Father of Baseball*, 50–51. Thorn notes that working men formed the Magnolia Club sometime before 1845 but that the team has been largely written out of the existing histories (31). East Coast elite colleges endeavored to create a unified set of rules in order to facilitate intercollegiate competition rather than to create a national football organization.

5. Thorn, *Baseball*, 43, 46.

6. Thorn lists publicity, gambling, and statistics as the three keys to baseball's rise (*Baseball*, 101).

7. The most thorough recent treatment of the Oneidas is Apostolov, "Les hauts," chap. 1.

8. Nancy Struna, *People of Progress*, 74.

9. Struna does not cite the original publication but instead relies on A. Hart, *Commonwealth History of Massachusetts*, 279–80.

10. Dunton, *John Dunton's Letters*, xi, quote xvi.

11. Ibid., 286n159. Whitmore cites many other examples where Dunton "borrowed" heavily from Williams; for example, 272n152, 277n155, 278n156, 283n158. As discussed in chapter 1, Williams's account, and subsequently Dunton's, is quite like that given by William Wood.

12. Struna, *People of Progress*, 67, 68.

13. Ibid., 131.

14. "Williamsburg," *Virginia Gazette* (Williamsburg), November 26, 1736.

15. Ledbetter, "Sports and Games," 32.

16. "Journal of Lieutenant Ebenezer Elmer," 22, 27, 31, 35, 98. Ledbetter notes that Elihu Clark played football in September 1775 ("Sports and Games," 37).

17. Morse, *American Universal Geography*, 317.

18. Struna, *People of Progress*, 69.

19. Struna, "Puritans and Sport," 9, 11, 12.

20. Trott, *Laws*, 231.

21. *Conductor Generalis*, 131.

22. *Several Rules*, 11; *Bylaws and Orders*, 10; "City of Boston," *Boston Daily Atlas*, December 16, 1844.

23. "A by-law in addition to a by-law relative to the highways and streets in the city of Hartford," *Hartford Courant*, May 5, 1818.

24. "Be it ordained by the Mayor . . .," *Hartford Courant*, May 10, 1825.

25. "Affairs in and About the City," *Boston Daily Atlas*, December 10, 1851.

26. The exact figure for the fine was $22.75. "An Expensive Court," *Louisville Daily Courier*, February 12, 1859.

27. "City Items," *Springfield (MA) Republican*, November 14, 1860.

28. "Communication," *Hartford Courant*, November 4, 1828.

29. "City Items," *Hartford Courant*, May 18, 1859.

30. "Jackson Square," *New Orleans Times-Picayune*, March 25, 1859. A February 26, 1859, *New Orleans Daily Delta* article voiced similar complaints.

31. "Nantucket," *Brooklyn Daily Eagle*, November 4, 1852.

32. "A Cincinnati paper say . . .," *Semi-Weekly Natchez (MS) Courier*, December 24, 1847.

33. "South Park," *San Francisco Chronicle*, September 3, 1868.

34. "Fatal Accident," *Boston Daily Atlas*, December 6, 1839.

35. "As Mrs. DeForrest and her daughter . . .," *Hartford Courant*, October 13, 1857.

36. *Youthful Recreations*, n.p.

37. Clarke, *Boy's Own Book* (1829), 17.

38. Clarke, *Boy's Own Book* (1881), 11.

39. Deming, "Three Ages of Football," 57, quotes 56, 58.

40. "Foot Ball," *Daily Illinois State Journal* (Springfield), April 2, 1859.

41. "Attention," *Baltimore Sun*, February 29, 1860. Given the probable age of the pair (Lemmon was nineteen in 1860 and working as a clerk) and the fact that there is no clear link to the college, the Mount Vernon Club is discussed in more detail in the chapter 3 ("United States Census, 1860," FamilySearch, accessed December 30, 2015, https://familysearch.org/pal:/MM9.1.1/M698-Z9Z).

42. "Quick-Step Foot-Ball Club," *Buffalo Commercial*, October 1, 1858. Curiously, a baseball club of the same name organized in May 1859, although none of the officers listed matched those of the football club ("The Quick-Step Base Ball Club . . .," *Buffalo Morning Express*, May 23, 1859).

43. "City Items," *Springfield (MA) Republican*, October 10, 1860.

44. "City Items," *Springfield (MA) Republican*, November 2, 1860. The match may have attracted press attention due to the presence of adults or because the son of a judge broke his arm during the match. The teams were baseball clubs that also played football. A day after the football games, the Hannibal and Atlantic squads along with another team called Olympics played a series of baseball games at the same location ("City Items," *Springfield (MA) Republican*, November 5, 1860).

45. Bundgaard, *Muscle and Manliness*, xi–xii, xvi, 11.

46. J. Lovett, *Old Boston Boys*, 75, quote 51–52.

47. Bundgaard calls the game "fundamentally soccer" while acknowledging that the sport was not codified until 1863 (*Muscle and Manliness*, 49). Apostolov attempts to sort out the features of the game the Oneidas played ("Native Americans, Puritans and 'Brahmins,'" 1263–65).

48. The crew usually wore blue handkerchiefs but none could be found so the stroke-oar Benjamin Crowninshield purchased silk ones of a color described as "nearly a crimson" (Crowninshield, "Boating," 253). Stephen Hardy cites this moment as the origin of Harvard's connection with the color crimson (*How Boston Played*, 6).

49. Hardy, *How Boston Played*, 5; Crowninshield, "Boating," 192. The more common explanation is that the football club was named after Lake Oneida, which was near to captain Gat Miller's hometown in Upstate New York. While D'Wolf gives no explanation for the name, another member of the team, Winthrop Scudder, wrote that it had been named for the lake. He explains that Oneida club member Cliff Watson, who later rowed Varsity crew and coached at Harvard, suggested the name. Scudder's account was not written down until 1923 (Scudder, "Historic Sketch.")

50. Sawyer, *History of Williston Seminary*, 90 (first quote), 136, 190 (second quote).

51. "Game of Foot Ball," *Boston Herald*, December 18, 1857.

52. "To the Students of Trinity College . . .," *Hartford Courant*, October 19, 1858.

53. "Local Affairs," *Hartford Courant*, November 6, 1858.

54. "The Game of Foot Ball," *Hartford Courant*, November 10, 1858.

55. "Foot Ball," *Hartford Courant*, November 13, 1858.

56. "Local Affairs," *Connecticut Courant* (Hartford), November 20, 1858.

57. The 1795 rules of Yale set a fine of eight cents for anyone playing football or handball in the college yard (Yale College, *Laws*, 26). A letter written to *Outing* magazine in 1889 claimed to be from an 1828 graduate of Yale. He wrote that it was customary for first-year students to provide footballs for the use of the college. He also described "great games" involving up to four hundred students divided into North Entries and South Entries. Such a pastime ended in 1828 ("Glances at our Letter File").

58. "The Battle of the Delta," *Harvard Register*, October 1827, 251. The poem was written by James Cook Richmond, then the editor of the *Register* (Prince, "Football at Harvard," 311).

59. "The Battle of the Delta," *Harvard Register*, October 1827, 252.

60. John Augustin, "The Foot-ball Game," *New York Clipper*, November 20, 1858; "Letter from First Private," *New Orleans Times-Picayune*, October 13, 1855.

61. "Foot Ball," *Boston Daily Advertiser*, November 1, 1859.

62. Heckel, *Who's Who*, 49. Lara O'Sullivan argues that the story was really intended to show how degenerate the Greeks had become that they were reduced to erecting statues to entertainers. Generally, ball games were not well valued in ancient Greek culture except by the Macedonians and Spartans, who may have seen them as good preparation for war ("Playing Ball," 18, 22–23, 28).

63. Hurd, *History of Yale Athletics*, 54.

64. Marsh, "Seventy-nine's Page of History," 350; A. McCabe, "Campus Events," 367.

65. Scott Meacham argues that there may have been as many as three different versions of football games played on college campuses during the nineteenth century ("Old Division Football").

66. Haswell, *Reminiscences*, 81–82; Wheeler, "President Wheeler's First impression," 300; Meacham, "Old Division Football."

67. Wertenbaker, *Princeton*, 245; Hurd, *History of Yale Athletics*, 54.

68. "Life in College," *Harvard Register*, February 1828, 379.

69. Prince, "Football at Harvard, 1800–1875," 316, quotes 322, 320.

70. Hurd, *History of Yale Athletics*, 55. P. Davis, for example, refers to him as a "Rugbeian" (*Football*, 54).

71. McKnight, "Football Beginnings at Yale." McKnight was a Yale alumnus ('76), and the information on Schaff's educational background came from a letter written by Schaff to McKnight (155).

72. Wertenbaker, *Princeton*, 163. Although he became interim president in 1822 and was hugely popular with students, he refused a permanent appointment and soon left the college, becoming president of the University of Knoxville in 1825 (Wertenbaker, *Princeton*, 164, 173).

73. Wertenbaker, *Princeton*, 280, 282; Henry and Scharff, *College as It Is*, xxii, xxiv.

74. Henry and Scharff, *College as It Is*, 80; W. Scott, "Statistics," 455.

75. Presbrey and Moffatt, *Athletics at Princeton*, 17.

76. Henry and Scharff, *College as It Is*, 250–51n18.

77. Stewart, "Foot-Ball," 443.

78. Henry and Scharff, *College as It Is*, 202.

79. Wertenbaker, *Princeton*, 278. The faculty contributed half the cost of the new gym (Presbrey and Moffatt, *Athletics at Princeton*, 20, 22).

80. P. Davis, *Football*, 41.

81. Strutt, *Sports and Pastimes*, 90; Aspin, *Ancient Customs*, 209.

82. P. Davis, *Football*, 14.

83. T. Collins, *How Football Began*, 118.

84. Strutt, *Sports and Pastimes*, 91.

85. P. Davis, *Football*, 41.

86. Edward Shippen, "Some Notes," 50. Shippen graduated from Princeton in 1845 and in 1900 wrote about his experiences as a student, but the memoir was not published until 1997. He also commented that his generation was physically stronger than those playing football at the time he was writing (50). Although unpublished until decades later, much of Shippen's account is quoted in Presbrey and Moffatt, *Athletics at Princeton*, and attributed to "an old Princetonian" (20).

87. Stewart, "Foot-Ball," 432.

88. Emphasis in the original. Presbrey and Moffatt, *Athletics at Princeton*, 21.

89. Henry and Scharf, *College As It Is*, 202.
90. Stewart, "Foot-Ball," 432.
91. Presbrey and Moffatt, *Athletics at Princeton*, 271.
92. Ibid., 271; Stewart, "Foot-Ball," 432.
93. Bernstein, *Football*, 6.
94. Putney, *Muscular Christianity*, 1, quote 12, 9.
95. Lucas, "Prelude," 53.
96. Blake, "Plea for Foot-Ball," 14, 10.
97. Thomas Wentworth Higginson, "Gymnasium, and Gymnastics," 187.
98. Winship, *American Literary Publishing*, table 3.3, p. 55.
99. Higginson, "Saints, and their Bodies," 584, quote 588.
100. "A Game of Football at Rugby," *New York Clipper*, December 25, 1858.
101. Putney, *Muscular Christianity*, 19, 23, 24.
102. Hardy, *How Boston Played*, 131.
103. R. Smith, *Sports and Freedom*, 72.
104. "Olla-podrida" (Feb. 1873), 208, 209.
105. "Olla-podrida" (Nov. 1873), 176–77.
106. McKnight, "Further Early Yale Football History," 182. R. Smith also quotes from Henry Grant's letter (*Sports and Freedom*, 74).
107. R. Smith, *Sports and Freedom*, 76–77. Smith tends to refer to the kicking games played at the colleges as "soccer." Although they were very similar to the association football rules, they were not the same game.
108. The earliest intercollegiate style game in school records was played in 1893. Lawrence University, "Records."

CHAPTER 3. MANLY GAMES OF CELEBRATION AND ESCAPE

1. Of these categories, only club football corresponds with Adrian Harvey's formal nonpublic school teams. Unlike his claims about England, such clubs were exceedingly rare in the United States before the 1880s (Harvey, "Public Schools," 273, 274). In contrast to Harvey, Tony Collins concludes that, even in England, "organised football matches were few and far between during the first half of the nineteenth century" (*How Football Began*, 14).
2. On the Oneidas, see Apostolov, "Native Americans, Puritans and 'Brahmins'" and Tallec Marston and Cronin, "Origins of Foot-ball."
3. Rotundo, *American Manhood*, 3.
4. Ibid., 55, 58, quote 192.
5. Intercollegiate or American football was heavily influenced by British models (T. Collins, *How Football Began*, chap. 15).
6. *Old Woodward*, 11, 13, 31, 40, 54.
7. Ibid., 71, 75, quote 74.
8. Ibid., 82ff, 88.

9. "A Challenge—Fall River vs. New Bedford," *Worcester (MA) Palladium*, November 28, 1855. The story originally appeared in the *New Bedford (MA) Standard*.

10. "A Rare Re-Union," *Boston Traveller*, August 22, 1857.

11. "An Extensive Game of Foot-ball," *New Orleans Daily Delta*, October 21, 1857.

12. "Quit Business and Gone to Play," *New Albany (IN) Daily Ledger*, October 29, 1857. The newspaper reprinted the story from an Indianapolis paper.

13. "Foot Ball on the Common," *Boston Herald*, November 25, 1853.

14. "City Intelligence," *Boston Courier*, November 26, 1855; "City Intelligence," *Boston Courier*, December 20, 1855; "Refusal to Pardon Coburn and Dalton," *Boston Evening Transcript*, July 8, 1856. Two men were ultimately convicted of assaulting William Sumner.

15. "City News," *Boston Herald*, December 1, 1848. Hay, Harvey, and Smith cite this as an example of a small-sided game played in the United States ("Football Before Codification," 162).

16. Greenberg, *Cause for Alarm*, 53. For examples involving the Hamiltons, see "Affairs About Home," *Boston Herald*, April 12, 1849; "A Card to Firemen," *Boston Herald*, June 27, 1849; and "A Card to Fireman," *Boston Herald*, June 30, 1849.

17. Greenberg, *Cause for Alarm*, 60, 63, quote 59.

18. Ibid., 76.

19. "City News," *Boston Herald*, December 1, 1848.

20. "From the New Haven Herald of Monday Evening," *Boston Courier*, November 4, 1841. The story appeared in a number of periodicals including the *Springfield (MA) Republican*, the *North American and Daily Advertiser* (Philadelphia), and the *Pennsylvania Inquirer and Daily Courier* (Philadelphia).

21. P. Davis, *Football*, 38.

22. "Various Items," *American Traveller* (Boston), November 26, 1859.

23. "Foot Ball," *New York Clipper*, December 26, 1857;; "Foot Ball in Philadelphia," *New York Clipper*, January 3, 1857; "Game of Foot Ball," *New York Clipper*, January 9, 1858.

24. "The Grand German Volksfest," *New Orleans Sunday Delta*, May 16, 1858.

25. "The City," *New Orleans Times-Picayune*, May 17, 1858.

26. Scott Crawford argues that the type of football played at the Volksfest was an early version of soccer. The fact that the event was open to anyone and that large crowds were present suggests that the football was likely similar to other types of mob-style games and therefore was not, as he contends, "a close parent of modern soccer" (*History of Soccer*, quote 25, 30).

27. "Boston Scottish Club," *Boston Herald*, September 27, 1861; "Affairs About Home," *Boston Herald*, December 5, 1863.

28. "New Year Sports," *New York Clipper*, December 30, 1854.

29. Swain, "Cultural Continuity and Football," 568, 569. For a critique of Swain's article, see R. Lewis, "Innovation not Invention."

30. Swain, "Cultural Continuity and Football," 568.

31. "Boston Gymnasium—Julien Hall," *Boston Daily Atlas*, September 15, 1843; "The Games and Sports at East Boston," *Boston Evening Transcript*, October 18, 1843; "Sheridan's Pistol Gallery," *Boston Daily Bee*, March 24, 1845.

32. "Amusement," *Boston Courier*, September 16, 1843.

33. "Athletic Games at East Boston," *Boston Evening Transcript*, October 20, 1843.

34. "Athletic Games," *Boston Daily Atlas*, October 21, 1843.

35. "Athletic Games at East Boston," *Boston Evening Transcript*, October 20, 1843.

36. "Athletic Games at the Cricket and Archery Ground," *Boston Evening Transcript*, November 1, 1843.

37. "Three Days Fete!," *Boston Evening Transcript*, July 18, 1844.

38. "Flower Queen!," *Buffalo Commercial*, August 4, 1863; "The Flower Queen Festival," *Buffalo Commercial*, August 8, 1863.

39. "Musical Card," *Buffalo Commercial*, February 7, 1851.

40. "The Flower Queen," *Buffalo Commercial*, June 11, 1856; "The Flower Queen," *Buffalo Commercial*, June 18, 1857; "Flower Queen!," *Buffalo Commercial*, August 4, 1863.

41. Van Buren, "Rules," 8.

42. US Sanitary Commission, *Report*, 40.

43. "The Supplies and General Arrangements," *New York Herald*, October 29, 1861.

44. Wiley, *Life of Billy Yank*, 170; Wiley, *Life of Johnny Reb*, 159. Specific examples of individual units playing football include Stevens, *Berden's United States Sharpshooters*, 20; Quint, *Record*, 52; "Camp Games," *Charleston (SC) Mercury*, April 3, 1862. One interesting report suggests that indoor football was one of the only recreations for federal soldiers held at Libby prison in Richmond, Virginia ("City Intelligence," *Richmond (VA) Enquirer*, February 2, 1864).

45. Haynes, *History*, 26–27.

46. Brady's National Photographic Portrait Galleries, "Camp Sports, 13th N.Y. Artillery Playing Ball before Petersburgh, Virginia," 1864–65, Library of Congress Prints and Photographs Division, https://www.loc.gov/item/2010648749/, accessed October 15, 2020. Details on the image in fig. 3.2 are as follows: "Petersburg, Virginia (vicinity). Playing ball. Camp of 13th New Heavy Artillery," 2 negatives (3 plates): glass, stereograph, wet collodion, Washington, D.C., Library of Congress Prints and Photographs Division, http://loc.gov/pictures/item/cwp2003004851/PP/, accessed June 22, 2017.

47. "13th Heavy Artillery Regiment Civil War," New York State Military Museum and Veterans Research Center, https://dmna.ny.gov/historic/reghist/civil/artillery/13thArtHvy/13thArtHvyMain.htm, accessed October 31, 2020.

48. "Camp Johnson."

49. Wiley, *Life of Billy Yank*, 47.

50. Alfred R. Waud, "Holiday in the camp of the 23 Penn. Vol. near Bladensburg, 1861, ca. December 25, Library of Congress Prints and Photographs Division, http://www.loc.gov/pictures/item/2004661360/, accessed June 22, 2017. "Holiday Sports in the Camp of the 23D Pennsylvania Volunteers, near Bladensburg," *New York Illustrated News*, January 11, 1862.

51. "Holiday in Camp." The issue also reports on Independence Day celebrations.

52. Quote from "A Sad Affair has occurred at Camp Stevens . . .," *Newport (RI) Mercury*, October 18, 1862. "Died of his Wounds," *Providence (RI) Evening Press*, October 17, 1862. James O'Niel (later reports spell it as O'Neal, and one gives his first name as John) was arrested for desertion and confessed that he had stabbed Simmons the previous autumn. He was eventually charged, convicted, and sentenced to life in prison for the murder ("State of Rhode Island and Providence Plantations," *Providence [RI] Evening Press*, October 24, 1862; "Examination of O'Niel," *Providence [RI] Evening News*, September 5, 1863; "Supreme Court," *Manufacturers' and Farmers' Journal* (Providence, RI), October 22, 1863; "The John O'Neal," *Newport [RI] Mercury*, January 16, 1864).

53. Betts, "Sporting Journalism," 40, 41, 42.

54. "Memorial Number," *New York Clipper*, February 1903.

55. Thorn, *Baseball*, 102, 104.

56. "Have we any Foot-ball players among us?," *New York Clipper*, December 13, 1856.

57. "Winter Sports," *New York Clipper*, December 20, 1856.

58. Ibid.; Stoneheng, *Manual of British Rural Sports*, 499–500.

59. "Winter Sports," *New York Clipper*, December 20, 1856.

60. "Foot Ball," *New York Clipper*, December 26, 1857.

61. Ibid.

62. John Augustin, "The Foot-ball Game," *New York Clipper*, November 20, 1858; "A Game of Football at Rugby," *New York Clipper*, December 25, 1858.

63. "The Game of Foot Ball," *New York Clipper*, December 3, 1859, emphasis in the original.

64. "Football in England," *New York Clipper*, December 26, 1863.

65. "Rules of Football," *New York Clipper*, December 3, 1864.

66. "Football," *Bell's Life in London*, November 28, 1863; "The Football Association," *Sporting Gazette*, November 28, 1863.

67. "Foot-Ball," *New York Evening Post*, February 9, 1864.

68. On the connection between cricket clubs and football in Scotland, see R. Young, *As the Willow Vanishes*.

69. Kilpatrick, "NYC Originals."

70. "The Cricket Match," *New York Tribune*, August 19, 1843; "A Cricket Match . . .," *New Orleans Times-Picayune*, September 7, 1843; "The Great Game of Cricket," *Philadelphia Public Ledger*, September 28, 1844.

71. "One Interested in the Club" and "St. George's Foot Ball Club," *Spirit of the Times*, October 7, 1854, 402; "St. George's Foot Ball Club," *New York Clipper*, October 15, 1854.

72. Kilpatrick, "NYC Originals"; "Sporting &C.," *New York Herald*, November 29, 1854.

73. "Clover Hill Foot Ball Club" and "The Clover Hill Foot Ball Club," *Brooklyn Daily Eagle*, December 2, 1859.

74. "Foot-Ball," *New York Clipper*, December 10, 1859.

75. "City Items," *Springfield (MA) Republican*, October 10, 1860; "New Club," *New Orleans Daily Delta*, September 14, 1859; "Foot Ball," *New Orleans Times-Picayune*, October 1, 1859.

76. "Attention Foot Ball," *Baltimore Sun*, September 14, 1859; "Attention," *Baltimore Sun*, February 29, 1860; "Notice—the Waverly Foot Ball Club," *Baltimore Sun*, September 8, 1860; "Attractive," *Baltimore Sun*, September 12, 1860. Waverly club listed no location and Cottage named no officers.

77. Bready, *Baseball in Baltimore*, 3, 6.

78. "United States Census, 1860," FamilySearch, https://familysearch.org/pal:/MM9.1.1/M698-Z9Z, accessed October 31, 2020.

79. University of Maryland, *Catalog*.

80. "City Intelligence," *Baltimore Daily Exchange*, September 11, 1860; "Base Ball Match Between the Excelsior and Waverly Clubs," *Baltimore Daily Exchange*, October 18, 1860.

CHAPTER 4. STEEL CITY SOCCER

1. Chadwick, *Beadle's dime book*.

2. Berthoff, *British Immigrants*, 5, 11.

3. Rosenzweig, *Eight Hours*, 39, 46, 55.

4. Ibid., 140–41.

5. Couvares, *Remaking of Pittsburgh*, 103, 104. Couvares names boxing and baseball as popular sports but does not discuss soccer (123).

6. Berthoff, *British Immigrants*, 21.

7. Crampsey, *First 100 Years*, 2–3.

8. Bueltmann, *Clubbing Together*, 5, 85. Soccer clubs played a similar role for Spanish immigrants to New York City in the 1920s (Bunk, "*Sardinero*").

9. The Scottish Football Association legalized professionalism in 1893 (McDowell, *A Cultural History*, 14).

10. In Scotland, the sport experienced similar challenges that Matthew McDowell calls "inter-organizational skullduggery" (*Cultural History*, 11).

11. Thomas Bell, *Out of this Furnace*, is a fictional account of the lives of Slovak immigrants based on the experience of his family. Interviews with workers and their families can be found in Bodnar, *Workers' World*.

12. "Sporting Notes," *Pittsburgh Post-Gazette*, October 7, 1885.

13. "Pittsburghers Failed to Show Up," *Pittsburgh Post-Gazette*, October 26, 1885.

14. "Sporting Notes," *Pittsburgh Post-Gazette*, August 29, 1887.

15. "Sporting Notes," *Pittsburgh Post-Gazette*, September 7, 1887.

16. "Sporting Notes," *Pittsburgh Post-Gazette*, February 20, 1888; "Sporting Notes," *Pittsburgh Post-Gazette*, March 19, 1888; "Sporting Notes," *Pittsburgh Post-Gazette*, March 26, 1888.

17. "The Sporting World," *Pittsburgh Post-Gazette*, May 26, 1888; "Braddock Claims Championship," *Pittsburgh Post-Gazette*, June 5, 1888; "The Weather Too Warm," *Pittsburgh Post-Gazette*, June 5, 1888.

18. William J. Barr, "It's a Great Game," *Pittsburgh Dispatch*, June 1, 1890.

19. "Clyde Football Club," *Pittsburgh Dispatch*, June 23, 1890; "Sporting Notes," *Pittsburgh Dispatch*, August 3, 1890. I have found no record that Clyde visited the United States as planned.

20. "A Football League," *Pittsburgh Dispatch*, November 17, 1890. Curiously, the initial list did not include McDonald or Braddock, although they eventually joined the competition. The teams named as possibilities were Eighteenth Ward, Homestead, Shadyside, East Liverpool, Lucyville, Monongahela City, Millvale, and Southside. Although not mentioned in connection with the league, the Allegheny Athletic Association also had a soccer team by this time.

21. "The Football League," *Pittsburgh Dispatch*, December 4, 1890.

22. This does not seem to refer to the western Pennsylvania championship from 1888 because the teams who played in that competition were not too distant from one another.

23. "Dates for Kickers," *Pittsburgh Dispatch*, December 10, 1890; "Thoroughly in Line," *Pittsburgh Dispatch*, December 13, 1890.

24. "Some Trouble in the Camp," *Pittsburgh Dispatch*, December 14, 1890.

25. "Want a Halt Called," *Pittsburgh Dispatch*, December 21, 1890.

26. "A Kick of New Castle," *Pittsburgh Dispatch*, December 16, 1890.

27. "Postponed their Dates," *Pittsburgh Dispatch*, January 8, 1891.

28. "Will have a New Name," *Pittsburgh Dispatch*, February 5, 1891; "The Kickers getting Organized," *Pittsburgh Dispatch*, February 8, 1891.

29. "Saturday's Football Games," *Pittsburgh Dispatch*, February 13, 1891.

30. "Football Players Meet," *Pittsburgh Dispatch*, March 5, 1891.

31. "The Football Clubs," *Pittsburgh Dispatch*, April 10, 1891.

32. "The Football Players," *Pittsburgh Dispatch*, April 5, 1891.

33. Byington, *Homestead*, 6. Similar characteristics in other areas also led to the development of footballing communities. Fall River, Massachusetts, one of the nation's earliest and most successful soccer-playing cities, attracted a great many workers from Lancashire, England (Berthoff, *British Immigrants*, 32; Allaway, *Rangers, Rovers, and Spindles*). The region, containing the cities of Preston, Bolton, Blackburn, and others, had long been a hotbed of association football. On the early sporting developments in Lancashire, see Harvey, *Football*, 59–64, and G. James, *Emergence of Footballing Cultures*.

34. "1910 United States Federal Census," Ancestry.com, accessed May 30, 2018; "1920 United States Federal Census," Ancestry.com, accessed May 30, 2018.

35. John Bodnar argues for the importance of family in the lives of industrial workers (*Workers' World*, 166–67).

36. "1880 United States Federal Census," Ancestry.com, accessed May 30, 2018. The parents of the McVicker boys had immigrated to Scotland from Ireland. These displaced communities took up soccer with the same passion as native-born Scots,

forming clubs such as Hibernian (Edinburgh), Celtic (Glasgow), and Harp (Dundee) (Crampsey, *First 100 Years*, 27).

37. *Pittsburgh, Pennsylvania, City Directory, 1891*, 543, U.S. City Directories, 1822–1995, Ancestry.com, accessed May 30, 2018; "1900 United States Federal Census," Ancestry.com, accessed May 30, 2018. See a record of the birth of Joseph Liddell in "Scotland Births and Baptisms, 1564–1950," FamilySearch, https://familysearch.org/ark:/61903/1:1:F77S-NBN, accessed July 24, 2018.

38. "Association Football To-Morrow," *Pittsburgh Daily Post*, January 15, 1897; "1871 England Census," Ancestry.com, accessed July 11, 2018; "1900 United States Federal Census," Ancestry.com, accessed July 11, 2018.

39. "A Football League," *Pittsburgh Dispatch*, November 17, 1890; "1900 United States Federal Census," Ancestry.com, accessed May 30, 2018; "A Great Team," *Pittsburgh Dispatch*, October 16, 1892.

40. "Soccer Football," *Pittsburgh Press*, November 16, 1910. The soccer-playing brothers were four of twelve children ("John Luxbacher Family Tree," FamilySearch, www.familysearch.org/tree/person/details/LXMC-M3N, accessed November 27, 2019).

41. "Association Football Team," *Pittsburgh Daily Post*, September 15, 1895.

42. "Getting into Line," *Pittsburgh Dispatch*, September 5, 1891.

43. "A Good Schedule," *Pittsburgh Dispatch*, September 27, 1891.

44. "Association Football," *Pittsburgh Dispatch*, October 25, 1891.

45. "An Awful Disruption," *Pittsburgh Dispatch*, November 11, 1891.

46. "They May Withdraw," *Pittsburgh Dispatch*, November 12, 1891.

47. "Settled Their Trouble," *Pittsburgh Dispatch*, November 21, 1891.

48. "Bloomfield's Treasurer Explains," *Pittsburgh Post*, January 19, 1894.

49. "Kicking Kickers," *Pittsburgh Daily Post*, October 28, 1891.

50. "Football Players at War," *Pittsburgh Press*, January 7, 1894; "Late Sporting Gossip," *Pittsburgh Press*, January 10, 1894; "General Sporting Notes," *Pittsburgh Press*, January 18, 1894.

51. "Will Have a League," *Pittsburgh Dispatch*, December 28, 1891.

52. "Amateur Sports," *Pittsburgh Press*, October 4, 1894; "Pittsburgh Rovers in Line," *Pittsburgh Daily Post*, October 24, 1897; "Great Struggles on the Gridiron," *Pittsburgh Daily Post*, November 24, 1897.

53. "Thistles were Beaten," *Pittsburgh Daily Post*, January 2, 1895.

54. "The Scotch are Beaten," *Pittsburgh Post-Gazette*, December 26, 1894.

55. Byington, *Homestead*, 14–15. She grouped Irish, German, Scottish, and English immigrants into the category of English-speaking groups.

56. Byington, *Homestead*, 16.

57. "Gathered to Rest," *Pittsburgh Press*, January 28, 1896; "Sporting Notes," *Pittsburgh Daily Post*, February 10, 1897; "Association Football," *Pittsburgh Daily Post*, August 9, 1897; "General Sporting Notes," *Pittsburgh Press*, January 7, 1893; "Amateur Sport,"

Pittsburgh Press, February 28, 1896. Beddoes had been captain of the Homestead squad and reportedly contracted the illness during a match.

58. W. B. McVicker, "What the Local Amateur Athletic Stars are Doing," *Pittsburgh Press*, March 23, 1913.

59. "Press League All-Star Team is selected for Big Game," *Pittsburgh Press*, December 15, 1912.

60. "Soccer Football," *Pittsburgh Press*, November 16, 1910. He may also have been arrested for public drunkenness while playing for Monongahela City in 1905 ("Newsy Notes," *Monongahela [PA] Daily Republican*, October 31, 1905).

61. Ralph Davis, "Ralph Davis' Column," *Pittsburgh Press*, January 3, 1913.

62. "'Jack' Robson, Soccer Star is Killed in Mine," *Pittsburgh Press*, March 14, 1913.

63. "Big Benefit for Robson's Family," *Pittsburgh Press*, March 23, 1913; "Robson Benefit at Beadling is Great Success," *Pittsburgh Press*, April 2, 1913.

64. "The Local Football Team Issue a Defi [*sic*] to Chicago," *Pittsburgh Dispatch*, January 7, 1891.

65. "After Our Kickers," *Pittsburgh Dispatch*, February 11, 1892.

66. "Was Quite a Battle," *Pittsburgh Dispatch*, February 23, 1892.

67. "The Western League," *Pittsburgh Dispatch*, October 2, 1892; "More New Players," *Pittsburgh Dispatch*, December 12, 1892.

68. "After Our Kickers," *Pittsburgh Dispatch*, February 11, 1892; "Getting in Line," *Pittsburgh Dispatch*, August 1, 1892.

69. "A Bold Challenge," *Pittsburgh Dispatch*, November 2, 1892.

70. "Win in Fine Style," *Pittsburgh Dispatch*, October 23, 1892; "A Great Team," *Pittsburgh Dispatch*, October 16, 1892; "To Tackle the Canadians," *Pittsburgh Dispatch*, November 20, 1892.

71. "The Canadians Won," *Pittsburgh Dispatch*, November 25, 1892.

72. "Another Tie Game," *Pittsburgh Dispatch*, December 27, 1892.

73. "Bloomfield's Treasurer Explains," *Pittsburgh Post*, January 19, 1894.

74. "A New Football Team," *Pittsburgh Press*, February 4, 1894; Poem in "Sporting in General," *Pittsburgh Press*, December 9, 1893.

75. "The Association Game," *Pittsburgh Press*, October 21, 1894.

76. J.H.G., "Sporting Gossip," *Pittsburgh Daily Post*, October 28, 1894. He is referring to the American League of Professional Football (ALPF). On the ALPF, see chapter 5.

77. "Sporting News of the Day," *Pittsburgh Daily Post*, December 2, 1895.

78. "Amateur Sports," *Pittsburgh Press*, September 8, 1894.

79. "Football Notes," *Pittsburgh Post-Gazette*, October 16, 1894; "Amateur Sports," *Pittsburgh Press*, October 11, 1894; "Sporting Notes," *Pittsburgh Daily Post*, October 10, 1894.

80. "There's Trouble in Sight," *Pittsburgh Post-Gazette*, December 11, 1894; "Grievance Committee Meeting," *Pittsburgh Post-Gazette*, December 18, 1894; "Pittsburgh Thrown Out," *Pittsburgh Post-Gazette*, December 20, 1894.

81. "Association Football League," *Pittsburgh Post-Gazette*, September 24, 1895; "Amateur Sports," *Pittsburgh Post-Gazette*, October 1, 1895; "Association Football," *Pittsburgh Daily Post*, October 8, 1895; "Amateur Sport," *Pittsburgh Press*, November 25, 1895.

82. "Homestead Scored," *Pittsburgh Daily Post*, December 1, 1895; "Homestead's Side," *Pittsburgh Daily Post*, December 2, 1895. "Association Football," *Pittsburgh Daily Post*, December 3, 1895.

83. "Football Notes," *Pittsburgh Daily Post*, November 5, 1896.

84. "Elected New Officers," *Pittsburgh Post-Gazette*, November 11, 1896; "M'Donald Wins the Cup," *Pittsburgh Daily Post*, February 7, 1897. Other teams in the area did not take part in the organized competition.

85. "Association Football," *Pittsburgh Daily Post*, September 26, 1897; "Cycling and Athletics," *Pittsburgh Press*, November 5, 1897.

86. "Cycling and Athletics," *Pittsburgh Press*, February 28, 1898. The protest was ultimately denied. "Association Football To-day," *Pittsburgh Daily Post*, March 26, 1898.

87. The five teams were East Pittsburg, Roscoe, Homestead, McDonald, and East Liverpool. "Great Struggles on the Gridiron," *Pittsburgh Daily Post*, November 24, 1898.

88. "No Association Football," *Pittsburgh Daily Post*, September 27, 1899.

89. "Champions Again in the Field," *Pittsburgh Daily Post*, October 31, 1903; "May form a League," *Pittsburgh Press*, September 4, 1904. The Roscoe Rangers claimed the title from 1900 to 1903.

90. "Another Star Team," *Pittsburgh Press*, November 25, 1900; "Association Football League," *Pittsburgh Daily Post*, November 23, 1900.

91. "East Liverpool Association Football," *Pittsburgh Daily Post*, September 10, 1901.

92. The list included not just historic clubs such as East Pittsburgh, McDonald, and East McKeesport but also newer teams such as Westinghouse AC, Standard Celtics, Moon Run, Cecil, Jeanette Swifts, and Swissvale.

93. "Association Football To-Day," *Pittsburgh Daily Post*, December 14, 1901.

94. "Association Football Game," *Pittsburgh Daily Post*, January 12, 1902.

95. "Association Football To-Day," *Pittsburgh Daily Post*, December 14, 1901. James McVicker was the manager of the Sturgeon team in 1902 ("Sturgeon Organizes Association Team," *Pittsburgh Daily Post*, October 26, 1902).

96. One of the rare accounts of the kind of trouble that afflicted the old league was when Bridgeville left the field in the sixtieth minute of a game because an offside call went against them ("Bridgeville Team Left Homestead Field," *Pittsburgh Daily Press*, November 2, 1902).

97. "East Pittsburgh is Angry," *Pittsburgh Daily Post*, December 20, 1903.

98. "Football Championship," *Pittsburgh Press*, December 30, 1900. "Capture Cup by One Goal," *Pittsburgh Daily Press*, January 14, 1906.

99. "1900 United States Federal Census," Ancestry.com, accessed August 4, 2019; "United States Federal Census," Ancestry.com, accessed August 4, 2019; "1930 United States Federal Census," Ancestry.com, accessed August 4, 2019.

100. "Interstate League is to be Formed," *East Liverpool (OH) Evening Review*, September 3, 1904.

101. "Rules to Govern New Association," *East Liverpool (OH) Evening Review*, September 20, 1904.

102. Ibid.

103. "Association Football," *Pittsburgh Daily Post*, October 29, 1904.

104. "Rugby Gains in Popularity," *Pittsburg Press*, December 11, 1904. Despite the headline, the story described association football.

105. The *Pittsburgh Daily Press* reported the figure as 3,000 ("Real Kickers Active," December 27, 1904), while the *Pittsburgh Weekly Gazette* wrote that it was "nearly 4,000" ("Roscoe Eleven is the Champion," December 27, 1904). Other numbers given included 1,200 at a Braddock vs. East Pittsburgh match and 300 at Roscoe on the final day of the season ("Real Kickers Finish a Successful Season on the Football Field," *Pittsburgh Daily Post*, January 3, 1904).

106. Hopkins, "Association Football," 63.

107. Adamson, "Pittsburgh and District Association Foot Ball League," 91, 80.

108. "East Pittsburgh is Eager to Win Out," *Pittsburgh Press*, October 12, 1910.

109. This was a rule of the Eastern Ohio and Western Pennsylvania League as well as the Pittsburgh Press League that began play in 1910–11 ("Rules Adopted for Soccer League," *Pittsburgh Press*, September 20, 1910).

110. "Teams in Press Soccer League had busy Week," *Pittsburg Press*, November 27, 1910.

111. "Westland has Dropped on of Press League," *Pittsburgh Press*, December 7, 1910.

112. "Press Soccer League," *Pittsburgh Press*, December 27, 1910; "Press Soccer League," *Pittsburgh Press*, January 5, 1911. When they realized they would not make it on time by train, the Dunlevy squad hired two cars to drive them, but despite the promises of the drivers they still arrived late.

113. "Morgan Team wins Strenuous Game," *Pittsburgh Press*, January 8, 1911; "Press Soccer Notes," *Pittsburgh Daily Press*, January 10, 1911; "100 Men are Probably Dead," *Daily Republican*, April 24, 1913. The explosion at the mine was likely due to an ignited gas leak ("Report of Explosion").

114. "The Western Socker [*sic*] League," *Pittsburgh Press*, October 24, 1905.

115. Cahill, "Review of Soccer."

116. "American Amateur Foot Ball Association," 39, 41.

117. "United States of America Foot Ball Association," 7, 9.

118. "Annual Report of the Treasurer," 10. "Fifth Annual Meeting," 13, 15, 17; "Eighth Annual Meeting," 18. Two figures are given for the organization's final balance in 1917. The "Auditor's Report" gives a final figure of $1,326.21, while the "Annual Report of the Treasurer" gives an ending balance of $1,347.43. One explanation is that the receipts for the fourth round of the National Challenge cup were not received by the time the financial committee submitted its report. Elsewhere in the guide, however,

those receipts appear as $107.96, so it does not totally explain the discrepancy (Cahill, *Spalding's Official "Soccer" Football Guide* [1917], 11, 32, 27).

CHAPTER 5. SOCCER GOES PRO

1. For a business-oriented analysis of the league and the causes of its failure, see Rasmussen, "Historical Analysis of Four Major Attempts to Establish Professional Soccer," 65–71.

2. The American Soccer League (ASL) began play in 1921. For discussion of the ASL, see chapter 9 and Jose, *American Soccer League*.

3. Jable, "Birth of Professional Football," 132, 143.

4. "General Sporting News of the Day," *Pittsburgh Dispatch*, October 3, 1892.

5. "A Review of Sports," *Pittsburgh Dispatch*, October 9, 1892.

6. "The Football Field," *Seattle Post-Intelligencer*, October 24, 1892.

7. "Professional Football Probable," *Buffalo Inquirer*, October 24, 1893.

8. "Notes and Comments," *New York Tribune*, November 5, 1893.

9. "Sporting News and Comment," *Washington Post*, July 30, 1894.

10. "The Proposed Professional Football League," *New York Tribune*, March 4, 1894.

11. "The Professional Football League," *New York Tribune*, March 2, 1894.

12. "A Professional Football League," *New York Tribune*, February 28, 1894.

13. The desire to keep costs low and maximize profits meant that other National League clubs were not invited to participate in the ALPF (Holroyd, "American League of Professional Football," 18).

14. Newspapers reported that people in Fall River were excited by the prospect of the league and hoped that their city would be represented ("The New Football Plan," *Fall River [MA] Daily Herald*, March 1, 1894). Others cautioned the owners, declaring that "it will be well for the newcomers to remember that they will have to cater on a different plan to baseball" ("The New Football Plan," *Fall River [MA] Globe*, March 1, 1894).

15. "Football League," *Elmira (NY) Daily Gazette and Free Press*, March 7, 1894. The owner of the Boston baseball team did not attend the meeting. The man present, Tim Murnane, was a former baseball player turned sportswriter described as "a mony-ed backer of sports." By the time the league began play in October, all the clubs, including Boston, were represented by the baseball club owners.

16. Holroyd, "First Professional Soccer League."

17. *Spalding's Official Base Ball Guide*, 23, 34, 40; Dennis Shea, "Letter from Brooklyn," *Fall River (MA) Globe*, October 4, 1894; "Professional Football," *Fall River (MA) Daily Herald*, July 26, 1894. Holroyd concludes that the league did use the reserve clause ("First Professional Soccer League").

18. *Spalding's Official Base Ball Guide*, 34, 49.

19. After the collapse of the league, Brooklyn and Baltimore played a three-game series "for the Championship of America." The matches took place in Fall River on November 1, 3, and 10. The teams drew in the first game before Brooklyn convincingly

won the next two 10–3 and 4–0. In the final match, fans of the Brooklyn team gathered near the net of opposing goalkeeper Stewart (who had had a shocker in the middle fixture) to hurl insults at him ("Professional Football," *Fall River [MA] Daily Herald*, October 31, 1894; "Great Football," *Fall River [MA] Daily Herald*, November 2, 1894; "Easy Work," *Fall River [MA] Globe*, November 5, 1894; "Dull Game," *Fall [MA] River Globe*, November 11, 1894). For more on the activities of teams following the collapse of the professional leagues, see Farnsworth, "After the Collapse."

20. "The Association Game," *Sporting Life*, October 20, 1894; "*Teutonic* Passenger Manifest," October 10, 1894, Statue of Liberty—Ellis Island Foundation, www.libertyellisfoundation.org, accessed May 27, 2018.

21. "The proposed Professional football league," *New York Tribune*, March 4, 1894.

22. "Adee on College Sports," *New York Evening World*, March 1, 1894.

23. "Oppose League Football," *Boston Daily Globe*, September 17, 1894.

24. Ross, *Great Baseball Revolt*, 13, 43, 184, 198. In 1894, *Sporting Life* wrote that losses in the 1890–91 season were closer to $500,000 ("Hub Happenings," *Sporting Life*, October 6, 1894).

25. Voight, *League That Failed*, 33, 188.

26. "The Association Game," *Sporting Life*, October 20, 1894.

27. At Eastern Park in Brooklyn, for example, college football games were scheduled on nine dates in October and six in November 1894 (Lucky's Amazing Sports Lists, "Football Games"). After the ALPF shut down, a friendly between Baltimore and Philadelphia had to be canceled because a horse show had made the field at the Orioles' Union Park unplayable (Czubinski, "First Professional Soccer League in America").

28. "Professional League," *Washington Post*, February 26, 1894; "Sporting news and Comment," *Washington Post*, October 14, 1894.

29. "General Sporting News of the Day," *Pittsburgh Dispatch*, October 3, 1892; "A Review of Sports," *Pittsburgh Dispatch*, October 9, 1892.

30. "Foot Ball," *Philadelphia Public Ledger*, August 25, 1894.

31. "Another Football League," *Fall River (MA) Globe*, August 29, 1894.

32. Farnsworth, "Clement Beecroft"; "Pennsylvania, Philadelphia Marriage Indexes, 1885–1951," FamilySearch, November 3, 2017, https://familysearch.org/ark:/61903/1:1:JJDY-78W.

33. Quoted in "Foot Ball," *Philadelphia Public Ledger*, August 25, 1894; "Association Football," *Newark Sunday Call*, September 16, 1894; "The Association Game," *Philadelphia Public Ledger*, October 13, 1894.

34. The top monthly wage was actually closer to sixty-five dollars ("Football Passes," *Fall River [MA] Evening News*, October 1, 1894).

35. "Foot Ball," *Philadelphia Public Ledger*, August 25, 1894.

36. "An Error Corrected," *Philadelphia Times*, October 16, 1894; "That New League," *Sporting Life*, October 6, 1894.

37. P. Williams, "Horace Fogel"; Voight, *League That Failed*, 195.

38. Murray, "History and Progress," 27.

39. Beecroft umpired in a benefit match played in Newark between select teams from that city and Paterson ("To-morrow's Football Game," *Paterson [NJ] Daily Guardian*, August 2, 1889).

40. "Foot Ball," *Philadelphia Public Ledger*, August 25, 1894. Farnsworth, "AAPF and the ALPF." Turner and Goldthorpe were elected in 1895 and 1896, respectively.

41. "American Football Association," *Paterson (NJ) Morning Call*, September 18, 1894; "The Realm of Sport," *Paterson (NJ) Daily Guardian*, October 2, 1894; "Association Football," *Newark Sunday Call*, September 16, 1894.

42. Farnsworth, "AAPF and the ALPF."

43. The Newark Caledonians won the 1895 American Cup; the first time since 1887 that a club from the area had captured the championship. The victory still resonated fifteen years later when C. K. Murray wrote that "The 'Calleys' won a glorious victory and brought the dear 'old mug' back to East Newark" ("History and Progress," 31). The 1895 competition was not without controversy. After losing to the Paterson True Blues in the semifinals, the Caledonians lodged a protest with the AFA. The association upheld the appeal and ordered a replay. The decision caused an uproar in the opposing city, prompting the *Paterson (NJ) Morning Call* to fume about a "Caledonian faction." The paper noted that the hearing was held in Newark and that it "was so corrupt the president refused to preside and retired from the room." After the first replay game ended in a draw, Newark won the second match 5–3 ("Football," *Paterson [NJ] Morning Call*, May 6, 1895; "Patersons Lose Again," *Paterson [NJ] News*, May 27, 1895).

44. "They are not Artists," *Boston Daily Globe*, October 19, 1894; "Foot Ball Schedule," *Boston Daily Journal*, September 17, 1894. Another complaint was that the pros would return from the three-month ALPF season to complete for clubs in the American Cup ("Footballists Convene," *Newark Sunday Call*, September 16, 1894).

45. "Byrne's Foot Ball Team," *Brooklyn Daily Eagle*, October 7, 1894; "Then Comes Football," *Washington Post*, August 5, 1894.

46. "Association Football," *Philadelphia Inquirer*, December 17, 1895; Farnsworth, "Philadelphia." The McKendrick brothers returned to Detroit and were eventually reinstated as amateurs ("Association Football," *Detroit Free Press*, April 3, 1895).

47. Farnsworth, "AAPF and the ALPF."

48. Czubinksi, "Dennis Shay." His surname was interchangeably spelled Shay or Shea. "Five Records Go," *Boston Daily Globe*, September 8, 1894.

49. "Football Passes," *Fall River (MA) Evening News*, October 1, 1894.

50. Farnsworth, "Philadelphia Phillies Soccer"; Czubinski, "First Professional Soccer League."

51. "Had an English Team," *Buffalo Morning Express*, December 31, 1894; "Another Pennant," *Baltimore Sun*, October 22, 1894.

52. "Now for Foot-Ball," *Baltimore Sun*, October 12, 1894.

53. "Association Football," *Detroit Free Press*, November 22, 1891. Prior to arriving in the United States, William McKendrick had lined up for Scottish club Greenock

Morton and A. W. Stewart had reportedly been with Glasgow Rangers. McKendrick was one of seven family members who played the sport; his younger brothers John and James joined him in Baltimore. Several of the McKendrick clan had previously played soccer in Minnesota, where, captained by John, their team Thistles won the local championship in 1889 ("Thistle Football Club Election," *Minneapolis Tribune*, April 12, 1889; "Thistles Win It," *St. Paul Daily Globe*, June 29, 1889).

54. "Sly Sullivan," *Sporting Life*, December 29, 1894, 1. The players later claimed that nobody met them at the ship on their arrival in New York (P. Brown, "Football Hustlers").

55. P. Brown, "Football Hustlers." Davis is sometimes spelled as Davies. Sullivan reportedly had agreements with several others who later backed out. The men who refused to come to the United States included Manchester City players Hugh Morris and George Mann. The two combined would make over one hundred appearances for City (Gary James, Twitter direct message to the author, April 21, 2020; "Football News and Notes," *Lancashire Daily Post*, October 4, 1894).

56. "An Alleged Violation of the Law," *Philadelphia Times*, October 20, 1894.

57. P. Brown, "Football Hustlers"; "*Teutonic* Passenger Manifest."

58. "An Alleged Violation of the Law," *Philadelphia Times*, October 20, 1894.

59. "Now for Foot-Ball," *Baltimore Sun*, October 12, 1894.

60. Barkey's first name remains a mystery, although Frederick Barkey and his brother George were both around the right age and lived in the Toronto area in 1891 and 1901 ("Census of Canada 1891" and "Census of Canada 1901," Library and Archives Canada, accessed April 10, 2020m www.bac-lac.gc.ca). The report of the match in Buffalo heaped praise on McKendrick, calling him "one of the greatest players in America today. His performance was simply brilliant" ("Beaten by Team Play," *Buffalo Evening News*, July 16, 1894). The paper refers to the fullback as "McHendrick," but a story in another newspaper gives the correct spelling ("Baseball and Football," *Buffalo Courier*, July 15, 1894).

61. "New York takes One," *Philadelphia Inquirer*, October 7, 1894.

62. "New Yorks Outkick the Longfellows," *Baltimore Sun*, September 23, 1894. Bootles FC was a club based in Liverpool, England; McKay made only one appearance for the side. I could not confirm that he played in any matches for Everton (Richard Gillham, e-mail to the author, July 1, 2019).

63. Farnsworth, "The AAPF and the ALPF"; Dennis Shea, "Captain Shea's Letter," *Fall River (MA) Globe*, October 20, 1894.

64. "Sporting News and Comment," *Washington Post*, October 9, 1894. Parr ultimately made only one appearance as a substitute.

65. "Players for Boston's Professional Team," *Baltimore Sun*, September 16, 1894. Various newspapers gave different spellings for the two players who despite all the reports did not play any matches for the team. The *Sun* names them as Joseph and Leonard Ellisham; the *Globe* has an alternative spelling of Ellesham; the *Boston Post* lists them as John and Leonard Allershaw ("Professional Football," *Boston Globe*, September 18, 1894; "Boston Footballists," *Boston Post*, September 18, 1894).

66. "Association Football," *Philadelphia Inquirer*, September 30, 1894; "Association Foot Ball," *Philadelphia Public Ledger*, October 1, 1894.

67. "American Association," *Philadelphia Public Ledger*, October 8, 1894.

68. "On Rugby Chalk Lines," *Paterson (NJ) Daily Guardian*, November 5, 1894; "The Game at Tioga," *Philadelphia Times*, October 14, 1894.

69. "Football Men Busy," *Newark Sunday Call*, September 23, 1894.

70. Farnsworth, "Philadelphia." Although the challenge was publicly accepted, there is no record the game was ever played.

71. "Professional Football," *Fall River (MA) Daily Herald*, October 8, 1894.

72. "They are not Artists," *Boston Daily Globe*, October 19, 1894.

73. Holroyd, "American League of Professional Football," 21.

74. "The Professional Football Game Postponed," *Baltimore Sun*, October 14, 1894.

75. For example, a Tuesday game at Philadelphia on May 8 drew 4,000, while a Wednesday match at Baltimore later in the season drew 3,700 spectators (Baseball Reference, "1894 Brooklyn Grooms Schedule").

76. Average per game based on figures given in Voight, *League That Failed*, 204. The numbers include the baseball teams that were not in the ALPF.

77. "Football," *Fall River (MA) Daily Evening News*, October 19, 1894; "Boston One Goal Ahead," *Inter Ocean*, October 19, 1894; "Brooklyn Vs. Philadelphia," *Evening World*, October 18, 1894; "Sporting in General," *Pittsburgh Press*, October 19, 1894; "They are not Artists," *Boston Daily Globe*, October 19, 1894; "Small Crowd at Polo Grounds," *Evening World*, October 18, 1894. Seifried and Pastore, "Temporary Homes," 267.

78. "The Professional Football League Disbands," *Baltimore Sun*, October 21, 1894.

79. Ross, *Great Baseball Revolt*, 30, 38.

80. Voight, *League That Failed*, 199.

81. "The Game at Tioga," *Philadelphia Times*, October 14, 1894.

82. "General Sporting Notes," *Philadelphia Public Ledger*, October 15, 1894; "An Error Corrected," *Philadelphia Times*, October 16, 1894. Beecroft canceled the match due to the poor condition of the field, and the *Philadelphia Public Ledger* argued that the referee misinterpreted the rules when awarding the game to the visitors. The stories leave unexplained why most of the team played an exhibition game on a bad field after the manager had called the match off.

83. Voight, *League That Failed*, 50; Westcott, *Philadelphia's Old Ballparks*, 75.

84. Seifried and Pastore, "Temporary Homes," 273.

85. "Hub Happenings," *Sporting Life*, October 6, 1894.

86. Voight, *League That Failed*, 190, 196.

87. "A Globe Day," *Boston Daily Globe*, October 25, 1894.

88. "Annual Earnings in Selected Industries and Occupations: 1890–1926," table Ba4320-4334, in Carter et al., *Historical Statistics*. Although the exact employment status of the players in 1894 is not known, later census data show that many of them did not work in high-paying jobs. As a mason, Arthur Puleston may have commanded decent wages, but some of the others probably earned much less: Henry Farrell worked

as a weaver, John Sunderland as a file cutter, and John Tobin as a fruit peddler. Fred Gregory, who turned down a contract because he feared injury, likely earned more than the others in his work as a purser ("United States Census, 1900" and "United States Census, 1910," FamilySearch, www.familysearch.org, accessed February 21, 2020).

89. "Football Players Get their Money," *Fall River (MA) Daily Evening News*, December 18, 1895. Puleston and John Sunderland received sixty-five dollars, Thomas Kenney and Patrick Farrell each got forty-five dollars. Another member of the team, Harry Cunliffe, reportedly did not receive his money, totaling $37.50, until January 1896 ("Local Lines," *Fall River [MA] Globe*, January 13, 1896).

90. Alec Wallace did not return with the other players arriving back in England on December 1, 1894. On December 22 he played for Newark Caledonians in a friendly against the Paterson True Blues ("Local Teams Win," *Paterson (NJ) Morning Call*, December 24, 1894). Although the players lined up for top clubs before leaving for the United States, none had much success after returning to Britain. Archie Ferguson eventually returned to settle permanently in the United States, but it is unknown if he continued to play soccer (P. Brown, "Football Hustlers"). Speaking with Fred Davis about his experiences, the *Sheffield (UK) Daily Telegraph* claimed that the returning players were "lamenting the evil fate which prompted them to pursue such a suicidal course." They also described the level of play in the ALPF as that of the Midland League, a semiprofessional competition that was a step below the English Football League ("The American Football Trip," December 6, 1894).

91. "Football League," *Elmira (NY) Daily Gazette and Free Press*, March 7, 1894.

92. The coach and players of Baltimore were surprised by the decision, but it is not known how the team's owner felt ("Another Pennant," *Baltimore Sun*, October 22, 1894; "The Football League Disbands," *Washington Post*, October 21, 1894).

93. "That New League," *Sporting Life*, October 6, 1894.

94. Voight, *League That Failed*, 212; "Alert League Men," *Sporting Life*, October 13, 1894.

95. "The Sporting Life's Position," *Sporting Life*, October 27, 1894.

96. Voight, *League That Failed*, 212.

97. "Girls on the Gridiron," *Los Angeles Herald*, December 4, 1893.

CHAPTER 6. COLLEEN BAWNS AND BONNIE LASSIES

1. J. Williams, *Contemporary History*, 10–16.

2. Cahn, *Coming on Strong*, 9.

3. Vertinsky, *Eternally Wounded Woman*, 40, 72.

4. The number of women attending college grew from 11,000 in 1870 to 85,000 in 1900 (Cahn, *Coming on Strong*, 13). For similar developments in Latin America, see Elsey and Nadel, *Futbolera*.

5. M. Lee, *History*, 76.

6. Cahn, *Coming on Strong*, 14, 15; Park, "Contesting the Norm"; Shattuck, *Bloomer Girls*, chap. 4.

7. Like some of the women who played in the first association football match, female high-wheel bike racers took their sport seriously and were skilled athletes (Hall, "Women's High-Wheel Bicycle Racing," 138).

8. J. Williams, *Contemporary History*, 17.

9. Shattuck, *Bloomer Girls*, 72–73.

10. Brennan, "'England' v. 'Scotland.'" See also Williamson, *Belles of the Ball*.

11. J. Lee, *Lady Footballers*, 24. The squad once attracted a crowd of fifteen thousand before the manager stole the profits and the operation collapsed (J. Williams, *Contemporary History*, 19).

12. See, for example, "Women Football Players," *New Haven (CT) Morning Journal and Courier*, March 14, 1895; "Woman and Home," *Sandusky (OH) Register*, March 11, 1895; "Football For Women," *Worcester (MA) Daily Spy*, April 6, 1895.

13. "Women at Football," *Buffalo Inquirer*, July 19, 1895; "Football for Ladies," *Brook (IN) Reporter*, June 28, 1895. The cartoons may have been originally published in England, but I could not locate copies in the British Newspaper Database.

14. *Harper's Bazaar*, August 28, 1869, 557.

15. "Currency," *Detroit Free Press*, September 23, 1874.

16. "Foot Ball in the Park," *National Police Gazette*, July 27, 1878.

17. "Last Evening a Goodly Number of Residents . . .," *Fort Wayne Sentinel*, April 13, 1882; "The City," *Fort Wayne Sentinel*, May 1, 1882.

18. "United States Census, 1880," FamilySearch, accessed February 6, 2018, https://familysearch.org/ark:/61903/1:1:MHM8-HW8.

19. "The Yale and Princeton lady football players," *Inter Ocean*, December 18, 1892.

20. "Matinee to-day at People's," *Cincinnati Inquirer*, October 8, 1894.

21. See, Shattuck, *Bloomer Girls*, esp. chap. 3.

22. "Girls on the Gridiron," *Los Angeles Herald*, October 25, 1894.

23. "Girl Foot-Ball Players," *Chicago Times*, November 13, 1894.

24. "Female Kickers," *San Francisco Call*, December 4, 1893. The second match ended as a goalless draw. "Football at Central Park," *San Francisco Call*, December 11, 1893.

25. "United States Passport Applications, 1795–1925," FamilySearch, https://familysearch.org/pal:/MM9.1.1/QV5Y-4PPC, accessed September 20, 2016; "United States Census, 1870," database with images, FamilySearch, https://familysearch.org/ark:/61903/1:1:MDS1–6J2, accessed September 20, 2016.

26. "Canadian Association," *Daily Alta California*, June 8, 1878; "Legal Intelligence," *Daily Alta California*, August 10, 1878; "Lacrosse Association," *Sacramento Daily Union*, March 22, 1879.

27. "The Sporting Park," *Daily Alta California*, September 29, 1884.

28. "The New Sporting Grounds," *Daily Alta California*, October 13, 1884.

29. "Athletic Tournament," *Daily Alta California*, November 22, 1884; "Central Park," *Daily Alta California*, November 22, 1884.

30. "Yesterday's Fires," *Daily Alta California*, May 14, 1887.

31. Franks, *Whose Baseball?*, 33, 43, 54, 55.

32. Spalding, *Always on Sunday*, 14.

33. Vermilyea, "Kranks' Delight," 39; K. Nelson, *Golden Game*, 20–21. Mone and his backers soon constructed a new facility in Alameda.

34. I calculated the 2020 value at "Measuring Worth," www.measuringworth.com, accessed November 16, 2020.

35. Spalding, *Always on Sunday*, 25, 27, 38, 45. By 1888 teams were spending an average of $17,000 a month in expenses, and in 1890 they played a 139-game schedule, up from just 30 in 1886.

36. "The City," *Daily Alta California*, March 21, 1886; quote in "Bat and Ball," *Daily Alta California*, April 5, 1886.

37. Franks, *Whose Baseball?*, 157, 163.

38. Sewell, *Women and the Everyday City*, xxii, xxvii, 95.

39. "Ladies," *Sacramento Daily Union*, October 4, 1884; "Hodge's Cloak and Suit House," *San Francisco Call*, June 15, 1890. On changes to women's tennis attire, see Schultz, *Qualifying Times*, 19–21.

40. Park, "British Sports and Pastimes," 306, 307, 308.

41. "Scottish Games," *Daily Alta California*, May 24, 1877; "Officers of the Caledonian Club," *Daily Alta California*, December 5, 1886.

42. "The World's International Contest and Baby Show," *San Francisco Call*, October 6, 1892; "Living Chess," *San Francisco Call*, November 27, 1892.

43. "In Possession," *Sacramento Daily Union*, February 18, 1882; "The Delegates," *Daily Alta California*, June 10, 1884.

44. "The Procession," *Daily Alta California*, July 5, 1887; "The Fourth of July," *Daily Alta California*, May 19, 1888.

45. Quotes in "The Ladies Day," *San Francisco Call*, October 9, 1893; "For the Fray," *San Francisco Call*, October 7, 1893. By 1903, the city had a women's shooting club called the San Francisco Damen Schützenverein. Park, "German Associational and Sporting Life," 60.

46. "Novel Football Game," *San Francisco Call*, November 6, 1893.

47. Shattuck, *Bloomer Girls*, 130–31.

48. "The Girl Ball Tossers," *Daily Alta California*, February 12, 1886. An article described Gutmann and his misdeeds at great length, including "the malarial aroma of his roseate gall" ("Victor E. M. Gutmann," *Daily Alta California*, August 11, 1886).

49. "Sporting in Central Park," *Daily Alta California*, February 15, 1886. The Blue Stockings defeated the Red Stockings 44–29.

50. "Champion Female Base Ball Game," *Daily Alta California*, February 12, 1886. The final score was 30–19 in favor of the Red Stockings.

51. "Sporting in Central Park," *Daily Alta California*, February 15, 1886.

52. "Female Ball-Tossing," *Sacramento Daily Union*, February 22, 1886.

53. Lee, *Lady Footballers*, 11.

54. "Victor E. M. Gutmann," *Daily Alta California*, August 11, 1886.

55. None of the newspapers reported any names of Red and Blue Stocking players, so it is impossible to guess what economic or ethnic groups they may have come from. By this time, male professional baseball players were drawn mainly from the working and lower-middle class (Franks, *Whose Baseball?*, 57).

56. "Football," *Daily Alta California*, March 20, 1888. A club called the California Rangers and a Stanford University team played using association rules in March 1888, with the former prevailing 4–0. In December that same year, a team of Scottish stonecutters recently employed by Stanford called the Mayfields defeated the Rangers 5–4 ("A Game of Football," *Los Angeles Herald*, December 26, 1888).

57. "A Football Association," *San Francisco Call*, August 13, 1892; "Association Football," *San Francisco Call*, October 22, 1892.

58. "Association Football," *San Francisco Call*, October 22, 1892.

59. "Football," *San Francisco Call*, January 1, 1893. Attempts to lure a team from Seattle apparently stalled due to the visitors demanding a $700 guarantee to make the trip ("Football," *San Francisco Call*, January 15, 1893).

60. "Growing Apace," *San Francisco Call*, January 11, 1893.

61. The nine senior clubs were: Oakland Athletic Club, Scottish Thistle, Pacific Wanderers, Alert Athletic Club, Rovers Association Football Club, Granites Football Club, American Eagle Association Football Club, Rangers, and Daltons. Only six figured in the Hilbert trophy competition: Thistles, Oakland, Wanderers, Rovers, Granites, and Rangers. The junior squads included: California Juniors, Golden State Rovers, California Violets, Southern Heights, Mission Rangers, and Golden City.

62. For example, "The Kickers," *San Francisco Call*, February 25, 1893; "Association Football," *San Francisco Call*, April 1, 1893.

63. Park, "British Sports and Pastimes," 306, 308.

64. "Kicks and Punts," *San Francisco Call*, January 4, 1893; "Football," *San Francisco Call*, February 5, 1893; "Football," *San Francisco Call*, July 1, 1894.

65. "Football," *San Francisco Call*, January 15, 1893.

66. Ibid.; "Football," *San Francisco Call*, January 22, 1893.

67. Profiles appeared in the *San Francisco Call* on the following dates in 1893: January 8, 15, 22; February 5, 12, 19; March 5, 26; April 16. No nationality was given for Private Fellows, who lined up for the Fort Mason army team, or for P. Kidd, who captained Rangers.

68. Franks, *Whose Baseball?*, 123.

69. "Sporting News," *San Francisco Call*, October 13, 1894.

70. "Won by Thistles," *San Francisco Call*, November 25, 1892.

71. "Won by Thistles," *San Francisco Call*, January 23, 1893.

72. "The Football Boom," *San Francisco Call*, November 24, 1892; "Association Football at Central Park" *San Francisco Call*, December 27, 1892. Such an event would have had teams composed of city residents from different nationalities competing in a tournament. It would not have involved national teams in the modern sense. An

exhibition game in Petaluma, California, on December 10, 1893, was billed as a match between England and America, with the Wanderers representing England and the Fort Mason army team the United States ("Americans Ahead," *San Francisco Call*, December 11, 1893).

73. Franks, *Whose Baseball?*, 62, 76. Prior to its collapse, the California State League had been renamed the Pacific Coast Baseball League.

74. "Novel Football Game," *San Francisco Call*, November 6, 1893. It is unclear what success he was referring to, since the earliest games in England had been played nearly a decade before and the more successful British Ladies FC did not begin play until 1895.

75. "Female Help Wanted," *San Francisco Call*, November 12, 1893.

76. "Sunday Football," *San Francisco Call*, November 13, 1893.

77. "Football," *San Francisco Call*, December 3, 1893.

78. "Female Kickers," *San Francisco Call*, December 4, 1893.

79. "Novel Football Game," *San Francisco Call*, November 6, 1893.

80. "Female Kickers," *San Francisco Call*, December 4, 1893.

81. For an example of a men's game report, see "Association Game," *San Francisco Call*, November 6, 1893.

82. "Female Kickers," *San Francisco Call*, December 4, 1893. For a discussion on the relationship between hairstyles and women's sport see Schultz, *Qualifying Times*, 1–8.

83. "Female Kickers," *San Francisco Call*, December 4, 1893. I reference the names as written in each article even though they do not match up across newspapers or even from articles published on different dates in the same paper.

84. "Girls kick the Ball," *San Francisco Chronicle*, December 4, 1893. The article claimed that Jimmy Tobin was the coach of the Lassies.

85. "Football at Central Park," *San Francisco Call*, December 11, 1893. The game ended in a 0–0 draw. A very short account of the second game appeared in "Girls Kick the Ball," *San Francisco Examiner*, December 11, 1893.

86. Sparks, *Capital Intentions*, 5.

87. Lee, *Lady Footballers*, xvii.

88. *Langley's San Francisco Directory*, n.p.

89. "Melancholy Day," *San Francisco Call*, November 27, 1893.

90. "Novel Football Game," *San Francisco Call*, November 6, 1893.

91. "United States Census, 1900," FamilySearch, https://familysearch.org/ark:/61903/1:1:M9GW-1CL, accessed November 21, 2016.

92. "Girls on the Gridiron," *Los Angeles Herald*, December 4, 1893.

93. *Langley's San Francisco Directory*, n.p.

94. "The Ladies," *Sacramento Daily Union*, September 12, 1896; "Miss Beyfuss' Injured Ankle Ends Contest," *San Francisco Call*, May 2, 1903.

95. "Athletic Sport," *San Francisco Call*, October 12, 1894; "Football Season," *San Francisco Call*, November 12, 1894; "Football," *San Francisco Call*, October 14, 1894.

96. "Scratch Teams," *San Francisco Call*, April 30, 1894.

97. "Football Season" *San Francisco Call*, November 12, 1894.

98. "Football across the Bay," *San Francisco Call*, February 23, 1895.

99. Pomeroy, "Oakland Hornets."

100. "For Lady Gymnasts," *San Francisco Call*, January 8, 1893.

101. "Physical Culture for Women," *San Francisco Call*, March 1, 1896.

102. "Potrero and South," *San Francisco Call*, June 14, 1895; "San Francisco Bicycle Riders as Disciples of Progress," *San Francisco Call*, July 26, 1896. The paper estimated that 5,000 riders participated in the protest and around 100,000 spectators witnessed the event.

103. "Girls to line up on the Gridiron," *San Francisco Call*, December 21, 1897.

104. Ibid.; "Ladies Football Game!," *San Francisco Call*, December 23, 1897.

105. "Girls to line up on the Gridiron," *San Francisco Call*, December 21, 1897.

106. "Ballet Deserts the Stage for the Gridiron," *San Francisco Call*, December 26, 1897.

107. "Bloomer Girls Kicked the Pigskin and Sowed the Ground with Hairpins," *San Francisco Chronicle*, December 26, 1897.

108. "Girls to Line Up on the Gridiron," *San Francisco Call*, December 21, 1897.

109. "Bloomer Girls Kicked the Pigskin and Sowed the Ground with Hairpins," *San Francisco Chronicle*, December 26, 1897. Hall notes that *pedestriennes* and bike racers often used pseudonyms in order to hide their real family name ("Women's High-Wheel Bicycle Racing in Nineteenth-Century America," 143).

110. "Ballet Deserts the Stage for the Gridiron," *San Francisco Call*, December 26, 1897.

111. See Sewell, *Women and the Everyday City*.

112. "How Girls Play Football," *San Francisco Call*, December 25, 1897.

113. "Charged with Vagrancy," *San Francisco Call*, January 10, 1898.

CHAPTER 7. WOMEN AND SOCCER IN THE EARLY TWENTIETH CENTURY

1. M. Lee, *History*, 76.

2. R. Smith, "Women's Control," 103, quote on 104, 105.

3. Ladda, "History of Intercollegiate Women's Soccer," 33.

4. J. Williams, *Beautiful Game*, 49, 51.

5. "Apologizes Feature in Girls Soccer Game," *Philadelphia Inquirer*, December 7, 1915; J. Williams, *Beautiful Game*, 49; Ladda, "History of Intercollegiate Women's Soccer," 53.

6. Hanschu, "Kansas State Normal Years," 20, 22, 24; "A new departure in athletics," *Emporia (KS) Gazette*, October 18, 1910.

7. "Miss Thayer of the Normal," *Emporia (KS) Gazette*, November 14, 1910.

8. "Girls' Soccer Tournament," *Emporia (KS) Gazette*, December 3, 1910. The game would not meet Shawn Renee Ladda's definition for a true intercollegiate match up since, at the time, soccer was not recognized as a varsity sport (Ladda, "History of Intercollegiate Women's Soccer," 4–5).

9. Quote in "Women's Soccer," *Seattle Star*, September 1, 1915; "Women to Play Soccer at College" *San Bernadino (CA) News*, September 2, 1915.

10. "University Girls Play Soccer," *Columbia Evening Missourian*, November 7, 1917; "United States Census, 1930," FamilySearch, https://familysearch.org/ark:/61903/1:1:X9QS-PXG, accessed March 4, 2018.

11. Quote in "Girl Students at M.A.C. will play Soccer, Hockey," *Port Huron (MI) Times Herald*, October 12, 1920; "Girls' Soccer Teams," *Omaha World-Herald*, November 17, 1920.

12. "Girl's Football Team for Seattle," *Seattle Star*, October 31, 1905.

13. "Success Assured for Girls Socker Team," *Seattle Star*, November 4, 1905.

14. "Sporting Notes," *Milwaukee Journal*, April 30, 1908.

15. "Brown Hair, Blue Eyes and Bloomers Prove Feature in Girls' Soccer Game," *Indianapolis Star*, December 26, 1913. "Women Play Soccer," *New York Times*, December 26, 1913; "Women's High Kick Feat Ends in Tie at Soccer," *New York Tribune*, December 26, 1913.

16. "Women Play Soccer," *New York Times*, December 26, 1913.

17. "Women's High Kick Feat Ends in Tie at Soccer," *New York Tribune*, December 26, 1913.

18. "United States Census, 1910," FamilySearch.org, https://familysearch.org/ark:/61903/1:1:M5HZ-CFT, accessed February 1, 2018.

19. "French Girls Play Soccer," *Ogden (UT) Standard*, June 3, 1918.

20. "Women War Workers are taking the Lead in All Masculine Sports," *Tacoma Times*, December 13, 1917.

21. Jean Williams makes a similar observation about the US tour of the Dick, Kerr Ladies team in 1922 (*Beautiful Game*, 47).

22. "Soccer Champions get Medals, Flowers, Cake," *Milwaukee Journal*, December 23, 1928.

23. "Maccabee Sport Club," *Brooklyn Daily Eagle*, September 13, 1927; quote in "Ladies' Soccer Team," *Brooklyn Daily Eagle*, October 17, 1928.

24. Danny Stevenson, "Soccerites Perform in Benefit Contest Today," *Los Angeles Times*, September 27, 1931; "Soccer Rivals in Tie Battle," *Los Angeles Times*, November 23, 1931.

25. "Form Women's Soccer Team," *Delaware County Daily Times* (Chester, PA), October 11, 1932.

26. Logan, *Early Years of Chicago Soccer*, 158.

27. "Southtown's Girl Soccer Team," *Southtown Economist* (Chicago), October 10, 1930.

28. Logan, *Early Years of Chicago Soccer*, 214–15.

29. Hugh Fullerton, "Hawthorne A. C. Biggest Athletic Club in World," *Chicago Tribune*, December 10, 1922. Western Electric's Hawthorne club had first organized a men's soccer team as early as 1910 (Logan, *Early Years of Chicago Soccer*, 107).

30. Logan, *Early Years of Chicago Soccer*, 158. See also Pesavento, "Sport and Recreation"; Pesavento and Raymond, "Men Must Play."

31. "California Death Index, 1940–1997," FamilySearch, https://familysearch.org/ark:/61903/1:1:VPHP-GDH, accessed November 26, 2014; "U.S., Social Security Applications and Claims Index, 1936–2007," Ancestry.com, accessed May 30, 2018.

32. "She Won the Pioneer Prize," *Anaconda (MT) Standard*, January 1, 1905. The essay was about the Lewis and Clark expedition.

33. "Win Gold Medals," *Billings Gazette*, December 9, 1904; "Montana News Brieflets," *Fort Benton (MT) River Press*, December 14, 1904; "Miss Doris Clark Won," *Marshalltown (IA) Evening Times-Republican*, January 16, 1905.

34. "Interstate Basket Ball," *San Francisco Call*, March 23, 1898.

35. "Co-Ed Sports and Pastimes," *San Francisco Call*, September 9, 1901

36. "Athletics."

37. "Women Seek Place on Student Body," *San Francisco Call*, February 23, 1910.

38. Bromley, "Gold 'C's' for the Women," 44–45.

39. "Gentler Sex to have Full Charge," *San Francisco Call*, February 22, 1910; "U.C. Soph and Senior Girls Win Out," *San Francisco Call*, February 23, 1913; *Blue and Gold Yearbook*, 1913, U.S., School Yearbooks, 1880–2012, Ancestry.com, accessed February 12, 2018. *Blue and Gold Yearbook*, 1914, U.S., School Yearbooks, 1900–1990, Ancestry.com, accessed February 12, 2018.

40. "Co-Eds to Appear in Light Opera," *San Francisco Examiner*, September 25, 1909; "Cast is Selected for Junior Plays," *San Francisco Call*, November 1, 1910; "Treble Clef to arrange Musicale," *San Francisco Call*, February 8, 1911.

41. "Mouse Breaks up Rehearsal, Two Kinds of Mischief Appear," *Oakland Tribune*, May 7, 1913.

42. "Mouse? Poof! Just Like That for Her," *San Francisco Examiner*, May 7, 1913.

43. "City Hall Notes," *Sacramento Bee*, June 9, 1913.

44. "City Hall Notes," *Sacramento Bee*, June 10, 1913, A slightly different salary range was reported in "Young Woman is Named to Playground Position," *Sacramento Union*, June 10, 1913.

45. "Oak Park Playground gains in Popularity," *Sacramento Union*, May 18, 1914; "Merchants to Purchase Suit for Ball Teams," *Sacramento Union*, May 20, 1914; "Easter Eggs to go Discovered in Park," *Sacramento Union*, April 23, 1916.

46. "Athletic Clubs Forming for the Benefit of School Girls," *Sacramento Bee*, March 21, 1917.

47. "Park Juveniles prepare for Season," *Sacramento Bee*, February 28, 1914; first quote in "Wanted: Girl's Team to Play Real Ball," *Sacramento Bee*, April 8, 1914; second quote in "Girls' Baseball Team is Out After Games and Bar None," *Sacramento Bee*, June 13, 1914.

48. "96,384 Persons Play at M'Kinley Park," *Sacramento Bee*, November 29, 1917.

49. "Plan under way to Control Court Hogs," *Sacramento Bee*, November 3, 1917; "Veterans Wage Battles on Oak Park Checker Boards," *Sacramento Bee*, November 25, 1914.

50. "Labor Men want Municipal Camp," *Sacramento Union*, August 30, 1918.

51. "Bee Basketball League Launched; Play Starts 18th," *Sacramento Bee*, January 4, 1919.

52. "Report on Soccer Dispute Due To-Night," *Sacramento Bee*, May 20, 1919.

53. "Commissioners Named to Control Destinies of Soccer League," *Sacramento Bee*, September 23, 1919. Several months later the *San Francisco Chronicle* declared Clark one of only two women soccer commissioners in the country. The other was likely Helen Clark ("Special Match of Soccer on Today," *San Francisco Chronicle*, April 4, 1920).

54. "Women's Soccer," *Seattle Star*, September 1, 1915; "Women to Play Soccer at College," *San Bernadino (CA) News*, September 2, 1915.

55. "Nineteen Teams Entered in School Soccer League," *Sacramento Bee*, October 27, 1917. Clark did not limit her efforts to promoting soccer; she also worked with high school coaches to form a gridiron football league in the city ("School Boys will Play American Football," *Sacramento Bee*, November 10, 1917).

56. John R. Young, "Many New Faces in the Line-Up of Soccer Teams," *Sacramento Bee*, October 19, 1918

57. John Young, "Two Games Scheduled for Cup Tie Play," *Sacramento Bee*, March 15, 1919.

58. "Rover and M'Kinley Park Clubs to Play off Cup Tie," *Sacramento Bee*, April 2, 1919.

59. "McKinley Park Team will take on Rovers," *Sacramento Bee*, March 1, 1919.

60. "Soccer Popular Sport with Local Athletes," *Sacramento Union*, February 1, 1919.

61. "Miss Doris Clark Resigns," *Sacramento Union*, July 8, 1919; *Crocker-Langley San Francisco City Directory* (1920), 498.

62. "Soccer Gossip," *Sacramento Bee*, February 11, 1920; "Soccer Gossip," *Sacramento Bee*, April 3, 1920.

63. John N. Young, "Soccer Season Looks Promising at this Time," *Sacramento Bee*, September 27, 1919.

64. Academical (pseud.), "McKinley Park Team," 150–51.

65. "Helen Clark is an Authority on Soccer and Basketball," *Bridgeport (CT) Evening Farmer*, January 20, 1919. Another Helen Clark of approximately the same age also lived in Connecticut around the same time. I was unable to confirm if her father was the George S. Clark who served in the state senate in 1903 (Connecticut General Assembly Database, last updated March 2019, https://www.ctatatelibrarydata.org/connecticut-general-assembly-members/). The *Spalding Soccer Football Guide* may have confused the two, writing that Helen Clark the soccer official was the daughter of a state senator ("Connecticut Women's Soccer").

66. New Haven Normal School of Gymnastics, *Catalogue*, 5, 24.

67. "Personals," *Bridgeport (CT) Evening Farmer*, October 29, 1918.

68. "Helen Clark is an Authority on Soccer and Basketball," *Bridgeport (CT) Evening Farmer*, January 20, 1919.

69. "Connecticut Women's Soccer." The story also includes photographs of the Bridgeport High School team and Swedish Ladies Soccer Football Club.

70. Photos of the Barnham team, Helen Clark, and Doris Clark are in Cahill, *Spalding's Official "Soccer" Football Guide* (1919), 62, 108. "First Woman to get Soccer Office Here," *Bridgeport (CT) Evening Farmer,* June 26, 1919.

71. "First Women's Soccer Game Played Today," *Bridgeport (CT) Evening Farmer,* November 29, 1919.

72. Booth, "Connecticut State Football League," 107. The Swedish team was likely affiliated with a men's club called Bridgeport Swedes who played in the city league.

73. Booth, "Girls will Play Soccer Game at Meadows Today," *Bridgeport (CT) Telegram,* May 1, 1920.

74. "Girl Soccer Teams Clash Today at Meadows," *Bridgeport (CT) Telegram,* December 4, 1920. The Esling Shield began in 1915 as a competition for junior soccer teams in Connecticut. It is unclear if this was the same trophy or a different one with the same name that would be given to the women's teams ("Joe Booth Chosen to Big Committee," *Hartford Courant,* February 28, 1915).

75. "Soccer Notes," *Hartford Courant,* February 15, 1920.

76. "Soccer Notes from Here, the State and Over There," *Hartford Courant,* March 5, 1920.

77. "Girl Soccer Teams to meet on Sunday," *Hartford Courant,* April 8, 1920.

78. "Girl Soccerites to Play Olympians," *Hartford Courant,* May 23, 1920. Unlike the *Hartford Courant* story from April 8, this article claims that the Olympians and Hartford City had played a month earlier to great acclaim. It may be that Hartford United was a men's teams made up of players from different teams competing in the city league ("Girls to Play United," *Hartford Courant,* April 20, 1920). A report titled "Women Soccer Teams Play," in the April 18, 1920, *Pittsburgh Press* noted that four women's teams from Bridgeport had organized a tournament, with a trophy to be awarded to the winners.

79. "Soccer Notes from Here, the State and Abroad," *Hartford Courant,* April 18, 1920.

80. "Girls' Soccer Club Officers Elected," *Hartford Courant,* October 10, 1920.

81. "Girl Soccerites Can't Get Games," *Bridgeport (CT) Evening Farmer,* December 17, 1921.

82. "Girl's Soccer Team," *Criterion* (Bridgeport High School), 1922, 99, "U.S., School Yearbooks, 1880–2012," Ancestry.com, accessed February 12, 2018. The Swedish men's league club had disbanded because some in the community viewed them as pro-German during World War I. Joe Booth, secretary-treasurer of the Connecticut State Football League, criticized such attitudes calling the Swedes "pro-Ally and . . . ever ready to assist whole heartedly in any patriotic movement." Likely the women's side was withdrawn at the same time (Booth, "Bridgeport Swedes," 111).

83. "No Girls Soccer Eleven at B.H.S.," *Bridgeport (CT) Evening Farmer,* October 4, 1922.

84. Doris Clark, "Just How Old is the Corset?," *San Francisco Chronicle*, September 20, 1914.

85. "Novel Day at California Club," *San Francisco Chronicle*, April 4, 1920; "Press Conference," *San Francisco Examiner*, September 23, 1923.

86. "Newspaper Girl Talks," *Santa Cruz Evening News*, July 18, 1922.

87. "Argonaut Disaster Reporters Organize," *Los Angeles Times*, July 4, 1923.

88. *Crocker-Langley San Francisco City Directory* (1920), 498; *Crocker-Langley San Francisco City Directory* (1921), 438; *Crocker-Langley San Francisco City Directory* (1922), 468; *Crocker-Langley San Francisco City Directory* (1923), 473; *Crocker-Langley San Francisco City Directory* (1924), 382.

89. "Marriages," *San Francisco Call*, August 1, 1923. The 1930 US Census listed Clark's occupation as "none" ("United States Census, 1930," FamilySearch, https://familysearch.org/ark:/61903/1:1:XCN3-8HH, accessed September 4, 2018).

90. "California Death Index, 1940–1997," FamilySearch, https://familysearch.org/ark:/61903/1:1:VPHP-GDH, accessed September 4, 2018.

91. "Find A Grave Index," FamilySearch, https://familysearch.org/ark:/61903/1:1:QVPS-PFM6, accessed September 4, 2018. An article from a few years later referred to her as "the late Helen Clark" who worked in the recreation department of the high school ("Track, Cage Star in High School," *Bridgeport [CT] Post*, August 22, 1948).

CHAPTER 8. SOCCER GOES TO WAR

1. *Official History*, 56, 58–59, 61, 65.

2. Hudson sailed for France on June 28, 1918, aboard the *Justicia* ("U.S., Naturalization Records, 1840–1957," Ancestry.com, accessed October 5, 2018; "U.S., Army Transport Service, Passenger Lists, 1910–1939," Ancestry.com, accessed March 11, 2020).

3. Cahill, foreword (1919).

4. Jose, *American Soccer League*.

5. On the origins of the National Challenge Cup, see Wangerin, "Foreign Bodies and Freezing Fans."

6. "United States World War I Draft Registration Cards, 1917–1918," FamilySearch, https://familysearch.org/ark:/61903/1:1:K68N-R93, accessed May 30, 2017. Family member Clyde Behrendt provided biographical information on Cunat (e-mail to the author, February 24, 2017).

7. Logan, *Early Years of Chicago Soccer*, 104, 121, 122.

8. J. G. Davis, "Soccer Football in Illinois."

9. Cummings, "Peel Challenge Cup Competition."

10. Joe Davis, "Two Soldiers Help Ranger Soccer Club Defeat Swedes, 2–0," *Chicago Tribune*, April 8, 1918; "Grant Eleven Ties Rockford," *Chicago Tribune*, April 14, 1918; "Brickies Eleven goes into Final," *Chicago Tribune*, April 29, 1918.

11. "Maurice John Hudson," United States World War I Draft Registration Cards, FamilySearch, https://www.familysearch.org/ark:/61903/1:1:KZV1-RQB

?from=lynx1UIV7, accessed November 22, 2019. *Crocker-Langley San Francisco Directory* (1917), 960.

12. "Football and Baseball," *San Francisco Call*, January 2, 1898.

13. J. Young, "Association Football in California" (1922), 143; J. Young, "San Francisco Football League," 144.

14. "Veteran Soccer Star Returns to Sport Tomorrow," *San Francisco Chronicle*, April 7, 1928.

15. "Barbarians," 209.

16. Pomeroy, "Oakland Hornets."

17. Goodman, "Association Foot Ball," 97.

18. "Barbarians," 209–10.

19. Cahill, *Spalding's Official Association "Soccer" Football Guide* (1912), 242.

20. "Barbarians Defeat Alameda Cricketers," *San Francisco Chronicle*, June 1, 1914; "Irish to Meet the All-Star at Soccer," *San Francisco Chronicle*, April 30, 1916.

21. "Barbarians Winners in Cup Tie Finals," *San Francisco Chronicle*, May 10, 1915; "Barb Soccerites Defeat S.F. in Cup Final," *San Francisco Examiner*, May 10, 1915.

22. On the development of sports within the military, see Pope, "Army of Athletes."

23. "Camp Dix Athletic Activity Plan to Enlist 10,526 Men in a Series," *Camp Dix News*, October 13, 1917.

24. "Hey Sam? Lamp what's on the Way for Soldiers," *Camp Sherman News*, August 14, 1918.

25. "Local Boys Enjoy Life in Camps," *Bristol (PA) Daily Courier*, February 26, 1918.

26. "Soccer Schedule Announced," *Gas Attack of The New York Division*, January 12, 1918; "Goebel Bros. were Cowboys in Arizona," *Camp Sherman News*, December 26, 1917.

27. "54th Pioneers Active in Sports," *Stars and Stripes*, March 21, 1919.

28. "323rd Field Artillery Battery," *Camp Sherman News*, November 28, 1917; "Goebel Bros. were Cowboys in Arizona," *Camp Sherman News*, December 26, 1917.

29. E. Johnson, *History of YMCA Physical Education*, 189.

30. "Y. M. C. A. Places Order for Athletic Goods," *Camp Sherman News*, February 20, 1918; "Athletics Hold Interest," *Camp Sherman News*, May 29, 1918.

31. The major groups included the YMCA, Young Women's Christian Organization, Young Men's Hebrew Organization, the Salvation Army, Knights of Columbus, War Camp Community Service, and the American Library Association (Steuer, "Service for Soldiers, 208).

32. "Athletics," *Camp Dix News*, January 9, 1918; "Soccer Game held in Spite of Rain," *Camp Crane News (Ambulance Service News)*, October 26, 1918.

33. Palmer, "Football Association," 97.

34. Mockler, "Soccer Football Chain Letter Fund"; Bagnall, "Activities."

35. Cahill, "Annual Report," 18.

36. Bius, "Damn Y Man," 17, 20.

37. *Summary*, first quote v, 10, second quote 145.

38. "Big Order for Sporting Goods," *Home Ties [Over the Top]*, September 7, 1918. The order also included replacement bladders for the soccer balls. Each ball cost five dollars (W. Johnson and E. Brown, *Official Athletic Almanac*, 164). Value in 2020 dollars computed at www.measuringworth.com.

39. The YMCA could afford to spend so much on soccer balls because it and other groups raised an extraordinary amount of money. During one campaign in November 1918, the organizations took in $203 million, of which $100.7 million went to the YMCA (Steuer, "Service for Soldiers," 252).

40. Wakefield, *Playing to Win*, 2–3, quote 6, 15, 23.

41. Pope, *Patriotic Games*, 148.

42. "The Value of Soccer," *Going Over*, August 5, 1918.

43. Cahill, foreword (1917), 3.

44. Thomas S. Rice, "Full Steam Ahead," *Going Over*, September 9, 1918.

45. "Soccer Schedule Announced," *Gas Attack of The New York Division*, January 12, 1918. *Official Athletic Almanac*, 117.

46. *Official Athletic Almanac*, 133.

47. "Baseball Leads All Sports with AEF in France," *Camp Sherman News*, April 3, 1919. In general, the YMCA counted total services provided even if the same solider was served more than once. It's likely that it used the same policy when counting participation and viewing figures (*Summary*, 8).

48. Hanson, *Inter-Allied Games*, 35. The total for baseball does not include indoor baseball which was higher than soccer at 646,066.

49. Riedi and Mason, "'Leather' and the Fighting Spirit," 486, 494, 495, 498.

50. Waquet, "Sport in the Trenches," 334, 339.

51. The process ran both ways, as Thierry Terret argues that French men learned a culture of masculinity based on team sports as a result of this "interculturality" ("American Sammys," 351).

52. Logan, *Early Years of Chicago Soccer*, 135.

53. "469th Aero Squadron," *Plane News*, December 21, 1918; "Americans Humble French," *Bulletin*, March 5, 1919; "French Soccer Team Beaten," *Stars and Stripes*, March 14, 1919.

54. "When Secretaries were Refugees," 22.

55. Terret, *Les jeux interalliés*, 31.

56. British participation in the games was minimal for reasons that remain unclear (Terret, *Les jeux interalliés*, 99–101).

57. Hanson, *Inter-Allied Games*, 242–43.

58. *United States Army in the World War*, 245. The organization of the tournament echoed that of similar competitions in the British army (J. Roberts, "Best Football Team," 39).

59. *United States Army in the World War*, 248.

60. Cunat is listed as "Cunard" in the almanac (*Official Athletic Almanac*, 117).

61. "Johnny Mackenzie Writes Pomeroy of Soccer in the Army," *San Francisco Chronicle*, June 21, 1919.

62. Hanson, *Inter-Allied Games*, 103. The results of the international friendlies are not known.

63. Photo published in Cahill, *Spalding's Official "Soccer" Football Guide* (1919), 151. The Canadian team manager also appears in the photograph, so perhaps it was taken on June 25, the day the United States and Canada played. Cunat's family has an unpublished photograph of the Czech team that may have been taken on June 26, the date they defeated the US team 8–2.

64. Grant, "YMCA and the US Army," 124, 132, 133.

65. Riess, "American Forces in Germany" (1921), 134.

66. Grant, "YMCA and the US Army," 133, 134. Belgium participated in the larger meet, but it is unclear whether it took part in the soccer tournament.

67. Riess, "American Forces in Germany" (1922), 255.

68. United States Army, "American Forces in Germany," 321.

69. Riess, "American Forces in Germany" (1922), 133; Riess, "American Forces in Germany" (1922), 255. It is not known how many of these matches took place as part of the Armies of Occupation Track and Field Championships. In that competition, the United States finished third behind Britain and France. Units stationed in Russia and the Philippines also played soccer (J. P. Campbell, "All Army Soccer Team Jumps to Third Place," *Here and There with the 31st*, March 1, 1922).

70. Cahill, foreword (1919).

71. Cahill, "Annual Report," 21. No edition was published for 1920–21.

72. Cahill, foreword (1922), 5.

73. Peel, "Annual Report," 14.

74. Healey, "Annual Report," 27.

75. Taylor, *Leaguers*, 228–29.

76. Keane, "National Challenge Cup Competition"; "National Challenge Cup Competition," 22; A. Brown, "National Challenge Cup Competition."

77. Spangler, "1920 National Challenge Cup Results"; Spangler, "1921 National Challenge Cup Results"; Cahill, foreword (1922), 6; Fernley, "Soccer's Progress," 36.

78. The format for the data is inconsistent, and not all leagues reported figures for all of the years. Some regions, including most of New England and California, did not consistently report on the number of teams involved in local competitions in those areas.

79. Logan, *Early Years of Chicago Soccer*, 152–53.

80. Hatfield, *History of Soccer*, 54, 57. The league would only last three seasons. Nonetheless, Hatfield calls the period 1920–32 soccer's golden age in the city.

81. Hakala, "US Open Cup Final: 1914 to the Present." The numbers include replays and two legged ties but exclude the 1924–25 season, when the ASL teams did not participate in the competition. Including that season would lower the average during the 1920s slightly to 12,161.

82. Hakala, "US Open Cup Final."

83. "Boston Triumphs 2–1, Before 17,000," *Boston Globe*, March 30, 1925. The Lewis Cup was contested only by American Soccer League Teams.

84. Data from the yearly summaries 1921–30 at the American Soccer History Archives, http://SoccerHistoryUSA/ASHA, accessed June 18, 2020.

85. Wangerin, *Soccer in a Football World*, 184.

86. Healey, "Annual Report of the President," *Spalding's Official "Soccer" Football Guide* (1922), 27.

87. G. Lewis, "World War I," 114.

88. Hollander, *American Encyclopedia of Soccer*, 36, 38.

89. See note 6.

90. "Rangers Eleven is Beaten by Olympics," *Chicago Tribune*, October 17, 1921; Joe Davis, "Pullman, 0; Rangers, 0," *Chicago Tribune*, May 8 1922; "Sparta Union to Tackle Kenosha Macwhytes," *Chicago Tribune*, February 4, 1923.

91. "Barbs Present Hudson with Watch," *San Francisco Chronicle*, March 27, 1921.

92. J. Young, "Association Football in California (1923), 147. The article in the guide states that popular sentiment was with the Barbs in the final because they had never won the cup before. The fact that they had triumphed in 1914–15 reveals again how fragile the history and memory of competitive soccer could be even among those who championed the sport.

93. "Barbs will Battle Vikings at Ewing," *San Francisco Chronicle*, January 31, 1926.

94. "U.S.I.V. Eleven Downs Espanola in Soccer Tilt," *San Francisco Chronicle*, April 9, 1928.

95. "Forty Clubs in Cup Ties Tournament," *San Francisco Chronicle*, December 16, 1935.

CHAPTER 9. ETHNIC AND INDUSTRIAL SOCCER

1. S. Hart, Chilton, and Donta, "Before Hadley," 45, 46, 51.

2. The ASL grew stronger and more competitive after the first season. It continued throughout the 1920s until internal disputes and economic pressures led to its collapse in 1931. A second ASL would soon be relaunched but it never achieved the level of success of the original circuit (Jose, *American Soccer League*).

3. Markovits and Steven L. Hellerman, *Offside*, 102. See also Abrams, "Inhibited."

4. For Chicago see Logan, *Early Years of Chicago Soccer*; Trouille, "Association Football to Fútbol." For the Boston area, see Apostolov, "Everywhere and Nowhere."

5. "Springfield," *Springfield (MA) Republican*, April 26, 1889; "To-Day," *Springfield (MA) Republican*, November 28, 1889; "Springfield," *Springfield (MA) Republican*, December 26, 1889.

6. "The Foot Ball League," *Worcester (MA) Daily Spy*, August 12, 1889; "Foot-Ball in this City," *Springfield (MA) Republican*, November 29, 1889.

7. In 1890 the *Fall River (MA) Daily Evening News* observed that Rangers were "comparatively a new club" ("Football," September 24, 1890). A story from later that year, however, claimed that the Holyoke team had played the Fall River Rovers as early as 1888 ("Rovers Again," *Fall River [MA] Daily Evening News*, December 1, 1890).

8. "Athletics on Holyoke's Park," *Springfield (MA) Republican*, July 6, 1890.

9. "Rovers Again," *Fall River (MA) Evening News*, December 1, 1890.

10. "Rangers win at Association Football," *Springfield (MA) Republican*, November 10, 1895; "Saturday's Football Games," *Springfield (MA) Republican*, November 18, 1890; "Football Games Wanted," *Boston Daily Globe*, October 26, 1903. The Ludlow Challenge Cup was a tournament between three teams: the Ludlows, Sons of Temperance (Ludlow), and Holyoke Rangers. It is not clear who won the trophy, but newspaper reports indicate that Rangers handily defeated both of the Ludlow squads. In 1894 the Rangers were scheduled to meet another Holyoke team called Thistle for "the disputed championship." No result or other information is available but it may have been the title of city champion ("Holyoke," *Springfield [MA] Republican*, November 29, 1894).

11. "Town Correspondence," *Vermont Watchman and State Journal* (Montpelier), September 2, 1896; "Labor Day," *Granite City Leader* (Barre, VT), September 12, 1896.

12. "Foot Ball Drawing," *Boston Daily Globe*, September 23, 1890; "1891 American Cup," Wikipedia, https://en.wikipedia.org/wiki/1891_American_Cup, accessed August 31, 2019.

13. "New Football League," *Springfield (MA) Republican*, August 26, 1904; "Will Present a Cup," *Holyoke (MA) Daily Transcript*, September 19, 1904.

14. "Will Present a Cup," *Holyoke (MA) Daily Transcript*, September 19, 1904. In later years the teams competed for the Walter Scott Cup.

15. "Football League Organized," *Holyoke (MA) Daily Transcript*, September 10, 1906; "Soccer League Standings," *Holyoke (MA) Daily Transcript*, October 7, 1907. It is not known what connection, if any, this Rangers squad had with the late nineteenth-century one.

16. "Schedule of Soccer League," *Springfield (MA) Republican*, September 26, 1911.

17. Hutner, *Farr Alpaca Company*, 3–5, 23.

18. Ibid., 57.

19. Ibid., 68. It is unclear when the field was created. Hutner discusses the company's granting of the field in the context of the creation of the Falco Athletic Association in 1914 (68). As noted, however, the soccer club had existed since 1909.

20. Mason, *Association Football*, 21, 90–91.

21. The American Writing Paper Company would also field a team, but only for the 1919–20 season.

22. "Champion Ludlow Beaten," *Holyoke (MA) Daily Transcript*, September 27, 1909.

23. "Big Soccer Game Tomorrow," *Holyoke (MA) Daily Transcript*, November 24, 1909. "Retain Chaloux Cup," *Holyoke (MA) Daily Transcript*, November 29, 1911. The first two editions of the challenge ended as draws, but Farr Alpaca won the cup each of the remaining years. After 1913 the teams no longer played on Thanksgiving Day.

24. "Farr Alpacas Nail Title," *Holyoke (MA) Daily Transcript*, November 28, 1910; "Alpacas take the Lead," *Holyoke (MA) Daily Transcript*, December 2, 1912; "One loss in three years," *Holyoke (MA) Daily Transcript*, February 2, 1913; "Alpacas clinch title," *Holyoke (MA) Daily Transcript*, November 28, 1913.

25. "Big Soccer Game Tomorrow," *Holyoke (MA) Daily Tribune*, November 24, 1909; "Pilgrims in a tie," *New York Tribune*, November 15, 1909. On the tour see Logan, "Pilgrims' Progress in Chicago."

26. *Holyoke City Directory 1912*, 270, 518, 519, 535. Photograph available at the Holyoke History Room.

27. Hutner, *Farr Alpaca Company*, 68n59.

28. "Big Game Arranged for Saturday," *Holyoke (MA) Daily Transcript*, November 21, 1913; *Holyoke City Directory 1914*, 419.

29. Hartford, *Working People of Holyoke*, 42.

30. "Alpacas Eliminated," *Holyoke (MA) Daily Transcript*, November 24, 1913.

31. "Bethlehem Teams Wins at Holyoke, Mass. Home Eleven Eliminates Bay State Team from American Cup Competition," *Bethlehem (PA) Globe*, November 24, 1913. Bethlehem Steel Soccer Club, http://bethlehemsteelsoccer.org/gl112413b.html, accessed July 1, 2020.

32. "Big Game for Alpacas," *Springfield (MA) Republican*, October 25, 1912.

33. Wording as in original. "Champion soccer team," *Springfield (MA) Republican*, December 31, 1911.

34. Some reports put the amount at $200 and others at $300. Quote in "Holyoke Springfield," *Springfield (MA) Republican*, April 22, 1915; "Sporting Comment" and "Farr Alpacas turned down," *Springfield (MA) Republican*, April 29, 1915; "Holyoke gets match," *Springfield (MA) Republican*, May 4, 1915. Burnett worked as a master mechanic at the Lyman Mills (*Holyoke City Directory 1916*, 213).

35. Keane, "Soccer in New England," 64; G. Collins, "Soccer in Massachusetts," 70; Scholefield, "Northern Massachusetts."

36. "Soccer league schedule," *Springfield (MA) Republican*, September 21, 1914.

37. "Soccer league schedule," *Springfield (MA) Republican*, September 21, 1914. The remaining sides were Gilbert & Brown, Athletics, Farr Alpaca, Three Rivers, Ludlow, Chicopee, and West Boylston. It seems that not all the clubs completed league play.

38. "Joy reigns in Holyoke," *Springfield (MA) Republican*, April 18, 1914; "Football standing announced," *Springfield (MA) Republican*, December 14, 1914; "Junior soccer league," *Springfield (MA) Republican*, September 25, 1916; "To boom soccer," *Springfield (MA) Republican*, March 6, 1916.

39. First quote in "Ludlow man suspended," *Springfield (MA) Republican*, March 7, 1916; "S. Lowe a 'pro,'" *Springfield (MA) Republican*, April 10, 1916; second quote in "Fredette barred," *Springfield (MA) Republican*, April 3, 1916.

40. "Soccer league to meet," *Springfield (MA) Republican*, August 18, 1916.

41. Since the league obviously had not objected to the Farr Alpaca team, it may be evidence that it was not a true "shop" team but rather a collection of workers.

42. "No worry here," *Springfield (MA) Republican*, November 17, 1916.

43. "Again bars Fisks," *Springfield (MA) Republican*, October 9, 1916; "Sporting news," *Springfield (MA) Republican*, November 3, 1916; "Soccer league not worried

over Fisks," and "No worry here," *Springfield (MA) Republican*, November 17, 1916; "Stand by state," *Springfield (MA) Republican*, November 25, 1916; "Soccer men meet," *Springfield (MA) Republican*, November 27, 1916; "Backs the ruling," *Springfield (MA) Republican*, December 5, 1916. The league countered by petulantly declaring that it could not be expelled since it had already voluntarily withdrawn from the state organization.

44. "Plan shop league," *Springfield (MA) Republican*, September 16, 1917.

45. "Burnett out for soccer presidency," *Springfield (MA) Republican*, June 19, 1921.

46. Fisk was based in Chicopee, Massachusetts; American Writing Paper was from Holyoke; and the others came from Springfield.

47. "Big field day," *Springfield (MA) Republican*, September 3, 1916.

48. Hutner, *Farr Alpaca Company*, 67, 68.

49. "Western Mass soccer schedule," *Springfield (MA) Republican*, October 22, 1920.

50. "Soccer To-day," *Springfield (MA) Republican*, March 19, 1921.

51. "Falco takes title in Soccer Final," *Boston Daily Globe*, April 24, 1921. Grey and Davis represented eastern Massachusetts

52. "Our best to go against Third Lanark on July 19," *Boston Daily Globe*, July 5, 1921.

53. George M. Collins, "Massachusetts scores inside of two minutes, but is beaten by Third Lanark," *Boston Daily Globe*, July 17, 1921. Third Lanark won the game 3–6.

54. Quote in "Falcos may enter league tonight," *Springfield (MA) Republican*, August 9, 1921; "Falcos vote to join new league," *Springfield (MA) Republican*, August 10, 1921.

55. "Soccer League Returns $550 to Bethlehem Team," *New York Tribune*, August 22, 1921. The $50 was an additional entrance fee.

56. "Professional Soccer Facing Greatest Crisis of Its Career," *New York Tribune*, September 4, 1921. "A swing along Athletic Row," *Bethlehem (PA) Globe*, August 31, 1921. Bethlehem Steel Soccer Club, http://bethlehemsteelsoccer.org/glo83121.html, accessed July 1, 2020.

57. C. Lovett, "First Big Professional League," 37.

58. "Professional Soccer Facing Greatest Crisis of Its Career," *New York Tribune*, September 4, 1921.

59. "Falcos get Coleman, Star Soccer Player," *Holyoke (MA) Daily Transcript*, October 4, 1921; "Changes in Soccer Teams," *Holyoke (MA) Daily Transcript*, October 5, 1921. Jose, *American Soccer League*, 21–22.

60. "Professional Soccer Facing Greatest Crisis of Its Career," *New York Tribune*, September 4, 1921. Lack of regular access to an adequate park contributed to the withdrawal of the Jersey City Celtics in November 1921 ("Jersey City Team Surrenders Berth in Soccer League," *New York Tribune*, December 11, 1921).

61. "Old baseball grounds sold," *Springfield (MA) Republican*, August 28, 1920. Information on the transaction can be found in item 21, *Deed Book 1873–1929*, Farr Alpaca Company Records, 6637, Kheel Center for Labor-Management Documentation and Archives.

62. Hutner, *Farr Alpaca Company*, 49, 50, 51.

63. Farr Alpaca's records held by the Kheel Center at Cornell University are not complete and some may have been disbursed after the company folded in 1940 while other materials may have been destroyed in a fire.

64. "Falcos to open season," *Holyoke (MA) Daily Transcript*, September 21, 1921.

65. Jose, *American Soccer League*, 23.

66. Cahill, *Spalding's Official "Soccer" Football Guide* (1922), 57; Jose, *American Soccer League*, 21. The second win came as a result of a forfeit when the clubs agreed to cancel the final two games of the season.

67. "Falcos defeat Abbots," *Holyoke (MA) Daily Transcript*, May 8, 1922.

68. George M. Collins, "Soccer teams ignore natives," *Boston Daily Globe*, June 29, 1926; George M. Collins, "Soccer due for a big year," *Boston Daily Globe*, July 23, 1926.

69. Green, *Holyoke Massachusetts*, 367.

70. Tischler, *Footballers and Businessmen*, 81.

71. "Games called off," *Holyoke (MA) Daily Transcript*, May 19, 1922.

72. "Soccer Snaps," *Boston Daily Globe*, June 28, 1922.

73. Hutner, *Farr Alpaca Company*, 73. The 2020 valuation is from https://www.measuringworth.com/.

74. "Todd's defeats Falcos by 4 to 1," *Springfield (MA) Republican*, October 30, 1921; "Falcos defeated by New Yorkers," *Springfield (MA) Republican*, November 20, 1921; "Falcos advance by 5–2 victory," *Springfield (MA) Republican*, November 27, 1921; "Phillies beat Falcos by 5–3," *Springfield (MA) Republican*, December 4, 1921; "Falcos get tie with Coats team," *Springfield (MA) Republican*, March 12, 1922; "Coats show more endurance in very last soccer game," *Holyoke (MA) Daily Transcript*, April 17, 1922; "Todds show real championship speed in Holyoke game," *Holyoke (MA) Daily Transcript*, April 20, 1922.

75. "Falcos and locals in 'no-decision,'" *Springfield (MA) Republican*, October 28, 1923.

76. The grounds may have limited crowd size since the facility had been built in 1904 as a baseball stadium with seating for just 1,250 fans ("Work begins today," *Holyoke [MA] Daily Transcript*, March 30, 1904). The field was sold in 1914 and supposedly the grandstand was removed ("Joy reigns in Holyoke," *Springfield [MA] Republican*, April 18, 1914). It is unclear what facilities were in place by 1921. A photograph of the Falcos from this period shows what appears to be a grandstand in the background so it is possible that the structure had either been rebuilt or was never torn down in the first place ("The Search for the Falcos," www.SoccerHistoryUSA.org /the-search-for-the-falcos/, accessed November 4, 2020).

77. Within a few years ASL games would regularly draw 5,000 and sometimes as many as 10,000 fans ("American Soccer League," in Allaway, Jose, and Litterer, *Encyclopedia of American Soccer History*, 10). Fall River opened a new stadium for the 1922 season that had a capacity of 15,000 (A. Foulds, *Boston's Ballparks and Arenas*, 155). For ticket prices, see Apostolov, "Everywhere and Nowhere," 6, 41n20.

78. "Treasurer's report read at the annual meeting of stockholders June 22, 1921," *Records Book 1914–1928*, Farr Alpaca Company Records, 6637, Kheel Center for Labor-Management Documentation and Archives.

79. Hartford, *Working People of Holyoke*, 157, 158.

80. Green, *Holyoke Massachusetts*, 367. The population figures are: 1880: 1,085; 1890: 2,175; 1900: 2,945; 1910: 2,957; 1920: 2,917. The percentages are: 1880: 4.95%; 1890: 9.92%; 1900: 8.26%; 1910: 5.12%; 1920: 4.85%.

81. Major League Soccer's New England Revolution face the same challenge (Moniz, "Adaptive Transnational Identity," 467–71).

82. Hartford, *Working People of Holyoke*, 35.

83. Green, *Holyoke Massachusetts*, 375.

84. Hartford, *Working People of Holyoke*, 49, 137.

85. DiCarlo, *Holyoke-Chicopee*, 371.

86. Hartford, *Working People of Holyoke*, 59; Green, *Holyoke Massachusetts*, 374.

87. "Springfield," *Springfield (MA) Republican*, March 6, 1890.

88. Hartford, *Working People of Holyoke*, 36.

89. "Stunts of Candlepin," *Springfield (MA) Republican*, January 17, 1913.

90. Mason, *Association Football*, 90–91.

91. Hartford, *Working People of Holyoke*, quote on 43, 44.

92. The club continued to sign players and in 1922 was victimized by "an old-country soccer player of considerable experience 'gone bad.'" The con-man vanished after receiving "a small advance in cash" from the club ("Confidence man hits Falcos," *Springfield [MA] Republican*, December 17, 1922).

93. George M. Collins, " 'Hubs' enter soccer league," *Boston Daily Globe*, October 23, 1925.

94. Hutner, *Farr Alpaca Company*, 73, 74.

95. Green, *Holyoke Massachusetts*, 366, 368.

96. "Falco Manager asks for Release after Six Years," *Springfield (MA) Republican*, February 21, 1926.

97. "Falco Soccer Team drops out of Triple A Loop," *Springfield (MA) Republican*, October 8, 1927. Lusitano's website is at http://www.gremiolusitano.com/, accessed June 19, 2020.

98. This was one reason for the sale of the stadium, see note 76. "Holyoke: Sports were always important," *Holyoke (MA) Daily Transcript-Telegram*, December 15, 1979.

99. Quoted in Green, *Holyoke Massachusetts*, 388–89.

CONCLUSION

1. E. Farnsworth and Bunk, "Gentlemen of Color"; see Bunk, "Barrow School"; T. McCabe, "Including Kearny's Leonard Raney."

2. "Metropolitan Areas—Population 1800–1900 (Part 1)," table A91034-1178, in Carter et al., *Historical Statistics*.

3. Interview with researcher Patrick Sullivan in Barron, "Before Atlanta United."

4. "Growing Apace," *San Francisco Call*, January 11, 1893; "Association Football," *Detroit Free Press*, September 12, 1895.

5. Table "Foreign-born Population, by Country of Birth: 1850–1990," table A9353-443, in Carter et al., *Historical Statistics*. The number of Scots arriving in the United States in 1890 was 242,231, and in 1900 it fell to 233,524. This contrasts with the significant growth of the previous decade when soccer expanded in the United States. Between 1880 and 1890 alone the number of arrivals from Scotland rose by 72,094.

6. See, for example, Bunk, "*Sardinero* and Not a Can of Sardines." The German-American League founded in 1923 and now known as the Cosmopolitan League is one of the oldest continuous soccer competitions in the country ("German American League," Wikipedia, https://en.wikipedia.org/wiki/German-American_Soccer_League, accessed June 7, 2020).

7. See Bunk, "Early Image of Black Soccer." Howard University would go on to have great success in intercollegiate soccer winning the men's national championship in 1971 (J. Scott, "Black School").

BIBLIOGRAPHY

ARCHIVES AND LIBRARIES

American Antiquarian Society, Worcester, MA.
American Soccer History Archives. www.SocchistoryUSA.org/ASHA.
Brooklyn Museum, Brooklyn, NY.
Carroll University Archives, Waukesha, WI.
Holyoke History Room, Holyoke Public Library, Holyoke, MA.
Kheel Center for Labor-Management Documentation and Archives, Martin P. Catherwood Library, Cornell University, Ithaca, NY.
Library and Archives Canada. https://www.bac-lac.gc.ca/eng/Pages/home.aspx.
Library of Congress Prints and Photographs Division, Washington, DC.
Special Collections and University Archives, University of Massachusetts, Amherst, MA.
The Statue of Liberty—Ellis Island Foundation. https://www.statueofliberty.org/statue-of-liberty/.

NEWSPAPER DATABASES

Accessible Archives (America and World War I, American Military Camp Newspapers, https://www.accessible-archives.com/collections/world-war-one-american-military-camp-newspapers/ and https://www.accessible-archives.com/collections/world-war-one-american-military-camp-newspapers-part-2/)
Bethlehem Steel Soccer Club (http://bethlehemsteelsoccer.org)

British Newspaper Archive (https://www.bl.uk/collection-guides/british-newspaper
-archive)

California Digital Newspaper Collection, Center for Bibliographic Studies and
Research, University of California, Riverside (http://cdnc.ucr.edu)

GenealogyBank (https://www.genealogybank.com/)

Google News Archive (https://news.google.com/newspapers)

Illinois Digital Newspaper Collections (https://idnc.library.illinois.edu/)

LA84 Foundation Digital Library Collections, the Sporting Life Collection (https://
digital.la84.org/digital/collection/p17103coll17)

Minnesota Historical Society, Minnesota Digital Newspaper Hub (https://www
.mnhs.org/newspapers/hub)

NewspaperArchive (https://newspaperarchive.com)

Newspapers.com (https://www.newspapers.com/)

Nineteenth-Century US Newspapers (Gale.com, https://www.gale.com/c/nineteenth
-century-us-newspapers)

Old Fulton New York Post Cards (https://fultonhistory.com/)

ProQuest Historical Newspapers (https://about.proquest.com/libraries/academic/
news-newspapers/pq-hist-news.html)

BOOKS AND OTHER SOURCES

Academical (pseud.). "McKinley Park Team, Sacramento." In Cahill, *Spalding's Official
"Soccer" Football Guide* (1922), 150–51.

Abrams, Nathan D., "Inhibited but Not 'Crowded Out': The Strange Fate of Soccer
in the United States." *International Journal of the History of Sport* 12, no. 3 (December
1995): 1–17.

Adamson, David C. "Pittsburgh and District Association Foot Ball League." In
Spalding's Official "Soccer" Foot Ball Guide, edited by Thomas W. Cahill, 91–93. New
York: American Sports Publishing, 1914.

Allaway, Roger. *Corner Offices and Corner Kicks*. Haworth, NJ: St. Johan Press, 2009.

———. *Rangers, Rovers, and Spindles: Soccer, Immigration, and Textiles in New England
and New Jersey*. Haworth, NJ: St. Johan Press, 2005.

Allaway, Roger, David Litterer, and Colin Jose. *The Encyclopedia of American Soccer*.
Lanham, MD: Scarecrow Press, 2001.

"American Amateur Foot Ball Association." In Cahill, *Spalding's Official Association
"Soccer" Foot Ball Guide* (1912), 39–41.

American Journeys. "Background." https://americanjourneys.org/aj-136/summary/
index.asp. Accessed October 29, 2020.

Anderson, Eric. "Waukesha: Birthplace of the U.S. Soccer?" *Wisconsin Soccer
Central*. October 9, 2012. https://www.wisconsinsoccercentral.com/news_article/
show/257454.

"Annual Report of the Treasurer." In Cahill, *Spalding's Official "Soccer" Football Guide*
(1917), 32.

"Annual Report of the Treasurer." In Cahill, *Spalding's Official "Soccer" Football Guide* (1923), 10.

Apostolov, Steven S. "Everywhere and Nowhere: The Forgotten Past and Clouded Future of American Professional Soccer from the Perspective of Massachusetts." *Soccer and Society* 13, no. 3 (May 2012): 1–47.

———. "Les hauts et les bas du *soccer* professionnel aux Etas-Unis à partir du cas du Massachusetts." PhD diss., Université Paris, 2011.

———. "Native Americans, Puritans and 'Brahmins': Genesis, Practice and Evolution of Archaic and Pre-Modern Football in Massachusetts." *Sport in Society* 20, no. 6 (2017): 1259–70.

Aspin, Jehoshaphat. *Ancient Customs, Sports, and Pastimes of the English.* London: John Harris, 1835.

"Athletics." *California Occident*, February 1909: 41.

"Auditor's Report." In Cahill, *Spalding's Official "Soccer" Football Guide* (1917), 11.

Bagnall, Thomas H. "Activities of the Chain Letter Fund." In Cahill, *Spalding's Official "Soccer" Football Guide* (1918), 39.

"The Barbarians." In *Spalding's Official Association "Soccer" Foot Ball Guide*, edited George W. Orton, 209–11. New York: American Sports Publishing, 1911.

Barrett, S. A. "The Washo Indians." *Bulletin of the Public Museum of Milwaukee* 2, no. 1 (1917): 1–53.

Barron, Brent. "Before Atlanta United: The Early History of Soccer in DeKalb County." *Dekalb Neighbor*, May 4, 2017. https://www.mdjonline.com/neighbor_newspapers/dekalb/sports/before-atlanta-united-the-early-history-of-soccer-in-dekalb-county/article_a2cb818c-30d8–11e7-bded-d71a93e8464d.html.

Bartram, William. *Travels Through North and South Carolina, Georgia, East and West Florida, the Cherokee Country, the Extensive Territories of the Muscogulges or Creek Confederacy, and the County of the Chactows.* Philadelphia: James & Johnson, 1791.

Baseball Reference. "1894 Brooklyn Grooms Schedule." www.baseball-reference.com/teams/BRO/1894-schedule-scores.shtml. Accessed May 28, 2018.

Belanger, Yale. "Towards an Innovative Understanding of North American Indigenous Gaming." In *First Nations Gambling in Canada*, edited by Yale Belanger, 10–34. Winnipeg: University of Manitoba Press, 2011.

———, ed. *First Nations Gambling in Canada.* Winnipeg: University of Manitoba Press, 2011.

Bell, Thomas. *Out of This Furnace.* 1941. Reprint, Pittsburgh: University of Pittsburgh Press, 1976.

Berkhofer, Robert F., Jr. *The White Man's Indian: Images of the American Indian from Columbus to the Present.* New York: Alfred A. Knopf, 1978.

Bernstein, Mark F. *Football: The Ivy League Origins of an American Obsession.* Philadelphia: University of Pennsylvania Press, 2001.

Berthoff, Rowland Tappan. *British Immigrants in Industrial America 1790–1950.* 1953. Reprint, New York: Russell and Russell, 1968.

Betts, John Rickards. "Sporting Journalism in Nineteenth-Century America." *American Quarterly* 5, no. 1 (Spring 1953): 39–56.

Bius, Joel R. "The Damn Y Man in WWI: Service, Perception, and Cigarettes." In *The YMCA at War: Collaboration and Conflict during the World Wars*, edited by Jeffrey C. Copeland and Yan Xu, 17–34. Lanham, MD: Lexington Books, 2018.

Blake, E. F. "A Plea for Foot-Ball." *Yale Literary Magazine* 24, no. 1 (October 1863): 10–16.

Block, David. *Baseball before We Knew It*. Lincoln: University of Nebraska Press, 2005.

Boas, Franz. *The Central Eskimo*. 1888. Reprint, Lincoln: University of Nebraska Press, 1964.

Bodnar, John. *Workers' World: Kinship, Community, and Protest in an Industrial Society, 1900–1940*. Baltimore, MD: Johns Hopkins University Press, 1982.

Bolsmann, Chris, and George Kioussis, eds. *Soccer Frontiers: The Global Game in the United States, 1863–1913*. Knoxville: University of Tennessee Press, 2021.

Booth, Joe. "Bridgeport Swedes Victims of Ignorance." In Cahill, *Spalding's Official Soccer Football Guide* (1919), 109–11.

———. "Connecticut State Football League." In Cahill, *Spalding's Official Soccer Football Guide* (1919), 105–7.

Bready, James H. *Baseball in Baltimore*. Baltimore, MD: Johns Hopkins University Press, 1998.

Brennan, Patrick. "'England' v. 'Scotland'—1881." Donmouth. Last updated March 9, 2020. http://www.donmouth.co.uk/womens_football/1881.html.

Bromley, Irma. "Gold 'C's' for the Women." *California Occident*, November 1908: 44–45.

Brown, Andrew. "National Challenge Cup Competition Committee Report." In Cahill, *Spalding's Official "Soccer" Football Guide* (1919), 9.

Brown, Paul. "Football Hustlers: The Doomed Attempts to Establish a Football League in the USA in the 19th Century." *Blizzard*, September 1, 2016. https://www.theblizzard.co.uk/article/football-hustlers.

Brown, Robert Perkins, Henry Robinson Palmer, Harry Lyman Koopman, and Clarence Saunders Brigham, eds. *Memories of Brown*. Providence, RI: Brown Alumni Magazine Company, 1909.

Brunet, Jacob. *Notes on the Early Settlement of the North-Western Territory*. New York: D. Appleton & Co., 1847.

Bueltmann, Tanja. *Clubbing Together: Ethnicity, Civility and Formal Sociability in the Scottish Diaspora*. Liverpool: Liverpool University Press, 2014.

Bundgaard, Axel. *Muscle and Manliness: The Rise of Sport in American Boarding Schools*. Syracuse, NY: Syracuse University Press, 2005.

Bunk, Brian D. "The Barrow School Socker Foot Ball Team." Society of American Soccer History. February 13, 2020. https://www.ussoccerhistory.org/the-barrow-school-socker-foot-ball-team/.

———. "An Early Image of Black Soccer in New York City?" Society for American Soccer History. February 11, 2020. https://www.ussoccerhistory.org/an-early-image-of-black-soccer-in-new-york-city/.

———. "*Sardinero* and Not a Can of Sardines: Soccer and Spanish Identities in New York City during the 1920s." *Journal of Urban History* 41, no. 3 (May 2015): 444–59.

Byington, Margaret F. *Homestead. The Households of a Mill Town.* 1910. Reprint, New York: Arno and the New York Times, 1969.

The Bylaws and Orders of the Town of Boston. Boston: Green and Russell, 1758.

Cahill, Thomas W. "Annual Report of the Honorary Secretary." Cahill, In *Spalding's Official "Soccer" Football Guide* (1919), 16–19.

———. Foreword. In Cahill, *Spalding's Official "Soccer" Football Guide* (1917), 3–4.

———. Foreword. In Cahill, *Spalding's Official "Soccer" Football Guide* (1919), 5.

———. Foreword. in Cahill, *Spalding's Official "Soccer" Football Guide* (1922), 5–7.

———. "Review of Soccer." In *Spalding's Official Association "Soccer" Foot Ball Guide,* edited by George W. Orton, 15–27. New York: American Sports Publishing, 1911.

———, ed. *Spalding's Official Association "Soccer" Foot Ball Guide.* New York: American Sports Publishing, 1912.

———, ed. *Spalding's Official "Soccer" Football Guide.* New York: American Sports Publishing, 1915.

———, ed. *Spalding's Official "Soccer" Football Guide.* New York: American Sports Publishing, 1917.

———, ed. *Spalding's Official "Soccer" Football Guide.* New York: American Sports Publishing, 1918.

———, ed. *Spalding's Official "Soccer" Football Guide.* New York: American Sports Publishing, 1919.

———, ed. *Spalding's Official "Soccer" Football Guide.* New York: American Sports Publishing, 1921.

———, ed. *Spalding's Official "Soccer" Football Guide.* New York: American Sports Publishing, 1922.

———, ed. *Spalding's Official "Soccer" Football Guide.* New York: American Sports Publishing, 1923.

Cahn, Susan. *Coming on Strong: Gender and Sexuality in Twentieth-Century Women's Sport.* New York: Free Press, 1994.

"Camp Johnson, near Winchester, Virginia—The First Maryland Regiment Playing Football before evening parade." *Harper's Weekly* 5, no. 244 (August 31, 1861): 557.

Carter, Susan B., Scott Sigmund Gartner, Michael R. Haines, Alan L. Olmsted, Richard Sutch, and Gavin Wright, eds. *Historical Statistics of the United States: Millennial Edition On Line.* New York: Cambridge University Press, 2006.

Cascio, Chuck. *Soccer U.S.A.* Washington, DC: Robert B. Luce, 1975.

Chadwick, Henry, ed. *Beadle's dime book of cricket and football: Being a complete guide to players, and containing all the rules and laws of the ground and games.* New York: Beadle and Adams Publishers, 1866.

Chappell, Edward. *Narrative of a Voyage to Hudson's Bay in His Majesty's Ship Rosamond.* London: J. Mawman, 1817.

Chief Clearwater. "Pasuckquakohowauog." *Narragansett Dawn* 1, no. 3 (July 1935): 14.

Cirino, Tony. *U.S. Soccer vs. the World.* Leonia, NJ: Damon Press, 1983.

Clarke, William. *The Boy's Own Book; A Complete Encyclopedia of all the Diversions, Athletic, Scientific, Recreative of Boyhood and Youth*. Boston: Munroe and Francis, 1829.

———. *The Boy's Own Book; A Complete Encyclopedia of all the Diversions, Athletic, Scientific, Recreative of Boyhood and Youth*. New York: James Miller, 1881.

Clements, William M. "Translating Context and Situation: William Strachey and Powhatan's 'Scornful Song.'" In *Born in the Blood: On Native American Translation*, edited by Brian Swann, 398–418. Lincoln: University of Nebraska Press, 2011.

Cohen, Kenneth. "A Mutually Comprehensible World? Native Americans, Europeans, and Play in Eighteenth-Century America." *American Indian Quarterly* 26, no. 1 (Winter 2002): 67–93.

Collins, George M. "Soccer in Massachusetts." In Cahill, *Spalding's Official "Soccer" Football Guide* (1915), 69–70.

Collins, Tony. "Early Football and the Emergence of Soccer, c. 1840–1880." *International Journal of the History of Sport* 32, no. 9 (2015): 1–16.

———. *How Football Began: A Global History of How the World's Football Codes Were Born*. London: Routledge, 2019.

———. "'Watching the Clock': Time, Contingency and Comparative Football History." Paper presented at the International Football history Conference, Manchester, UK, June 2019.

Conductor Generalis or the Office, Duty and Authority of Justices of the Peace, High-Sheriffs, Under-Sheriffs, Goalers, Coroners, Constables, Jury-Men, and Overseers of the Poor. Philadelphia: Benjamin Franklin, 1749.

Conn, Steven. *History's Shadow: Native Americans and Historical Consciousness in the Nineteenth Century*. Chicago: University of Chicago Press, 2004.

"Connecticut Women's Soccer." In Cahill, *Spalding's Official "Soccer" Football Guide* (1921), 90.

Couvares, Francis G. *The Remaking of Pittsburgh. Class and Culture in an Industrializing City, 1877–1919*. Albany: State University of New York Press, 1984.

Crampsey, Bob. *The First 100 Years*. Glasgow: Scottish Football League, 1990.

Crawford, Scott. *A History of Soccer in Louisiana 1858–2013*. N.p.: LAPrepsoccer, 2013.

Crocker-Langley San Francisco City Directory. San Francisco: H. S. Crocker Co., 1920–24.

Crowninshield, Benjamin William. "Boating." In *The Harvard Book*, edited by F. O. Vaille and H. A. Clark, 2:191–267. Cambridge, MA: Welch, Bigelow, and Company University Press, 1875.

Culin, Stewart. *Games of Chance*. Vol. 1 of *Games of the North American Indians*, 1907. Reprint, Lincoln: University of Nebraska Press, 1992.

———. *Games of Skill*. Vol. 2 of *Games of the North American Indians*, 1907. Reprint, Lincoln: University of Nebraska Press, 1992.

Cummings, W. R. "Peel Challenge Cup Competition." In Cahill, *Spalding's Official "Soccer" Football Guide* (1918), 89.

Curry, Graham. ed. *The Early Development of Football. Contemporary Debates*. London: Routledge, 2019.

Czubinksi, Grant. "Dennis Shay: Patriarch of American Goalkeepers." *A Moment of Brilliance: An American Soccer History Blog.* February 12, 2016. http://amofb.blogspot.com/2016/02/dennis-shay-americas-goalkeeper.html.

———. "The First Professional Soccer League in America and the Senators of Washington, Part Three." *A Moment of Brilliance: An American Soccer History Blog.* January 17, 2014. www.amofb.blogspot.com/2014/01/the-first-professional-soccer-league-in_17.html.

Davis, J. G. "Soccer Football In Illinois." In Cahill, *Spalding's Official "Soccer" Football Guide* (1917), 82.

Davis, John. *The Voyages and Works of John Davis the Navigator.* Edited by Albert Hastings Markham. London: Hakluyt Society, 1880.

Davis, Parke H. *Football: The American Intercollegiate Game.* New York: Scribner and Sons, 1911.

Dawson, Melanie. "The Miniaturizing of Girlhood: Nineteenth-Century Playtime and Gendered Theories of Development." In *The American Child. A Cultural Studies Reader,* edited by Caroline F. Levander and Carol J. Singley, 63–84. New Brunswick, NJ: Rutgers University Press, 2003.

d'Azevedo, Warren L., Introduction. In d'Azvedo, "Washo Indians of California and Nevada," 1–7.

d'Azevedo, Warren L., ed. "The Washo Indians of California and Nevada." Special issue, *Anthropological Papers* 67 (August 1963).

Delsahut, Fabrice. "From Baggataway to Lacrosse: An Example of the Sportization of Native American Games." *International Journal of the History of Sport* 32, no. 7 (2015): 923–38.

Delsahut, Fabrice, and Thierry Terret. "First Nations Women, Games, and Sport in Pre- and Post-Colonial North America." *Women's History Review* 23, no. 6 (2014): 976–95.

Deming, Clarence. "Three Ages of Football." *Outing* 41, no. 1 (October 1902): 56–59.

Denton, Daniel. *A Brief Relation of New York, with the Places thereunto Adjoyning, the New Netherlands, &c.* London, 1670.

DePasquale, Paul W. "'Worth the Noting': European Ambivalence and Aboriginal Agency in *Meta Incognita*." In *Reading beyond Words: Contexts for Native History,* 2d ed., edited by Jennifer S. H. Brown and Elizabeth Vibert, 5–38. Peterborough, ON: Broadview Press, 2003.

Dewey, Edward H. "Football and the American Indians." *New England Quarterly* 3, no. 4 (October 1930): 736–40.

DiCarlo, Ella Merkel. *Holyoke-Chicopee. A Retrospective.* Holyoke, MA: Transcript-Telegram, 1982.

Downey, Allan. *The Creator's Game: Lacrosse, Identity, and Indigenous Nationhood.* Vancouver: UBC Press, 2018.

Dunton, John. *John Dunton's Letters from New England.* Edited by W. H. Whitmore. Boston: Publications of the Prince Society, 1858.

Dure, Beau. *Why the U.S. Men Will Never Win the World Cup: A Historical and Cultural Reality Check.* Lanham, MD: Roman & Littlefield, 2019.

Egede, Hans. *A Description of Greenland*. London: T. and J. Allman, 1818.

"Eighth Annual Meeting." In Cahill, *Spalding's Official "Soccer" Football Guide* (1921), 10–18.

Eisen, George. "Games and Sporting Diversions of the North American Indians as Reflected in American Historical Writings of the Sixteenth and Seventeenth Centuries." *Canadian Journal of History of Sport* 9, no. 1 (1978): 58–85.

Elsey, Brenda, and Joshua Nadel. *Futbolera: A History of Women and Sports in Latin America*. Austin: University of Texas Press, 2019.

Farnsworth, Ed. "The AAPF and the ALPF: The Beginnings of Professional League Soccer in the United States." Society for American Soccer History, July 24, 2018. http://www.ussoccerhistory.org/the-aapf-and-the-alpf-the-beginnings-of -professional-league-soccer-in-the-united-states/.

———. "After the Collapse: ALPF vs. ALPF in Baltimore and Fall River, 1894–96." Society for American Soccer History, April 27, 2020. https://www.ussoccerhistory .org/after-the-collapse-alpf-vs-alpf-in-baltimore-and-fall-river-1894-96/.

———. "Clement Beecroft: The Father of League Soccer in Philadelphia." Philly Soccer Page, December 3, 2009. http://www.phillysoccerpage.net/2009/12/03/ clement-beecroft-the-father-of-league-soccer-in-philadelphia/.

———. "Philadelphia and the Other First Professional Soccer League in the U.S." Philly Soccer Page, October 23, 2015. http://www.phillysoccerpage.net/2015/10/23/ philadelphia-and-the-other-first-professional-soccer-league-in-the-u-s/.

———. "The Philadelphia Phillies Soccer Connection—Part 2." Philly Soccer Page, April 1, 2010. www.phillysoccerpage.net/2010/04/01/the-philadelphia-philliesphilly- soccer-connection-part-2/.

Farnsworth, Ed, and Brian D. Bunk. "Gentlemen of Color: Oliver and Fred Watson, the Earliest known African American Soccer Players in the United States." Society for American Soccer History, December 8, 2020. https://www.ussoccerhistory.org/ gentlemen-of-color-oliver-and-fred-watson-the-earliest-known-african-american -soccer-players-in-the-united-states/.

Fausz, J. Frederick. "An 'Abundance of Blood Shed on Both Sides': England's First Indian War, 1609–1614." In *Virginia Reconsidered: New Histories of the Old Dominion*, edited by Keven R. Hardwick and Warren R. Hofstra, 11–47. Charlottesville: University of Virginia Press, 2003.

———. "Middlemen in Peace and War: Virginia's Earliest Indian Interpreters, 1608– 1632." *Virginia Magazine of History and Biography* 95, no. 1 (January 1987): 41–64.

Fernley, John A. "Soccer's Progress and Prospects." In Cahill, *Spalding's Official "Soccer" Football Guide* (1923), 36–37.

"Fifth Annual Meeting." In Cahill, *Spalding's Official "Soccer" Football Guide* (1918), 13–17.

Fisher, Donald M. *Lacrosse: A History of the Game*. Baltimore, MD: Johns Hopkins University Press, 2002.

———. "Contested Ground: North American Cultures and the History of Lacrosse." PhD diss., State University of New York at Buffalo, 1997.

Fossett, Reneé. *In Order to Live Untroubled: Inuit of the Central Arctic, 1550–1940*. Winnipeg: University of Manitoba Press, 2001.

Foulds, Alan. *Boston's Ballparks and Arenas*. Hanover, NH: University Press of New England, 2005.

Foulds, Sam, and Paul Harris. *America's Soccer Heritage*. Manhattan Beach, CA: Soccer for Americans, 1979.

Franks, Joel S. *Whose Baseball? The National Pastime and Cultural Diversity in California, 1859–1941*. Lanham, MD: Scarecrow Press, 2001.

Freed, Stanley A., and Ruth S. Freed. "The Persistence of Aboriginal Ceremonies among the Washo Indians." In d'Azvedo, "Washo Indians of California and Nevada," 25–40.

"Glances at our Letter File." *Outing* 8, no. 5 (February 1889): 465.

Gleach, Frederic W. "Controlled Speculation and Constructed Myths: The Saga of Pocahontas and Captain John Smith." In *Contexts for Native History*, 2d ed., edited by Jennifer S. H. Brown and Elizabeth Vibert, 39–74. Peterborough, ON: Broadview Press, 2003.

Goodman, Sam. "Association Foot Ball in California." In *Spalding's Official Association "Soccer" Foot Ball Guide*, 93–103. New York: American Sports Publishing, 1909.

Grant, Larry. "The YMCA and the US Army in Post-World War I France and Germany." In *The YMCA at War: Collaboration and Conflict during the World Wars*, edited by Jeffrey C. Copeland and Yan Xu, 123–41. Lanham, MD: Lexington Books, 2018.

Green, Constance McLaughlin. *Holyoke Massachusetts: A Case History of the Industrial Revolution in America*. 1939. Reprint, Hamden, CT: Archon Books, 1968.

Greenberg, Amy S. *Cause for Alarm: The Volunteer Fire Department in the Nineteenth-Century City*. Princeton, NJ: Princeton University Press, 1998.

Hager [Hagar], Stansbury. "Micmac Customs and Traditions." *American Anthropologist* 8, no. 1 (January 1895): 31–42.

Hakala, Josh. "The US Open Cup Final: 1914 to the Present." TheCup.us, September 30, 2011. https://thecup.us/2011/09/30/the-open-cup-final-1914-present/.

Hall, M. Anne. "Women's High-Wheel Bicycle Racing in Nineteenth-Century America: More than Salacious Entertainment." *Sport History Review* 50 (2019): 137–58.

Hanschu, Steven. "The Kansas State Normal Years: 1863–1923." *Emporia State Research Studies* 49, no. 1 (2013): 19–28.

Hanson, Joseph Mills ed. *The Inter-Allied Games: Paris 22nd June to July 6th 1919*. Paris: Games Committee, 1919.

Hardy, Stephen. *How Boston Played: Sport, Recreation, and Community, 1865–1915*. Boston: Northeastern University Press, 1982.

Hart, Albert Bushnell, ed. *Commonwealth History of Massachusetts*. Vol. 2. New York: States History Company, 1927–30.

Hart, Siobhan M., Elizabeth S. Chilton, and Christopher Donta, "Before Hadley: Archaeology and Native History, 10,000 BC to 1700 AD." In *Cultivating a Past: Essays on the History of Hadley, Massachusetts*, edited by Marla R. Miller, 43–67. Amherst: University of Massachusetts Press, 2009.

Hartford, William F. *Working People of Holyoke: Class and Ethnicity in a Massachusetts Mill Town, 1850–1960*. New Brunswick, NJ: Rutgers University Press, 1990.

Harvey, Adrian. *Football: The First Hundred Years: The Untold Story*. New York: Routledge, 2005.

———. "The Public Schools and Organized Football in Britain: Fresh Perspectives on Old Paradigms." *International Journal for the History of Sport* 33, no. 3 (2016): 272–88.

Haswell, Charles H. *Reminiscences of an Octogenarian*. New York: Harper and Brothers, 1896.

Hatfield, Thomas. *The History of Soccer in Greater Cleveland from 1906 until 1981*. Denver, CO: Outskirts Press, 2014.

Hay, Roy, Adrian Harvey, and Mel Smith. "Football before Codification: The Problems of Myopia." *Soccer and Society* 16, no. 2 (2014): 156–68.

Haynes, E. M. *A History of the Tenth Regiment VT. Vols*. Rutland, VT: Tuttle Company, 1894.

Healey, George. "Annual Report of the President." In Cahill, *Spalding's Official "Soccer" Football Guide* (1922), 26–28.

Heckel, Waldemar, ed. *Who's Who in the Age of Alexander the Great: Prosopography of Alexander's Empire*. Malden, MA: Blackwell, 2006.

Henry, James Buchanan, and Christian Henry Scharff. *College as It Is, or the Collegian's Manual in 1853*. Edited by J. Jefferson Looney. Princeton, NJ: Princeton University Libraries, 1996.

Higginson, Thomas Wentworth. "The Gymnasium, and Gymnastics in Harvard College." In *The Harvard Book*, edited by F. O. Vaille and H. A. Clark, 2:186–90. Cambridge, MA: Welch, Bigelow, and Company University Press, 1875.

———. "Saints, and their Bodies." *Atlantic Monthly Magazine* 1, no. 5 (March 1858): 582–95.

Hinderaker, Eric. *Elusive Empires: Constructing Colonialism in the Ohio Valley*. Cambridge: Cambridge University Press, 1997.

"Holiday in Camp—Soldiers Playing 'Foot-Ball.'" Print. *Harper's Weekly* 9, no. 446 (July 15, 1865): 444.

Hollander, Zander, ed. *The American Encyclopedia of Soccer*. New York: Everest House, 1980.

Holroyd, Steve. "The American League of Professional Football, 1894." *Soccer History* 14 (Spring 2006): 17–22.

———"The First Professional Soccer League in the United States: The American League of Professional Football." American Soccer History Archives. Last updated September 4, 2000. www.SoccerHistoryUSA.org/ASHA/alpf.html.

Holyoke City Directory 1912. Holyoke, MA: Transcript Publishing Co., 1912.

Holyoke City Directory 1914. Holyoke, MA: Transcript Publishing Co., 1914.

Holyoke City Directory 1916. Holyoke, MA: Transcript Publishing Co., 1916.

Hopkins, Ivor A. "Association Football in Western Pennsylvania." In *Spalding's Official "Soccer" Foot Ball Guide, 1909*. New York: American Sports Publishing, 1909.

Hume, Ivor Noël. *The Virginia Adventure: Roanoke to James Towne: An Archaeological and Historical Odyssey*. New York: Alfred A. Knopf, 1994.

Hurd, Richard Melancthon. *A History of Yale Athletics, 1840–1888*. New Haven, CT: R. M. Hurd, 1888.

Hutner, Frances Cornwall. *The Farr Alpaca Company: A Case Study in Business History*. Northampton, MA: Smith College History Department, 1951.

"Inuit Games." *Tumivut* 2 (1991): 15–43.

Jable, J. Thomas. "The Birth of Professional Football: Pittsburgh Athletic Club Ring in Professionals in 1892." *Western Pennsylvania Historical Magazine* 62, no. 1 (1979): 131–47.

James, Gary. *The Emergence of Footballing Cultures: Manchester, 1840–1919*. Manchester: Manchester University Press, 2019

Johnson, Elmer L. *The History of YMCA Physical Education*. Chicago: Association Press, 1979.

Johnson, Wait C., and Elwood S. Brown, eds. *Official Athletic Almanac of the American Expeditionary Forces 1919: A.E.F., Championships, Inter-Allied Games*. New York: American Sports Publishing Company, 1919

Jose, Colin. *The American Soccer League, 1921–1931: The Golden Years of American Soccer*. Lanham, MD: Scarecrow Press, 1998.

"Journal of Lieutenant Ebenezer Elmer." *Proceedings of the New Jersey Historical Society* 3, no. 1 (1848): 21–90.

Keane, Albert. "The National Challenge Cup Competition." In *Spalding's Official "Soccer" Foot Ball Guide*, edited by Thomas W. Cahill, 51. New York: American Sports Publishing Company, 1914.

———. "Soccer in New England." In Cahill, *Spalding's Official "Soccer" Football Guide* (1915), 64–65.

Kilpatrick, David. "NYC Originals: Thanksgiving Games of the St. George's Foot Ball Club." Society for American Soccer History, November 22, 2018. http://www.ussoccerhistory.org/nyc-originals-thanksgiving-games-of-the-st-georges-foot-ball-club/.

Kioussis, George. "Exceptions and Exceptionalism: The United States Soccer Football Association in a Global Context, 1950–74." PhD diss., University of Texas at Austin, 2015.

Kroeber, A. L. "Games of the California Indians." *American Anthropologist* 22, no. 3 (July–September 1920): 272–77.

Ladda, Shawn Renee. "The History of Intercollegiate Women's Soccer in the United States." PhD diss., Teacher's College, Columbia University, 1995.

Lanfranchi, Pierre, and Matthew Taylor. *Moving with the Ball: The Migration of Professional Footballers*. New York: Berg, 2001.

Lange, Dave. *Soccer Made in St. Louis: A History of the Game in America's First Soccer Capital*. St. Louis, MO: Reedy Press, 2011.

Langill, Ellen. *Carroll College: The First Century*. Waukesha, WI: Carroll College Press, 1990.

Langley's San Francisco Directory. San Francisco: Geo. B. Wilbur, 1894.

Lawrence University. "Records." https://s3.amazonaws.com/vikings.lawrence.edu/documents/2020/4/23/footballrecords.pdf. Accessed July 6, 2020.

Ledbetter, Bonnie S. "Sports and Games of the American Revolution." *Journal of Sport History* 6, no. 3 (Winter 1979): 29–40.

Lee, James F. *The Lady Footballers: Struggling to Play in Victorian Britain.* New York: Routledge, 2008.

Lee, Mabel. *A History of Physical Education and Sports in the U.S.A.* New York: John Wiley, 1983.

Lewis, Guy. "World War I and the Emergence of Sport for the Masses." *Maryland Historian* 4, no. 2 (1973): 109–22.

Lewis, R. W. "Innovation not Invention: A Reply to Peter Swain Regarding the Professionalization of Association Football in England and Its Diffusion." *Sport in History* 30, no. 3 (2010): 475–88.

Lockerby, Earle. "Ancient Mi'kmaq Customs: A Shaman's Revelations." *Canadian Journal of Native Studies* 24, no. 2 (2004): 403–23.

Logan, Gabe. *The Early Years of Chicago Soccer, 1887–1939.* Lanham, MD: Lexington Books, 2019.

———. "Pilgrims' Progress in Chicago: Three English Soccer Tours to the Second City, 1905–09." *Soccer and Society* 11, no. 3 (May 2010): 198–212.

Loskiel, George Henry. *History of the Mission of the United Brethren among the Indians of North America.* Translated by Christian Ignatius LaTrobe. Piccadilly: Brethren's Society for the furtherance of the Gospel, 1794. Originally published as *Geschichte der Mission der Evanglischen Bruder unter den Indianern in Nordamerika.* Leipzig, 1789.

Lovett, Charles A. "First Big Professional League Launched." In Cahill, *Spalding's Official "Soccer" Football Guide* (1921), 37–38.

Lovett, James D'Wolf. *Old Boston Boys and the Games they Played.* Riverside Press, 1906.

Lowie, Robert H. "Ethnographic Notes on the Washo." *University of California Publications in Archaeology and Ethnography* 36, no. 5 (1939): 301–52.

Lucas, John A. "A Prelude to the Rise of Sport: Ante-bellum America, 1850–1860." *Quest* 11 (1968): 50–57.

Lucky's Amazing Sports Lists. "Football Games at Eastern Park, Brooklyn." Last modified March 1, 2007. www.luckyshow.org/football/ep.htm.

Lyon, George. *The Private Journal of Captain G. F. Lyon of H.M.S. Hecla.* London: John Murray, 1824.

Mancall, Peter C. "The Raw and the Cold: Five English Sailors in Sixteenth-Century Nunavut." *William and Mary Quarterly* 70, no. 1 (January 2013): 3–40.

Markham, Clements R. *A Life of John Davis the Navigator 1550–1605, Discoverer of the Davis Straits.* New York: Dodd, Mead and Co., 1889.

Markovits, Andrei, and Steven Hellerman. *Offside: Soccer and American Exceptionalism.* Princeton, NJ: Princeton University Press, 2001.

Marsh, Edward. "Seventy-Nine's Page of History." In R. Brown et al., *Memories of Brown*, 350–55.

Mason, Tony. *Association Football and English Society, 1863–1915*. Brighton, UK: Harvester Press, 1980.

McCabe, Anthony. "Campus Events in the Eighties." In R. Brown et al., *Memories of Brown*, 366–84.

McCabe, Thomas A. "Cooper's Block: America's First Soccer Neighborhood." *Soccer and Society* (2016): 1–10.

———. "Including Kearny's Leonard Raney." Society for American Soccer History. February 25, 2020. https://www.ussoccerhistory.org/including-kearnys-leonard -raney/.

McDowell, Matthew L. *A Cultural History of Association Football in Scotland, 1865–1902*. Lewiston, NY: Edward Mellen Press, 2013.

McFadden, Doris Loa, Mildred Dunham Van Dyke, and Eileen Luz Johnston. *The Presbyterian Church of Basking Ridge, New Jersey, Founded Circa 1717: A History*. 1898. Reprint, n.p.: Johnston Letter Company, 1961.

McKnight, Everett J. "Football Beginnings at Yale." *Yale Alumni Weekly*, November 3, 1911, 155–56.

———. "Further Early Yale Football History." *Yale Alumni Weekly*, November 19, 1911, 182–84.

Meacham, Scott. "Old Division Football, the Indigenous Mob Soccer of Dartmouth." Dartmo. Last updated November 5, 2006. http://www.dartmo.com/football/.

Mitchell, Andy. "A Transatlantic Football Game in 1873." Scottish Sport History. October 11. 2017. http://www.scottishsporthistory.com/sports-history-news-and- blog/a-transatlantic-football-game-in-1873.

Mitchell, Michael Kanentakeron. *Teiontsikwaeks (Day yoon chee gwa ecks): Lacrosse, the Creator's Game*. Akwesasne, ON: Ronathahonni Cultural Centre, 2010.

Mitchell, Peter. "'A Horse Race Is the Same All the World Over': The Cultural Context of Horse Racing in Native North America." *International Journal for the History of Sport* (May 2020): 1–20.

Mockler, E. L. "Soccer Chain Letter Fund." In Cahill, *Spalding's Official "Soccer" Football Guide* (1918), 39.

Moniz, Miguel. "Adaptive Transnational Identity and the Selling of Soccer: The New England Revolution and Lusophone Migrant Populations." *Soccer and Society* 8, no 4 (October 2007): 459–77.

Morgan, Lewis H. *League of the Ho-dé-no-sau-nee or Iroquois*. 1851. Reprint, New York: Dodd, Mead and Company, 1922.

Morse, Jedidiah. *The American Universal Geography*. Boston: Isaiah Thomas and Ebenezer T. Andrews, 1793.

Murray, C. K. "History and Progress of the American Football Association," in *Spalding's Official Association "Soccer" Foot Ball Guide*, 27–38. New York: American Sports Publishing, 1910.

Nash, Alice. "'Antic Deportment and Indian Postures': Embodiment in the Seventeenth-Century Anglo-Algonquian World." In *A Centre of Wonders: The Body in Early America*, edited by Janet Moore Lindman and Michele Lise Tarter, 163–76. Ithaca, NY: Cornell University Press, 2001.

"The National Challenge Cup Competition, 1915–16." In Cahill, *Spalding's Official "Soccer" Football Guide* (1915), 22–23.

Nelson, Edward William. *The Eskimo about the Bering Strait.* 1899. Reprint, Washington, DC: Smithsonian Institution Press, 1983.

Nelson, Kevin. *The Golden Game: The Story of Baseball in California.* Lincoln: University of Nebraska Press, 2004.

New Haven Normal School of Gymnastics. *Catalogue.* New Haven, CT: New Haven Normal School of Gymnastics, 1919.

New York State Division of Military and Naval Affairs: Military History. "13th Heavy Artillery Regiment Civil War." New York State Military Museum and Veterans Research Center. Last modified February 8, 2018. https://dmna.ny.gov/historic/reghist/civil/artillery/13thArtHvy/13thArtHvyMain.htm.

Nuttall, Mark. "Arsarnerit: Inuit and the Heavenly Game of Football." In *The Global Game: Writers on Soccer*, edited by John Turnbull, Thom Satterlee, and Alon Robb, 274–81. Lincoln: University of Nebraska Press, 2008.

The Official Guide to Gaelic and Association Football. New York: American Sports Publishing, 1893.

The Official History of the Eighty-Sixth Division. Chicago: States Publication Society, 1921.

Old Woodward: A Memorial relating to Woodward High School, 1831–1836 and Woodward College, 1836–1851 in the City of Cincinnati. Cincinnati: Old Woodward Club, 1884.

"Olla-podrida." *Nassau Literary Magazine* 28, no. 3 (February 1873): 208–11.

"Olla-podrida." *Nassau Literary Magazine* 29, no. 2 (November 1873): 156–59.

O'Sullivan, Lara. "Playing Ball in Greek Antiquity." *Greece and Rome* 50, no. 1 (2012): 17–33.

Oxendine, Joseph B. *American Indian Sports Heritage.* Lincoln: University of Nebraska Press, 1995.

Palmer, William. "Football Association of Eastern Pennsylvania and District." In Cahill, *Spalding's Official "Soccer" Football Guide* (1919), 96–98.

Paraschak, Victoria. Review of Stewart Culin, Games of the North American Indians, Vol. 1—Games of Change, Vol. 2—Games of Skill." *Canadian Journal of History of Sport* 26 (1995): 91–93.

Park, Roberta J. "British Sports and Pastimes in San Francisco 1848–1900." *British Journal of Sports History* 1, no. 3 (1984): 300–317.

———. "Contesting the Norm: Women and Professional Sports in Late Nineteenth-Century America." *International Journal for the History of Sport* 29, no. 5 (April 2012): 730–49.

———. "German Associational and Sporting Life in the Greater San Francisco Bay Area, 1850–1900." *Journal of the West* 26 (1987): 47–64.

Parry, William Edward. *Journal of a Second Voyage for the Discovery of a North-west Passage from the Atlantic to the Pacific.* London: John Murray, 1824.

————. *Journal of a Voyage for the Discovery of a North-west Passage from the Atlantic to the Pacific.* London: John Murray, 1821.

Peel, Peter J. "Annual Report of the President." In Cahill, *Spalding's Official "Soccer" Football Guide* (1919), 14–15.

Pesavento, Wilma J. "Sport and Recreation in the Pullman Experiment, 1880–1900." *Journal of Sport History* 9, no. 2 (Summer 1982): 38–62.

Pesavento, Wilma J., and Lisa C. Raymond. "'Men Must Play; Men Will Play': Occupations of Pullman Athletes, 1880 to 1900." *Journal of Sport History* 12, no. 3 (Winter 1985): 233–51.

Pomeroy, Edgar. "Oakland Hornets." In *Spalding's Athletic Library Association Foot Ball Guide*, edited by Jerome Flannery, n.p. New York: American Sports Publishing, 1905.

Pope, Steven W. "An Army of Athletes: Playing Fields, Battlefields, and the American Military Sporting Experience, 1890–1920." *Journal of Military History* 59 (July 1995): 435–56.

————. *Patriotic Games: Sporting Traditions in the American Imagination 1876–1926.* New York: Oxford University Press, 1997.

Presbrey, Frank, and James Hugh Moffatt, eds. *Athletics at Princeton: A History.* New York: Frank Presbrey Co., 1901.

Price, John A. "Some Aspects of Washo Life Cycle." In d'Azvedo, "Washo Indians of California and Nevada," 96–114.

————"Washo Prehistory: A Review of Research." In d'Azvedo, "Washo Indians of California and Nevada," 78–95.

Prince, Morton H. "Football at Harvard, 1800–1875." In *The H Book of Harvard Athletics 1852–1922*, edited by John A. Blanchard, 311–71. Cambridge, MA: Harvard Varsity Club, 1923.

Prins, Harald E. L. *The Mi'kmaq: Resistance, Accommodation, and Cultural Survival.* Fort Worth, TX: Harcourt Brace College Publishers, 1996.

Putney, Clifford. *Muscular Christianity: Manhood and Sports in Protestant America, 1880–1920.* Cambridge: Harvard University Press, 2001.

Quint, Alonso H. *Record of the Second Massachusetts Infantry: 1861–1865.* Boston: James P. Walker, 1867.

Rasmussen, Knud. *Intellectual Culture of the Igulik Eskimos.* Vol. 7 of *Report of the Fifth Thule Expedition 1921–24.* Translated by W. Worster. Copenhagen: Gyldendalske Boghandel,Nordisk Forlag, 1929.

Rasmussen, Wayne Douglas. "Historical Analysis of Four Major Attempts to Establish Professional Soccer in the United States of America between 1894 and 1994." PhD diss., Temple University, 1995.

Rementer, Jim. "Pahsahëman—The Lenape Indian Football Game." *Official Website of the Delaware Tribe of Indians* (blog), June 27, 2013. www.delawaretribe.org/blog/2013/06/27/pahsahman-the-lenape-indian-football-game/.

Report of Explosion in the Cincinnati Mine of the Pittsburgh Coal Company Courtney, PA. April 23, 1913. (1914.)

Riedi, Eliza, and Tony Mason, "'Leather' and the Fighting Spirit: Sport in the British Army." *Canadian Journal of History/Annales canadiennes d'historie* 41 (2006): 485–516.

Riess, Lew. "American Forces in Germany." In *Spalding's Official Athletic Almanac*, 251–55. New York: American Sports Publishing, 1922.

———. "American Forces in Germany." In Cahill, *Spalding's Official "Soccer" Football Guide* (1921), 133–34.

Roberts, James. "'The Best Football Team, the Best Platoon': The Role of Football in the Proletarianization of the British Expeditionary Force, 1914–1918." *Sport in History* 26, no. 1 (April 2006): 25–46.

Roberts, Mike. *Before Codification.* Vol. 1 of *The Same Old Game: The True Story of the Ancient Origins of Football.* Barcelona: RobertsBCN Publications, 2011.

———. *Codification.* Vol. 2 of *The Same Old Game: The True Story of the Ancient Origins of Football.* Barcelona: RobertsBCN Publications, 2011.

Robinson, James. "The History of Soccer in the City of St. Louis." PhD diss., St. Louis University, 1966.

Rosenzweig, Roy. *Eight Hours and What We Will: Workers and Leisure in an Industrial City, 1870–1920.* Cambridge: Cambridge University Press, 1985.

Ross, Robert B. *The Great Baseball Revolt: The Rise and Fall of the 1890 Players League.* Lincoln: University of Nebraska Press, 2016.

Rotundo, E. Anthony. *American Manhood: Transformations in Masculinity from the Revolution to the Modern Era.* New York: Basic Books, 1993.

Rountree, Helen C. *The Powhatan Indians of Virginia: Their Traditional Culture.* Norman: University of Oklahoma Press, 1989.

———. "The World of the Algonquian-Speaking Peoples." In *John Smith's Chesapeake Voyages, 1607–1609*, edited by Helen C. Rountree, Wayne E. Clark, and Kent Mountford, 25–55. Charlottesville: University of Virginia Press, 2007.

Rubertone, Patricia E. *Grave Undertakings: An Archaeology of Roger Williams and the Narragansett Indians.* Washington D.C.: Smithsonian Institution Press, 2001.

Runkel, Phillip M. "A Peculiar Scene: Football in 1866." *Landmark* 20, no. 2 (Summer/Autumn 1977): 2–3.

Salter, Michael Albert. "Games in Ritual: A Study of Selected North American Indian Tribes." PhD diss., University of Alberta, 1972.

Sawyer, Joseph Henry. *A History of Williston Seminary.* Easthampton, MA: Published by the Trustees, 1917.

Schiff, Andrew J. *The Father of Baseball: A Biography of Henry Chadwick.* Jefferson, NC: MacFarland, 2008.

Scholefield, James E. "The Northern Massachusetts and New Hampshire Association." In Cahill, *Spalding's Official "Soccer" Football Guide* (1915), 73.

Scholes, Tom. *Stateside Soccer: The Definitive History of Soccer in the United States.* Worthing, UK: Pitch Publishing, 2019.

Scott, Jermaine. "'A Black School Is Not Supposed to Win': Black Teamwork at Howard University, 1970–74." *Journal of Sport History* 46, no. 3 (2019): 347–62.

Scott, William B. "Statistics." In *The Princeton Book*, 453–57. Cambridge, MA: Riverside Press, 1879.

Schultz, Jaime. *Qualifying Times: Points of Change in U.S. Women's Sport.* Urbana: University of Illinois Press, 2014.

Scudder, Winthrop S. "An Historical Sketch of the Oneida Football Club of Boston 1862–1865." N.p.: Massachusetts Historical Society, 1926.

Seifried, Chad, and Donna Pastore. "The Temporary Homes: Analyzing Baseball Facilities in the United States Pre-1903." *Journal of Sport History* 37, no. 2 (Summer 2010): 257–82.

Several Rules, Orders, and By-laws Made and Agreed upon by the Free-holders and inhabitants of Boston of the Massachusetts [sic] at their Meeting May 12 and September 22, 1701. Boston: Bartholomew Green and John Russell, 1701.

Sewell, Jessica Ellen. *Women and the Everyday City: Public Space in San Francisco, 1890–1915.* Minneapolis: University of Minnesota Press, 2011.

Shattuck, Debra A. *Bloomer Girls: Women Baseball Pioneers.* Urbana: Illinois University Press, 2017.

Shippen, Edward. "Some Notes about Princeton." *Princeton University Library Chronicle* 59, no. 1 (Autumn 1997): 15–57.

Simmons, William S. *The Narragansett.* New York: Chelsea House, 1989.

Smith, Melvin. *Evolvements of Early American Foot Ball.* N.p.: AuthorHouse, 2008.

Smith, Ronald A. *Sports and Freedom. The Rise of Big-Time College Athletics.* Oxford: Oxford University Press, 1988.

———. "Women's Control of American College Sport: The Good of Those Who Played or an Exploitation of Those Who Controlled?" *Sport History Review* 29 (1998): 103–20.

Spalding, John E. *Always on Sunday. The California Baseball League, 1886–1915.* Manhattan, KS: Ag Press, 1992.

Spalding's Official Base Ball Guide and Official League Book for 1880. Chicago: A. G. Spalding and Bros., 1880.

Spangler, Adam. "1920 National Challenge Cup Results." TheCup.us, January 16, 2009. https://thecup.us/2009/01/16/1920-national-challenge-cup-results/.

———. "1921 National Challenge Cup Results." TheCup.us, January 16, 2009. https://thecup.us/2009/01/16/1921-national-challenge-cup-results/.

Sparks, Edith. *Capital Intentions: Female Proprietors in San Francisco, 1850–1920.* Chapel Hill: University of North Carolina Press, 2006.

Spelman, Henry. *Relation of Virginia.* London: Chiswick Press, 1872. Online facsimile edition at www.americanjourneys.org/aj-136/. Accessed August 20, 2014.

"Sport and Recreation." *Inuktituk* 57, no. 1 (1984): 54–60.

Steuer, Kenneth. "Service for Soldiers: The Experience of American Welfare Agencies." In *Personal Perspectives: World War I*, edited by Timothy C. Dowling, 205–58. Santa Barbara, CA: ABC-CLIO, 2006.

Stevens, C. A. *Berden's United States Sharpshooters in the Army of the Potomac 1861–1865.* St. Paul, MN, 1892.

Stewart, David. "Foot-Ball." In *The Princeton Book*, 432–440. Cambridge, MA: Riverside Press, 1879.

Stonehenge [John Henry Walsh]. *Manual of British Rural Sports.* 2nd ed. London: G. Routledge & Co., 1856.

Strachey, William. *The Historie of Travelle into Virginia Britania (1612).* Edited by Louis B. Wright and Virginia Freud. 1849. Reprint, London: Hakluyt Society, 1953.

Struna, Nancy L. *People of Prowess: Sport, Leisure, and Labor in Early Anglo-America.* Urbana: University of Illinois Press, 1996.

———. "Puritans and Sport: The Irretrievable Tide of Change." *Journal of Sport History* 4, no. 1 (1977): 1–21.

Strutt, Joseph. *The Sports and Pastimes of the People of England.* London: Methen and Co., 1801.

Summary of the World War Work of the American YMCA. N.p.: International Committee of the Young Men's Christian Associations, 1920.

Swain, Peter. "Cultural Continuity and Football in Nineteenth-century Lancashire." *Sport in History* 28, no. 4 (2008): 566–582.

Szymanski, Stefan, and Andrew Zimbalist. *National Pastime: How Americans Play Baseball and the Rest of the World Plays Soccer.* Washington, DC: Brookings Institution Press, 2005.

Szymanski, Stefan, and Silke-Maria Weineck. *It's Football, not Soccer (and Vice Versa): On the History, Emotion, and Ideology Behind One of the Internet's Most Ferocious Debates.* Self-published, 2018.

Tallec Marston, Kevin. "An International Comparative History of Youth Football in France and the United States (c. 1920-c. 2000): The Age Paradigm and the Demarcation of the Youth Game as a Separate Sector of Sport." PhD diss., De Montfort University, 2012.

Tallec Marston, Kevin, and Mike Cronin. "The Origins of Foot-ball in America: Foundation Myths, Memorialization and Rethinking the Oneida Football (Soccer) Club." In *Soccer Frontiers: The Global Game in the United States, 1863–1913*, edited by Chris Bolsmann and George N. Kioussis. Knoxville: University of Tennessee Press, 2021.

Taylor, Matthew. *The Leaguers: The Making of Professional Football in England, 1900–1939.* Liverpool: University of Liverpool Press, 2005.

Terret, Thierry. "American Sammys and French *Poilus* in the Great War: Sport, Masculinities and Vulnerability." *International Journal of the History of Sport* 28, nos. 3–4 (March 2011): 351–71.

———. *Les jeux interalliés de 1919. Sport, guerre et relations internationales.* Paris: L'Harmattan, 2002.

Thorn, John. *Baseball in the Garden of Eden.* New York: Simon and Schuster, 2011.

Tischler, Steven. *Footballers and Businessmen: The Origins of Professional Soccer in England.* New York: Holmes and Meier, 1981.

Tomlinson, Brett. "The Birth of Football . . . Or Not." *Princeton Alumni Weekly*, October 23, 2019. https://paw.princeton.edu/article/birth-football-or-not.

Trott, Nicholas. *The Laws of the Province of South-Carolina*. Charles-town: Lewis Timothy, 1736.

Trouille, David. "Association Football to Fútbol: Ethnic Succession and the History of Chicago-Area Soccer, 1890–1920." *Soccer and Society* 9, no. 4 (October 2008): 455–76.

United States Army. "American Forces in Germany." *American Representation in Occupied Germany, 1920–21*, vol. 2, n.p. 1921.

United States Army in the World War, 1917–1919: Bulletins, GHQ, AEF. Vol. 17. 1948. Reprint, Washington, DC: U.S. Army Division of Military History, 1988.

"United States of America Foot Ball Association." In *Spalding's Official Association "Soccer" Foot Ball Guide*, edited Thomas W. Cahill, 7–9. New York: American Sports Publishing, 1913.

US Sanitary Commission. *A Report to the Secretary of War of the Operations of the Sanitary Commission, and Upon the Sanitary Conditions of the Volunteer Army, its Medical Staff, Hospitals, and Hospital Supplies*. Washington, DC: McGill and Withrow, 1861.

University of Maryland. *Catalog*. 1858. Ancestry.com. Accessed May 1, 2017.

Van Buren, W. H. "Rules for Preserving the Health of the Soldiers." In *Military Medical and Surgical Essays Prepared for the United States Sanitary Commission*, 159–71. Washington DC, 1865.

Vennum, Thomas. *American Indian Lacrosse: Little Brother of War*. Washington, DC: Smithsonian Institution Press, 1994.

Vermilyea, Natalie. "Kranks' Delight: California Baseball 1858–1888." *Californian*, March–April 1991, 32–41.

Vertinsky, Patricia A. *The Eternally Wounded Woman: Women, Doctors, and Exercise in the Late Nineteenth Century*. Urbana: University of Illinois Press, 1989.

Voight, David Quentin. *The League That Failed*. Lanham, MD: Scarecrow Press, 1998.

Wakefield, Wanda Ellen. *Playing to Win: Sports and the American Military, 1898–1945*. Albany: State University of New York Press, 1997.

Wallis, Wilson D., and Ruth Sawtell Wallis. *The Micmac Indians of Eastern Canada*. Minneapolis: University of Minnesota Press, 1955.

Wangerin, David. "Foreign Bodies and Freezing Fans: The Births of the USFA and the National Challenge Cup." In *Distant Corners: American Soccer's History of Missed Opportunities and Lost Causes*, 34–57. Philadelphia: Temple University Press, 2014.

———. *Soccer in a Football World*. Philadelphia: Temple University Press, 2008.

Waquet, Arnaud "Sport in the Trenches: The New Deal for Masculinity in the France." *International Journal of the History of Sport* 28, nos. 3–4 (March 2011): 331–50.

Wertenbaker, Thomas. *Princeton: 1746–1896*. Princeton, NJ: Princeton University Press, 1946.

Westcott, Rich. *Philadelphia's Old Ballparks*. Philadelphia: Temple University Press, 1996.

Wheeler, Benjamin Ide. "President Wheeler's First impression of Brown." In R. Brown et al., *Memories of Brown*, 292–300.

"When Secretaries were Refugees." *For the Millions of Men Now Under Arms*, no. 14 (March 1919): 19–23.

Wiley, Bell Irvin. *The Life of Billy Yank*. Book 1 of *The Common Soldier in the Civil War*. New York: Grosset and Dunlap, 1952.

———. *The Life of Johnny Reb*. Book 2 of *The Common Soldier in the Civil War*. New York: Grosset and Dunlap, 1952.

Williams, Jean. *A Beautiful Game: International Perspectives on Women's Football*. Oxford: Berg, 2007.

———. *A Contemporary History of Women's Sport. Part One: Sporting Women, 1850–1960*. New York: Routledge, 2014.

Williams, Phil. "Horace Fogel." Society for American Baseball Research. https://sabr.org/bioproj/person/4a35828d. Accessed June 5, 2018.

Williams, Roger. *A Key into the Language of America*. Edited by John J. Teunissen and Evelyn J. Hinz. 1643. Reprint, Detroit: Wayne State University Press, 1973.

Williamson, David J. *Belles of the Ball*. Devon, UK: R & D Associates, 1991.

Winship, Michael. *American Literary Publishing in the Mid-Nineteenth Century: The Business of Ticknor and Fields*. Cambridge: Cambridge University Press, 1995.

Wood, William. *New England's Prospect*. Edited by Alden T. Vaugh. 1634. Reprint, Amherst: University of Massachusetts Press, 1977.

Yale College. *The Laws of Yale-College, in New Haven, in Connecticut, enacted by the President and Fellows the Sixth Day of October, A. D. 1795*. Thomas Green and Son, 1800.

Young, J. N. "Association Football in California." In Cahill, *Spalding's Official "Soccer" Football Guide* (1922), 143–44.

———. "Association Football in California." In Cahill, *Spalding's Official "Soccer" Football Guide* (1923), 145–49.

———. "San Francisco Football League." In Cahill, *Spalding's Official "Soccer" Football Guide* (1922), 144–45.

Young, Richard S. *As the Willow Vanishes: Glasgow's Forgotten Legacy*. n.p.: Consilience Media, 2014.

Youthful Recreations. Philadelphia: J. Johnson, c. 1816.

INDEX

BRIAN D. BUNK is a senior lecturer in the history department at the University of Massachusetts. He is the author of *Ghosts of Passion: Martyrdom, Gender, and the Origins of the Spanish Civil War* and coeditor of *Nation and Conflict in Modern Spain: Essays in Honor of Stanley G. Payne*.

SPORT AND SOCIETY

The University of Illinois Press
is a founding member of the
Association of University Presses.

———————————————

University of Illinois Press
1325 South Oak Street
Champaign, IL 61820-6903
www.press.uillinois.edu